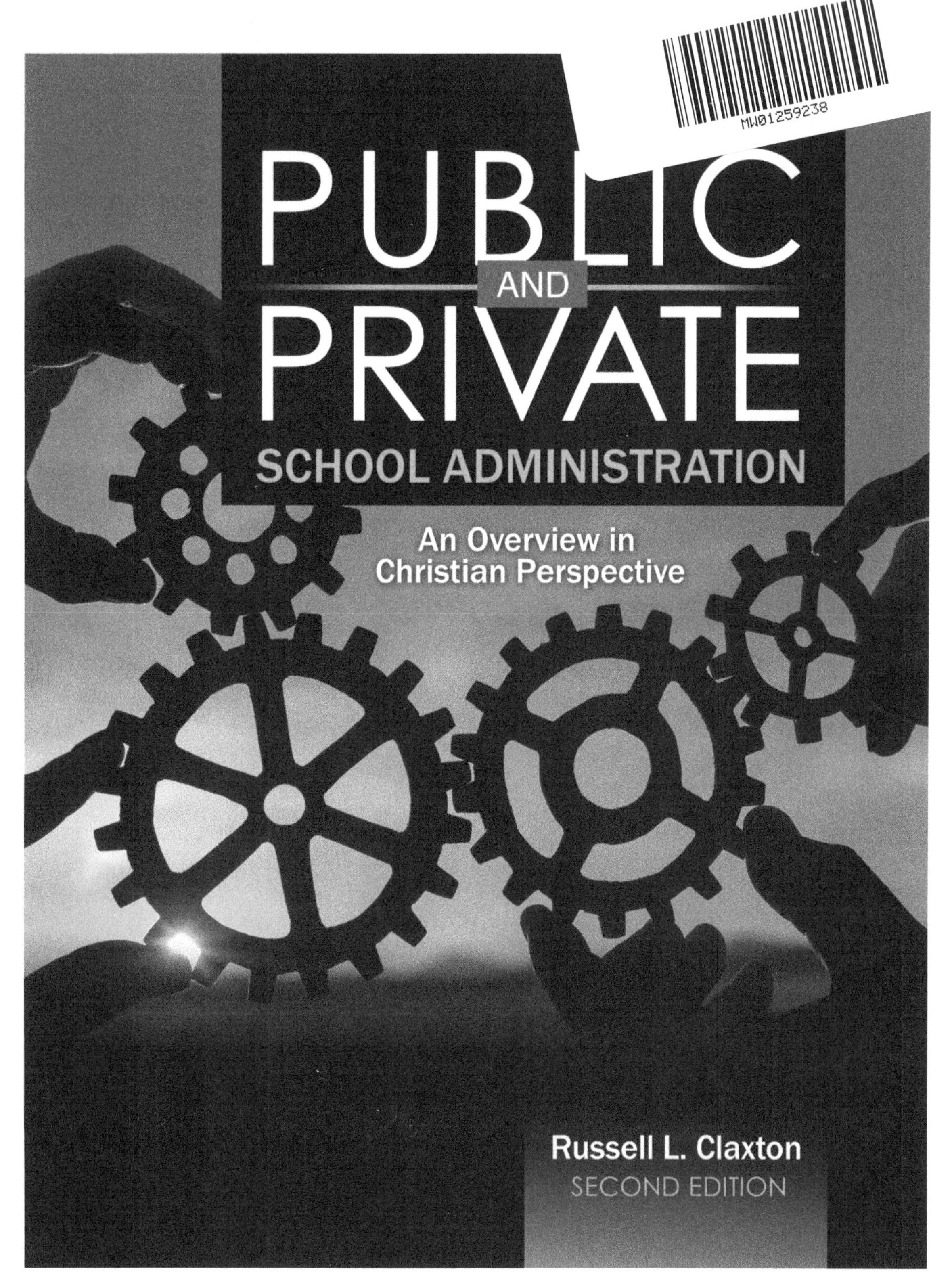

Contributing Authors:
Bunnie Claxton, Mark A. Angle, John C. Bartlett, Andrea P. Beam, Russell L. Claxton, Shanté Moore-Austin, Leldon W. Nichols, Connie L. Pearson, Samuel J. Smith, and James A. Swezey

Kendall Hunt
publishing company

www.kendallhunt.com
Send all inquiries to:
4050 Westmark Drive
Dubuque, IA 52004-1840

ISBN 978-1-5249-8765-7

Published in the United States of America

CONTENTS

INTRODUCTION

Russell L. Claxton

Not everyone should be a teacher, and not every teacher should be a school leader. But for those educators that are called and equipped to lead, it can be a fulfilling and rewarding career. The purpose of this book is to expose current and future school leaders to the most common aspects of school administration. Many textbooks address public school leadership, and some even address leading a private school, but few books address both, while comparing and contrasting the two. Furthermore, the Christian Perspective aspect of the book addresses biblical principles that apply to both the public and private school settings.

Each chapter of this book addresses topics that are relevant to licensure standards, is written by an author that has extensive experience in that area, and addresses the topic from a biblical worldview. Although one book can barely scratch the surface of what a school leader should know and be able to do, I hope that reading this book will transform your leadership as you take another step toward your leadership goals.

SCHOOL ADMINISTRATION

The Title

If asked to describe the position of a principal, most people will broadly define this position as the person who leads or "runs" a school. But if asked to define the roles and responsibilities of the principal position, the response requires much detail and can become quite complex. Even the title of a school leader can vary based on the setting (e.g. headmaster, lead administrator, director, president) . The term principal is commonly used to describe the leader of a public school, although some people may generically refer to all school administrators as principals. School leaders may also serve in secondary roles such as assistant or vice principal, dean, administrative assistant, or various other department or content leadership roles. In a private school, the leader's title may be head master or superintendent, while others on the administrative team can carry school specific titles. Although this book may often refer to a school leader a principal, you may one day find yourself leading a school under a different title.

The Path

There are many paths to the principal's office, and there are many different job descriptions once you arrive. In the residential leadership courses I teach, I am fortunate to meet students who are already serving as school leaders, and I enjoy hearing stories about their leadership journeys. It is interesting how vastly different leadership preparation can be. Some leaders spend years serving in various leadership roles as teachers, to then complete an internship or training program, next acquiring diverse experience as an assistant principal, and eventually being selected as a principal. These school leaders often spend years gaining the experience and knowledge needed to lead a school, and can still feel unprepared. To the other extreme, I remember one student who had a vastly different experience. She was completing her second year as a teacher in a small private school and had just been informed that she was selected to serve as the school principal in the upcoming school year. She was "cramming" to learn as much as possible prior to assuming her new role, but I am not even sure she had the experience to "know what she didn't know." Some educators know that they want to be leaders early in their careers and take advantage of opportunities to prepare for a leadership position, while others find themselves in leadership roles sometimes unexpectedly. How you get to a leadership position is not nearly as important as what you do once you get there.

In most public schools, obtaining a job as an administrator includes the minimum requirements of teaching experience and a graduate degree in school administration. From there, the qualifications can vary between states, districts, and even schools. Some leadership qualifications are determined at the state level through licensure requirements, while districts and schools can determine their own additional qualifications and preferences. Although districts cannot require less of their administrators than what the state requires, many can, and do, require more.

Private schools have much more flexibility regarding the requirements of a school leader. Although private school leaders may serve without a leadership degree or state license, many are still required to attain such qualifications for accreditation purposes.

The Task

Defining the roles and responsibilities of school administrator is much like describing the roles and responsibilities of a teacher. A teacher can be broadly described as someone who provides instruction to students, but the specifics can vary greatly based on grade level, school, state, community, etc. Likewise, a school administrator leads a school, but beyond that, the specifics can be affected by many factors.

The role of the school leader continues to evolve. You may have heard the phrase "principals are no longer building managers, but are now instructional leaders." Although it is true that the principal's role in instruction has increased over the years, someone still has to manage the building. However, given the variety of learning environments, defining what that job looks like can be difficult.

So what makes the day-to-day experience of one school leader so much different than another? Here are a few differences to consider:

Grade Level – The difference in leading an elementary school and a high school goes far beyond the age of the students. Yes, the interaction with students will be different, but so will interactions with teachers, parents, and the community. Some of the topics in this book may seem more relevant to one level than another.

State, District, and School – As mentioned previously, requirements to become a school administrator vary between states and districts, and so do the expectations once you get the job. Many of your day-to-day activities and priorities will be dictated to you by someone else, and expectations can be formal or informal.

Community – Leading a school in a small rural town can be very different from leading a school in a large city. Although it would be difficult to define the differences, there would likely be many. School funding, transportation, parent involvement, and transiency, to name a few, are all factors that can affect schools from one community to the next.

Public or Private – No two schools are the same, and some private schools are more similar to public schools than they are different, but in most cases, the differences are significant. Funding sources, religious affiliation, educator qualifications, and curriculum choices are some of the areas where public and private schools may differ.

The People – Two schools can be almost identical in many ways, and still be very different in other ways. Similar buildings, curriculum, communities, and funding do not necessarily result in similar situations. Every group of students is different, as is every faculty. Leaders can also make a significant impact on the climate and culture.

CONCLUSION

This book contains independent contributions from multiple authors with the intent of exposing current and potential school leaders to diverse backgrounds and experiences. As a group, the authors have many years of experience in educational administrations as teachers, building level leaders, district leaders, and educational leadership professors. Experiences include leadership in public and private schools, and at the elementary, middle, and high school levels. I hope you will find some common themes that will indicate important aspects of leadership in various settings, as well as aspects of school leadership that are different from one setting to another.

Whether you serve in a public, private, or Christian school, I hope you will find this book practical and useful in preparing for whatever role God has for you. You may find that leading a school is the hardest job you will ever love.

Chapter 1

Creating and Communicating a Shared Vision

James A. Swezey

Vision without action is merely a dream. Action without vision just passes the time. Vision with action can change the world.
—Joel A. Barker—

OVERVIEW

There is little argument that with the advent of No Child Left Behind in 2001, U.S. school systems and school districts have been under constant pressure to seek continual improvement (Bernhardt, 2004). Few, if any, school administrators would argue that their own schools do not possess several areas in which they can improve upon the educational services they offer their students. This need for improvement is a clarion call for change within every school campus and every school system in the country. The question is, "Whose vision of change is going to be embraced?" At the national level, some cast a vision wherein education simply needs to be reformed through minor—or even major—changes within the existing system (Berliner & Biddle, 1995; Ravitch, 2010), whereas others are calling for a completely new vision of education that will radically transform our current system (Kohn, 2011; Kozol, 2005; Marshall, 2006). Schlechty (2009) contrasts school reform and transformation this way:

> Transformation by necessity includes altering the beliefs, values, and, meanings—the culture—in which programs are embedded, as well as changing the current system of rules, roles, and relationships—social structure—so that the innovations needed will be supported. Reform, in contrast, means only installing innovations that will work within the context of the existing structure and culture of school. (p. 3)

Whether one believes that schools need to be radically transformed or simply reformed, the key ingredient to bringing about any degree of change is a shared vision that is effectively communicated to constituent stakeholders so that all will be drawn into the process. Therefore, this chapter will seek to examine the details of shared vision from a variety of perspectives, including biblical principles, scholarly research, and practical applications.

Objective

By the end of this chapter the reader should be able to:

1. Collaboratively develop a shared educational mission and vision.
2. Identify, articulate, and cultivate core values that define the organization's culture.
3. Develop an action plan to achieve the vision.
4. Monitor and evaluate the mission and vision and revised as needed to address changes in circumstances and opportunities.

INTRODUCTION

Many people enjoy excellent eyesight early in life. But with age, things begin to change. I noticed it for the first time as I approached my 47th birthday when I tried to read the newspaper one morning. I complained to my wife that the print on this particular copy must be poor because it appeared to be fuzzy. She only chuckled knowingly and recommended that I might want to see an optometrist to have my eyes checked. I scoffed and declared it could not be a problem with my vision because it had always been 20/20. Slowly, though, over time, I began to notice that it was increasingly difficult to read any printed page and then even my computer screen. My distorted vision eventually made work difficult and then impossible. My vision had become inadequate to get the job done, and I needed a new set of lenses through which to view my world.

Poor eyesight might be an inconvenience, but when it comes to school leadership, poor vision is a critical disability. Vision is absolutely necessary to lead a school effectively in the 21st century. A properly implemented shared vision provides all stakeholders with a lens through which they can clearly perceive events that affect the school. As Leech and Fulton (2008) noted, "Increased involvement of employees and other stakeholders in organizational decision making is a practice that has gained much popularity over the past two decades" (p. 632). Vision is of such great importance that when school leadership books are written, or leadership standards developed, promoting a shared vision is often listed as one of the first and most prominent responsibilities of a school leader.

> Vision is absolutely necessary to lead a school effectively in the 21st century.

BACKGROUND

There is no shortage of historical perspectives regarding the evolution of shared leadership and vision, as much has been written about these topics, especially in the past 25 years (Northouse, 2012). The concepts of leadership and vision casting, however, are as old as recorded human history. Pearce and Conger (2010) distinguished between shared leadership and traditional views in that shared models promote influence processes that are "more than just downward influence on subordinates . . ." but rather are "broadly distributed among a set of individuals instead of centralized in hands of a single individual who acts in the role of a superior" (p. 167). They noted that, historically, leadership was viewed in the singular—the leader. Eventually, researchers would emerge who defined leadership as an action or a set of behaviors. Pearce and Conger outlined the extensive evolution of shared leadership dating back to the 1920s with Follett's (1924) law of the situation, which turned the focus of leadership away from the individual in authority toward the particulars of the situation at hand. Other paradigms along the way included co-leadership and social exchange theory, which were popular in the 1950s; participative decision making in the 1970s; self-managing work teams and empowerment in the 1980s; and shared recognition and connective leadership in the 1990s. Kantabutra (2010) explained that before the 1980s, "vision was mostly a concept of researchers who studied political leadership, and the leadership of social or religious movements. It was rarely considered within the leadership literature. Only in the past couple of decades has vision been extensively discussed in the leadership discipline" (p. 259).

Vision is not easily defined, and even when there are attempts to do so, definitions are often not agreed upon (Kantabutra, 2010). According to Hallinger and Heck (as cited in Kantabutra, 2010), "Mission or shared vision exist when personal visions of a critical mass of people cohere in a common sense of purpose within a community" (p. 260). Collins and Porras (1994) described vision as two complementary forces engaged together: core identity and envisioned future. Kantabutra summed up the various scholarly perspectives this way: "Vision is about the future, induces people to act towards a common goal, provides a sense of direction, and is important for strategy and planning" (p. 261). Kantabutra listed the various attributes of vision as brevity, clarity, future orientation, stability, challenge, abstractness, and an ability to inspire (p. 263).

Vision is not easily defined, and even when there are attempts to do so, definitions are often not agreed upon

Smith and Lucas (2000) describe a shared vision as

> a process of involving everyone together in deciding and developing the future of the school system. It doesn't mean taking people's input, selecting some of it, and discarding the rest. It means establishing a series of forums where people work together to forge the future direction of the school. . . . [to] get outcomes they respect and can make a commitment to. (p. 290)

BIBLICAL PERSPECTIVES

Vision and God's Word

What does the Bible have to say about vision? Apparently, a great deal! As Boa (2012) noted:

> In fact, it could be said that the entire Bible is a vision-casting book that invites us not only to look ahead to God's promises for the future, but also to participate in their realization. God has granted us the immeasurable privilege of participating in his work, and he offers us "a slice of the action" that will have enduring consequences. (para. 15)

The word *vision* appears 121 times in the New American Standard Bible (NASB). All too often, though, people take the Scriptures out of context or simply parrot something they have heard without proper understanding (Malone, n.d.). A common example of this is the misapplication of Proverbs 29:18 (NASB): "Where there is no vision, the people are unrestrained, but happy is he who keeps the law." Christians use this verse to make the case that believers need to establish goals for the future and put plans in place. Sometimes they will even summon the old King James Version (KJV) to link this lack of goals and plans to the verbiage of people perishing: "Where there is no vision, the people perish" (KJV). What is typically overlooked, however, is a proper understanding of the context of the verse. In the case of a proverb like this, "vision" is in parallel to "the law": "Where there is no *vision*, the people are unrestrained, but happy is he who keeps *the law*" (NASB; emphasis added). This is a common use of ancient, proverbial wisdom literature.

So, vision in this case does not refer to a future goal, but rather to God's Word. Thus, the Amplified Bible (AMP) reads: "Where there is no vision [no redemptive revelation of God], the people perish; but he who keeps the law [of God, which includes that of man]—blessed (happy, fortunate, and enviable) is he." The point of this passage, and many others throughout the Scriptures, is that God's Word is meant to be the guiding vision for all people.

The psalmist elegantly captured the thought that God's Word should guide vision when he wrote, "Your word is a lamp to my feet and a light to my path" (Psalm 119:105, NASB). Without the light of God's Word shed on the path of life, how can people know whether or not they are headed in the right direction? It is an intimate relationship with God that must direct the vision for life, not an individual's own finite wisdom and understanding. Consider further Proverbs 3:5–6: "Trust in the Lord with all your heart and do not lean on your own understanding. In all your ways acknowledge Him, and He will make your paths straight." A vision for the education of children should be based, as much as possible, on God's Word. Vision can be expressions of both personal and corporate alignment with Scripture.

Personal Vision

In his groundbreaking book on learning organizations, *The Fifth Discipline*, Peter M. Senge (1994) began with the concept of personal mastery and built upon it by encouraging his readers to develop an individual, personal vision. For some educators, a personal vision involves a call to serve in public, charter, urban, or international schools. That is the case for several of the other contributing authors to this book. My own personal vision, however, led me to serve in Christian schools. The guiding vision for my professional life grew out of my personal relationship with God and my understanding of His Word. My original plans to teach in California public schools changed when I came to understand in a new light a well-known passage of Scripture called the Great Commission:

© Rawpixel.com/Shutterstock.com

> Go therefore and make disciples of all the nations, baptizing them in the name of the Father and the Son and the Holy Spirit, teaching them to observe all that I commanded you; and lo, I am with you always, even to the end of the age. (Matthew 28:19–20)

At first reading, it appeared to me that the imperative verb was *Go*. I then learned from a college professor that the imperative verb is actually *make disciples* and that all the other verbs in the passage—as you are going, baptizing, and teaching—support the Commission. Since that time, I have adopted this verse as a key guiding vision. After graduation, I began to interview for teaching positions and, after much prayer, believed that I could be most effective making disciples in Christian schools. Within Christian schools, I could openly share my faith, teach from the Scriptures, disciple, and pray with my students. Understandably, for those whom God has given a heart for the public school, the making of disciples must be approached in a different manner. In whatever way Christians choose to articulate the call to make disciples, all are to be witnesses to the Gospel of Jesus Christ: "But you will receive power when the Holy Spirit has come upon you; and you shall be My witnesses both in Jerusalem, and in all Judea and Samaria, and even to the remotest part of the earth" (Acts 1:8).

Christians can be witnesses through both word and deed. According to Boa (2012), "We are active participants in that last phrase; we are witnesses charged with taking the life of Christ 'to the ends of the earth.'" The ends of the earth must include those in our public schools. Christian educators in public schools can take the life-giving love of Christ with them through their words, attitudes, and actions: "Let your light shine before men in such a way that they may see your good works, and glorify your Father who is in heaven" (Matthew 5:16).

Corporate Vision

In corporate situations, educational leaders may draw upon biblical principles as well. For example, the great worth of all children is alluded to in passages such as Psalm 139:13–14: "For You formed my inward parts; You wove me in my mother's womb. I will give thanks to You, for I am fearfully and wonderfully made; wonderful are Your works, and my soul knows it very well." Also, the value of children is implicit in Jesus' rebuke of His disciples when they attempted to stop children from approaching Him: "But Jesus called for them, saying, 'Permit the children to come to Me, and do not hinder them, for the kingdom of God belongs to such as these'" (Luke 18:16). Clearly, a vision for education must include a high view of the worth and value of children.

When the Lord prepared Moses to lead Hebrew slaves out of bondage in Egypt, He cast an enticing vision, using lush agrarian imagery, that appealed to them. Through His prophet Moses, God Almighty told them of a land flowing with milk and honey:

> The LORD said, "I have surely seen the affliction of My people who are in Egypt, and have given heed to their cry because of their taskmasters, for I am aware of their sufferings. So I have come down to deliver them from the power of the Egyptians, and to bring them up from that land to a good and spacious land, to a land flowing with milk and honey. . . ." (Exodus 3:7–8a)

The Lord also cast a vision of a Promised Land for New Testament believers. He revealed to the apostle John a vision of paradise:

> Then I saw a new heaven and a new earth; for the first heaven and the first earth passed away, and there is no longer any sea. And I saw the holy city, new Jerusalem, coming down out of heaven from God, made ready as a bride adorned for her husband. And I heard a loud voice from the throne, saying, "Behold, the tabernacle of God is among men, and He will dwell among them, and they shall be His people, and God Himself will be among them, and He will wipe away every tear from their eyes; and there will no longer be any death; there will no longer be any mourning, or crying, or pain; the first things have passed away." (Revelation 21:1–4)

These visions are meant to (1) bring comfort to God's people when they face trials and tribulations, (2) inspire those who follow Him to a life of sacrifice, (3) encourage Christians to complete the good works He has prepared for them, and (4) offer an eternal reward, the heart of which is to spend eternity in perfect fellowship with Him. All Christians should be attracted to a vision such as this, and all Christian leaders can help create visions that reflect principles from God's Word!

THEORETICAL FRAMEWORKS

A Christian Framework

Few Christians have written more popular works on leadership than John Maxwell. He is an entrepreneur and the author of dozens of books on the topic of leadership, millions of which have sold around the world in 50 different languages. He is among the most widely recognized experts in the field, especially within the Christian community, and has successfully extended his reach into the secular business world. In one of his earlier works, *Developing the Leader Within You*, Maxwell (1993) defined leadership with a single word: influence. He explained, "After more than four decades of observing leadership within my own family and many years of developing my own leadership potential, I have come to this conclusion: Leadership is influence. That's it. Nothing more; nothing less" (p. 1). Maxwell viewed integrity as the most important ingredient of leadership, but he claimed vision was leadership's most indispensable quality. He wrote, "Without [vision], energy ebbs low, deadlines are missed, personal agendas begin to surface, production falls, and people scatter" (p. 139). He placed people into four categories when it comes to vision. The first are the wanderers who never see the vision. The second are the followers who do see it but never pursue it on their own. The third are the achievers who both see and pursue it. Finally, there are the leaders who see it, pursue it, and then help others to see it. If Maxwell were to be criticized for any shortcomings in his views, it might be that he often persists in a singular vision of the leader and—by extension—the leader's singular vision, developed in isolation from others. Blackaby and Blackaby (2011) expressed suspicion of such leader-driven visions and argued that they may better reflect a worldly perspective.

Another prolific Christian author on the topic of leadership is George Barna, founder of the market research firm the Barna Group. The firm primarily works with private, nonprofit religious organizations but also extends its reach into the secular world. It "is widely considered to be a leading research organization focused on the intersection of faith and culture" by offering "a range of customized research, resources and training to serve churches, non-profits, businesses and leaders. The company provides primary research; diagnostic tools; print and digital resources; leadership development; training and keynote talks; and organizational enhancement" (Barna Group, n.d.). The author of dozens of books, Barna dedicated one of his early efforts in 1992 entirely to the topic of vision. In *The Power of Vision: Discover and Apply God's Plan for Your Life and Ministry*, Barna (2009) defined a vision for ministry as "a clear mental image of a preferable future imparted by God to His chosen servants and is based on an accurate understanding of God, self and circumstances" (p. 26). One of the keys to understanding vision from this Christian perspective is that vision is God-centered and people-oriented.

In the now-famous words of evangelical pastor Rick Warren (2002), "It's not about you" (p. 17). A Christian's God-centered vision for the ministry of education must begin with an intimate relationship with God. Barna (2009) explained that "any vision based upon [Christian leaders'] capacities will be flawed and limited" (p. 61) because of their finite, fallen, and sinful natures. He argued that God's vision for life and ministry is perfect, blessed, and inspired. In order to capture this God-centered vision, Barna pointed out that individuals must pursue a relationship with God through prayer, the study of the Bible, and even such spiritual disciplines as fasting. Blackaby and Blackaby (2011) also argued that a Christian's vision must begin with God:

> Yet many Christian leaders adopt the world's approach to vision and miss out on God's way. In seeking to serve God, they inadvertently try to take on the responsibility of God. The truth is, God is on a mission to redeem humanity. He is the only one who knows how to do it. Leaders must understand, as Christ did, that their role is to seek the Father's will and to adjust their lives to him. (p. 70)

For Christian administrators, any vision for their personal lives, and then—by extension—their professional lives, must flow out of their relationship with God.

For Christian administrators, any vision for their personal lives, and then—by extension—their professional lives, must flow out of their relationship with God.

Research and Other Theoretical Frameworks

If it is to be assumed that the foundation for vision is formed in the spiritual realm out of the core of personal faith, how might this vision be built upon in practice and applied in such a way as to serve professional educators? What may the Christian administrator learn from the world of secular research and scholarship that might align itself with God's vision for work and ministry? The good news is that there is plenty to draw upon.

It is enticing to think that every administrator might be a Joe Clark (see *Lean on Me* [DVD], 1989), who seemed to single-handedly turn around a struggling school. Although movie heroes such as Clark may be based on actual people and events, it is more than likely that even these lone rangers needed help along the way, especially in regard to others embracing a shared vision of a changed future. It is clear from experience that a singular model of the leader-as-hero is neither ideal, nor optimal, nor sustainable for 21st-century school systems (Siccone, 2012). Kouzes and Posner (2007) wrote, "It's not just the leader's vision. It's a shared vision" (p. 105). Our country has changed over the course of the past 50 years, and our collective views of leadership rarely allow for autocratic dictators.

Whereas shared vision may be the exception rather than the rule within ecclesiastical leadership, it is becoming widely accepted within education, and—if Barna (2009) and Blackaby and Blackaby (2011) are correct—stakeholders have a right, and perhaps even a duty, to be suspicious of leaders who claim to be the singular possessor of a vision for everyone else. Is it possible that the biblical principle of humility as seen in the heart of servant leadership might compel us to seek out others as to how we might express a vision for a school? A shared vision might be exactly the type of vision to which God has called administrators to develop at their schools.

Shared vision encompasses far more than simply a vision statement (Senge, 1994). Shared vision is an expression of shared leadership, which can be defined as "a dynamic, interactive influence process among individuals in groups for which the objective is to lead one another to the achievement of group or organizational goals or both" (Pearce & Conger, 2010, p. 167). It begins "by calling people to come together to think and act, with the power they already

Shared vision encompasses far more than simply a vision statement have, about the things that are important to them" (Smith & Lucas, 2000, p. 291). Northouse (2012) described vision as a picture of a better future than the present, a change that moves the organization toward something more positive, an embracing of values that people find worthwhile or desirable, a map with directions that guide followers and affirm that they are on the right track, and a challenge to stakeholders to "transcend the status quo to do something to benefit others" (p. 113).

Ideally, a shared vision should be reached by consensus. Most people confuse making a decision by consensus with taking a democratic vote and allowing the majority to rule. Although consensus decision making is called a radical form of democracy (Mitchell, 2006), the two have very little in common. Democracy is the making of decisions by the majority, whereas consensus requires unanimity. Quaker institutions, for example, have a tradition of decision making by consensus, which is reached when everyone in the group can live with the decision without feeling compromised. A danger inherent when attempting to reach actual consensus is that goals such as "educate all children to full potential" may become bland and vacuous in an effort to appeal to and appease all stakeholders (Hargreaves, 1995).

Although not strictly the "Quaker Way," good consensus decisions mean that all participants contribute resources, accept the use of one another's resources and opinions, and view "different" as helpful rather than as a hindrance. Consensus means that everyone involved can paraphrase the issue, everyone has a chance to describe his or her feelings about the issue, those who continue to disagree indicate publically that they are willing to go along for an experimental try for a prescribed period of time, and all share in the final decision (Young, 2004, p. 93). Brave administrators will resist the temptation to abuse their power and forgo manipulation when employing this approach to developing a shared vision.

These brave leaders choose to build what are called *authentic partnerships*. Auerbach (2012) explained, "Authentic partnerships are respectful alliances that value relationship building, dialogue, and sharing power as part of socially just schools" (p. 34). The shared goals are based on mutual interests, equity, social justice, dialogue, and empowerment. The first key to building authentic partnerships is respect. Respect is built when the organization affirms the culture and views of others. It avoids what Auerbach called deficit thinking, which views poor, minority, and immigrant families as uncaring, uninvolved, and lacking strong parenting skills. According to McEwan (2003b), principals who embrace a shared vision are not ladder climbers; they want to make a difference by bringing healing to ailing schools. They work for equity and excellence. To these administrators, leadership evokes a sense of religious calling.

According to Smith and Lucas (2000), the process of developing a vision has three purposes: (1) it addresses pent-up tensions over current problems and concerns, (2) it allows people to talk about their deepest hopes and desires for their children and community, and (3) it performs the action of re-creating the school together as a group (pp. 290–291). As a part of a 9-year conversation with parents at his K–8 school, Lucas took his stakeholders through an exercise that required administrators to consider three different images of the school. It began with student interviews regarding their hopes and desires for their school. The next step involved the teachers' perceptions, and then finally the parents'. After the various perspectives were gathered and the data organized, the school held a meeting where all the views were unveiled and then compared and contrasted. The resulting discussion served as the basis for developing a shared vision in which all participants' voices were heard.

Once a shared vision is arrived at, the administrator's job has just begun. The first thing to attend to is to communicate the vision to all stakeholders (Green, 2010). Young (2004) wrote, "Effective principals articulate a clear vision about what is expected of adults and students. They do this more than once at the beginning of the year. . . . They motivate, inspire, provide direction, and celebrate excellence" (p. 33). Communicating the vision, though, is not enough; leaders must be able to accomplish the vision through hard work (McEwan, 2003b). Neuman and Simmons (2000) explained that the principal's "responsibilities are to provide direction and guidance for the implementation of that vision, to keep it constantly evident in their own words and actions, and to help the school community remain faithful to the vision in its daily practice" (p. 11). Finally, administrators must possess the resolve (strength of character in face of opposition), goals, and "lifevision" (an overall, deep commitment to ideals and values) needed to see it through to completion (McEwan, 2003b). It is the lifevision that sustains the principal during times of difficulty; it brings joy, and energizes and renews the spirit and soul (McEwan, 2003b).

The benefits of shared vision are critical to morale in that "people excel and learn, not because they are told to do so, but because they want to" (Senge, 1994, p. 9). Kouzes and Posner (2007) wrote, "When visions are shared they attract more people, sustain higher levels of motivation, and withstand more challenges than those that are singular" (p. 105). A growing body of literature clearly suggests that school leaders have a key role in developing strong and effective school climates (Devos & Bouckenooghe, 2009; Marzano, Waters, & McNulty, 2005). Devos and Bouckenooghe wrote, "Effective leaders are committed, able to motivate staff and students, and able to create and maintain conditions necessary for the building of professional learning communities within schools" (p. 177). They posited several dimensions identified as characteristics of effective and strong school climates, including goal-orientedness, which reflects the extent to which the school vision is clearly formulated and shared by the school members. Professional learning communities (PLCs) are cornerstones for building effective schools, and a shared vision is critical to their formation. "Learning community teachers and administrators enhance their effectiveness so that students benefit through five key organizational structures: supportive, shared leadership; collective creativity; shared values and vision; supportive conditions; and shared personal practice" (Doolittle, Sudeck, & Rattigan, 2008, p. 305).

A shared vision is at the heart of Sergiovanni's (1992) virtuous school, based on a community covenant. He explained that the virtuous school becomes a learning community in and of itself. The stakeholders believe that every student can learn, and they do everything in their power to see that every student does learn. The virtuous school seeks to provide for the whole student—academically, physically, and socially—and honors respect. In such an organization, parents, teachers, community, and school are partners with reciprocal and interdependent rights to participate and benefit and with obligations to support and assist.

Vision in the News

Schools in Columbus, Mississippi, worked to formulate a new vision that would guide the district into the future (Sisson, 2012a, 2012b). The Columbus district had struggled to raise student performance on state accountability tests, with the district as a whole meriting a "D" designation classification from the state. Columbus High School earned an "F" and reported low test scores as well as low graduation rates in 2010–2011. Sisson (2012b) reported that only two of the district's seven schools improved their ranking.

The process of developing a new vision for the district included a set of three strategic planning sessions at which various members of the community were encouraged to engage each other actively. Those invited included more than 60 teachers, administrators, and community leaders, including the mayor and the police chief. They met with representatives from an outside agency who were present to guide them through the process. Participants worked in small groups to discuss the core values that would inform the vision. The former state superintendent "encouraged the district to write a vision statement that is focused on results and is achievable, measurable, simple and clear" (Sisson, 2012a). The district superintendent noted that the development of the new vision "is more involved—and more inclusive—than previous efforts" (Sisson, 2012a).

Many of the teachers applauded the effort, claiming that they appreciated being part of the planning process and that the process would increase morale and build a greater sense of community. One unique aspect of the Columbus effort was its plan to hold a "gallery walk-through" (Sisson, 2012b), during which numerous rough drafts of the vision statements were posted and participants were asked to rate them on a scale of one to five.

Common Mistakes

There are several common mistakes administrators make when trying to provide leadership to their schools. The first, and perhaps most common, is simply a lack of vision. These schools may have a vision statement, a mission statement, and a statement of core values, but this does not mean that the leader has a vision—let alone a shared vision embraced by all stakeholders. Kouzes and Posner (2007) wrote,

> Call it what you will—*vision*, *purpose*, *mission*, *legacy*, *dream*, *aspiration*, *calling*, or *personal agenda*—the point is the same. If we are going to be catalytic leaders in life, we have to be able to imagine a positive future. . . . [Leaders] are able to develop an *ideal and unique image of the future for the common good.* (p. 105)

Leaders who lack a sense of vision are what may be called chameleon leaders (McEwan, 2003a): "The chameleon leader is as adaptable as a one-size-fits-all pair of socks—no definition, no limits, and no parameters. Just tell me what you want and I'll do it" (p. 68). These leaders are often ineffective and do not last long in their positions.

Another common mistake made by both leaders and followers is to think that vision is solely the responsibility of the school principal, the superintendent, or the school board. There are still some who advocate for a top-down approach. Collins (2001) posited that his effective Level 4 leader "catalyzes commitment to and vigorous pursuit of a clear and compelling vision, stimulating higher performance standards" (p. 20), and the Level 5 leader "builds enduring greatness through a paradoxical blend of personal humility and professional will" (p. 20). According to Collins, the Level 4 leader first establishes the vision (the what) and then enlists others (the who), and the Level 5 leader enlists the right people (the who) and then determines where to go (the what). "But visions based on authority are not sustainable" (Smith et al., 2000, p. 72)—eventually, stakeholders may grow weary of following a vision perceived as being imposed on them. Most followers innately desire to hear how their hopes and dreams will be fulfilled. "They want to see themselves in the picture of the future that the leader is painting. The very best leaders understand that their key task is inspiring a *shared* vision, not selling their own idiosyncratic view of the world" (Kouzes & Posner, 2007, p. 117).

Other leaders confuse mission with vision by failing to align the two. McEwan (2003a) defined vision as "a driving force reflecting the instructional leaders' image of the future, based on their values, beliefs and experiences" (p. 67), whereas "mission, on the other hand, is the direction that emerges from the vision and guides the day-to-day behavior of the organization" (p. 67). Administrators who fall into this trap make the mistake of failing to link their day-to-day decisions, processes, procedures, and policies (mission) with the end in mind (vision). Virtually every aspect of the school may be scrutinized in light of the vision. The question needs to be asked on a regular basis, "How does this decision guide us towards the school's vision?"

Dreamers and idealists tend to cast visions that are disconnected from reality. These detached visions eventually lead to cynicism, frustration, and discouragement among stakeholders. Government bureaucrats tend to be good at this. Consider Goals 2000, for instance. Many younger educators may not even remember or know about the Goals 2000: Educate America Act (P.L. 103-227) and how it served as a predecessor to No Child Left Behind. In 1994, President Clinton signed the act into law, and among the goals to be achieved in 6 short years were (1) all children in America will start school ready to learn, (2) high school graduation rates will reach 90%, (3) U.S. students will be first in the world in mathematics and science achievement, and (4) every school in the United States will be free of drugs, violence, and the unauthorized presence of firearms and alcohol

and will offer a disciplined environment conducive to learning. Although all of these are laudable goals and every educator would desire to see the nation's schools achieve them, few people were foolish enough to embrace a vision they knew would never be realized.

A mistake common to novice administrators is misreading their new school's culture and misinterpreting the school's ability to embrace change (Green, 2010). When dramatic change is needed and stakeholders resist, leaders may need to exercise singular power to bring about needed change (Yukl, 2010, p. 168). Even Sergiovanni (1992), author of *Moral Leadership*, recognized that there are occasions in which creating a shared vision is impractical and the leader needs to "define the needs of those to be served" when "students, parents, and teachers are not ready or able to define their own needs" (p. 125). Ideally, the principal would eventually work with other stakeholders to forge a new culture in which everyone would see the value of shared leadership and embrace their mutual responsibility to the community and, ultimately, to the children.

Maxwell (1993) explained that the failure of vision is usually predicated upon human shortcomings, what he called "people problems" (p. 150). He identified types of people who might stand in the way of the vision of an organization. Among them are the following:

- *Limited Leaders:* either lack vision or lack the ability to communicate it to others.
- *Concrete Thinkers:* "doers" who can only see what is, not what could be.
- *Dogmatic Talkers:* stakeholders who cannot move beyond their own narrow beliefs.
- *Continual Losers:* those who perhaps once attempted something, but failed and then allowed their fear of failure to keep them from ever trying again.
- *Satisfied Sitters:* reside in the comfort of security, but as Maxwell noted, with comfort comes complacency.
- *Problem Perceivers:* "see a problem in every solution" (p. 153). Self-seekers will undermine the vision when it serves their own self-interest.

EXEMPLARY VISION STATEMENTS

Following is a variety of sample vision statements that attempt to capture the spirit of the different types of schools they might represent. They exemplify the ideal that every school is different; therefore, every vision for each individual school should be unique. A properly written vision statement should assist the reader in imagining what the school would look like, what its halls would sound like, and how teachers and students would interact across the campus.

Horace Mann Elementary School

Our vision for Horace Mann Elementary School is to create an encouraging environment where students are inspired to reach their academic potential. Our aim is to foster a collaborative effort among parents, faculty, staff, students, and the community. Through cooperation with all our stakeholders, we will work to ensure that children receive an appropriate education that meets their needs. We will do this by providing them with a differentiated curriculum aligned with their unique learning styles. Our ultimate goal is to help them become self-directed, lifelong learners.

West Side High School

West Side High School will provide an education that will afford an optimistic future for its students. It will be a school where students are motivated to learn with the assistance of exceptional instruction and innovative technology. Students will graduate with the knowledge, skills, and dispositions to succeed in an increasingly technological world. West Side will collaborate with the community to prepare knowledgeable citizens for the future. As students contribute to their own well-being and to that of the community, society will become a better place for all.

Epic Charter School

Epic Charter School is a primary-grade school (K–3) that strives for every child to develop an awareness of their own individuality, recognizing their own strengths and weaknesses. Epic ensures that students develop their full potential in an environment where they enjoy learning and build strong self-esteem. Their interests and needs drive the curriculum as instructors capitalize on student strengths while they help them remediate their weaknesses. We educate the whole child—socially, emotionally, physically, and academically.

Evangelical Christian School

Evangelical Christian School (CCS) is committed to fulfilling the Great Commission by educating students to become disciples of Jesus Christ. Our goal is to provide an excellent education based upon a Christian worldview, enabling students to reach their full potential in all aspects of life: spiritually, academically, physically, and socially. Our approach to education is both biblical and relational, seeking to partner with parents in the education of their children.

Best Practices

Creating a shared vision is a difficult, complex, time-consuming, and stressful task (Casey, 2005; Leech & Fulton, 2008). It can take many paths, and much has been written to guide administrators down these paths. For instance, Kouzes and Posner (2007) recommended that leaders listen deeply to others, determine what is meaningful to others, make it a cause for commitment, and be forward looking in times of rapid change (pp. 118–124). Yukl (2010) noted, "Before people will support radical change, they need to have a vision of a better future that is attractive enough to justify the sacrifices and hardships the change will require" (pp. 309–310). Kouzes and Posner also suggested a strategy for enlisting the support of others: "appeal to common ideals, connect to what is meaningful to others, take pride in what makes the organization unique, and align your dream with the dreams of others" (pp. 133–137). Agee (2011) added that effective visionary leaders are teachers, listen to others, and work to understand their perspectives, but, most important, love the people and the organizations they serve.

Green (2010) suggested three steps to take when creating a shared vision. Administrators should begin by deepening their understanding of the school organization and by establishing positive interpersonal relationships with stakeholders. Next, school leaders must understand the process of school improvement and effectively explain the process to various stakeholders. Finally, they must be able to communicate the need for change to faculty and staff. The dialogue can begin with questions such as the following:

- What are our core beliefs, values, and goals?
- What do we want the school to look like in 5 years?
- What are our strengths and areas needing improvement?
- What changes need to occur in order for us to meet the needs of all the students we serve?

Yukl (2010) added a few more nuanced steps when he recommended that leaders involve important stakeholders, pinpoint strategic objectives with broad appeal, identify still-applicable elements from the old ideology, connect the vision to core competencies, gauge the credibility of the vision, and regularly assess and refine the vision (p. 313).

It is important to remember that creating a shared vision is not a one-shot deal. "School leaders should implement a plan for the continuous communication of the vision so that it gains power and does not lose its momentum over time" (Green, 2010, p. 179). McEwan (2003a) suggested starting by communicating the vision to teachers: "Your job as an instructional leader is continually explain, teach, share, demonstrate, model, facilitate, persuade, and cajole" (pp. 68–69). Specific steps might include keeping an open-door policy, maintaining a visible presence, and constantly engaging in dialogue. This communication must extend to students as well. McEwan

It is important to remember that creating a shared vision is not a one-shot deal.

posited that effective school administrators "can be seen wherever students are congregated: playgrounds, athletic events, concerts and plays, bus stops, cafeterias, and hallways" (p. 72). Diligent administrators will maximize the value of school assemblies, written communication, informal conversations, school newspapers, and student councils. Finally, parents often feel like the neglected partner in their children's education, and school leaders must do more to reach out to them. School leaders can communicate the vision to parents through weekly or monthly newsletters that focus on student learning and encourage parental support in informal gatherings where parents are invited to meet with the administrative team to discuss vision, websites, and back-to-school nights (McEwan, 2003a). Even informal home visits might be appropriate in some cases.

POLICY IMPLICATIONS

Policy implications for individual schools and systems are readily apparent based on the material within this chapter. One of the most obvious implications is that school boards need to reflect on the current cultures of leadership embodied in their schools. If their schools are being led by autocratic leaders who are imposing their own visions on a powerless constituency, it is their responsibility to work to change the culture. Because the local board in many school systems exercises final authority over matters such as vision development, they should take the lead in creating a culture wherein all stakeholders are invited to participate and have their voices heard.

A more practical policy implication is the need for school leaders to be trained as to how they can effectively build a culture in which a shared vision is the norm. After school leaders are adequately trained, they need to be assessed regarding their effectiveness in developing a shared vision and—if one is already in place—their effectiveness in carrying out that vision through administrative duties. Too often, administrator evaluations are cursory in nature or even completely neglected. This benign neglect is often the case when schools are perceived as functioning efficiently. For such a school, it is only when it is in crisis or a problem arises that the principal receives a thorough evaluation. A careful examination of a principal's leadership regarding shared vision must include a 360-degree assessment from a variety of constituents, including—when appropriate—teachers, staff, parents, and students.

CONCLUSION

If you are reading this book, it is likely that you have sensed God's call to the field of education and specifically to school administration. It is also likely that this is not a passing occupational fad but you but a career to which you may dedicate the majority of your working years. This is not just another job to pass the time until something else comes along; this is something about which you care deeply. Your responsibility is to match your passion with a vision that will help sustain you when difficult times come, and—be assured—if they have not already come, they will. Kouzes and Posner (2007) captured it this way:

> In the final analysis, what you envision for the future is really all about expressing your passion. It's all about what gets you up in the morning and won't let you sleep at night. It's all about something that you find so important that you're willing to put in the time, suffer the inevitable setbacks, and make the necessary sacrifices. (p. 113)

Discussion Questions

1. How would you describe your vision for your personal life?

2. How does your "lifevision" inform your professional life?

3. What Scriptures help shape your vision for life and work?

4. Maxwell (1993) defined leadership simply as "influence." How do you define leadership?

5. How would you describe the pros and cons of shared leadership?

6. How well does your school incorporate various stakeholders in the development of the school's vision?

7. What mistakes have you seen leaders make when crafting a shared vision?

Activities

Activity 1: Create a Shared Vision in a Picture

Purpose: This exercise guides a group through the process of creating a shared vision using images and pictures rather than words. The drawing of a picture keeps people from writing down clichés or abstractions that have little personal meaning or fail to inspire them.

Step 1. *Create a picture of a desired future state for your school.* Divide the participants into small groups of four to six people. Ask everyone to dream about the future of his or her group or organization. Have each participant make a quick sketch of an image that comes to mind.

Step 2. *Share drawings with other group members.* Ask the participants to show and explain their images to the others in their group.

Step 3. *Prepare one drawing per group.* Ask each group to prepare one large drawing that captures the collective dream of the members in their group.

Step 4. *Present small-group drawings.* Ask each group to present its large drawing to the other groups. While the small groups present their drawings, summarize the elements and concepts that the drawings portray on a separate board or wall chart.

Step 5. *Review the elements and concepts represented in the drawings.* When all the groups have completed their presentations, review the elements and concepts that you recorded.

Activity 2: Marriage of Ideas

Purpose: This exercise can be used to guide a very large group through the process of creating a shared vision.

Step 1. *Imagine the future.* Ask each participant to envision a preferred future for the school by identifying two or three aspects of the school that can be improved and recording them as sentences or phrases.

Step 2. *Share each vision.* Participants will form pairs and share their visions with the other person. Together, they will discuss each of their conceptions and attempt to reach consensus ("marriage of ideas") on two or three aspects on which they can agree. This step will be repeated in groups of four and then groups of eight. It can be repeated as many times as is necessary until there are two groups remaining that report to each other.

Step 3. *Record key elements of the vision statements from the two groups.* Ask each group to record the key elements or phrases of its vision statement.

Step 4. *Organize elements and key phrases into categories.* Representatives from each group match similar and then compatible aspects of each group's vision statement until consensus can be reached.

Step 5. *Draft a shared vision statement.* Have a small team synthesize the messages that pertain to each aspect and write a statement that reflects the shared vision.

Step 6. *Present the draft shared vision statement for comment and discussion.*

CASE STUDIES

Case 1: Going Nowhere Fast

In recent years, Lincoln High School and its surrounding community have fallen on hard times. With the downturn in the economy and subsequent layoffs and falling property taxes, the urban-fringe community of Lincoln Heights has resisted raising local taxes or passing bond measures to raise funds to make much-needed repairs to the high school. Along with problems of an aging physical plant, Lincoln has failed to close the gaps between the academic success rates for those who are identified as economically disadvantaged or minority and their more affluent white classmates. To top it off, there has been a revolving door in the principal's office, with three new administrators coming and going in the span of just 4 years. Each administrator publically expressed frustration with the district office and school board. An exasperated superintendent and school board realize the school is headed in the wrong direction and that fundamental changes need to be made but cannot agree on how to move forward. At recent board meetings, a vocal group of affluent parents called for the board to hire the head football coach, whom they perceive as a strong, charismatic leader who could lead the school in its return to its former glory of years past, as the new principal. They want the principal to be empowered to make any and all changes he feels are needed. Another equally vocal group of parents, largely comprised of poor, working-class households, advocates for someone outside the district who will bring a new perspective and fresh ideas. If you were hired as a consultant to this district, how would you advise the parties to proceed?

Case 2: Trouble in Paradise

Paradise Christian Academy (PCA) is a growing PS2–8 Christian school affiliated with a large nondenominational church located in the suburbs. The school only admits students from families where at least one parent or guardian professes a relationship with Christ and regularly attends church, but the church is a "seeker-sensitive" church with active outreach programs to non-Christians. For the first 20 years of its existence, PCA was led by its founding principal, Mrs. Thomas, and a volunteer parent advisory board. Historically, the church allowed the school to operate largely independent of any oversight by the pastor or the board of elders. The recent growth in enrollment has led some parents to accuse the school of losing it sense of identity as an "extended family." These same parents are also concerned that the school's focus on student spiritual growth is being watered down as new families enroll who are pushing for higher academic standards and more extracurricular activities. At the fall back-to-school program, Mrs. Thomas announced her plans to retire at the end of the school year. Over the summer, the church pastor had stated publically that he planned to become more involved in the leadership and operation of the school and that he wanted to open enrollment to non-Christian families to bring the school into alignment with the vision of the church. The parent advisory board is disappointed in the pastor's announcement and is concerned that they will be excluded from expressing a voice in the school's future. Some of the parents vented their frustrations and are threatening to withdraw their students. If you were a church elder, how would you advise the pastor to proceed?

REFERENCES

Agee, B. R. (2011). Leadership, vision, and strategic planning. In D. S. Dockery (Ed.), *Christian leadership essentials: A handbook for managing Christian organizations* (pp. 46–64). Nashville, TN: B & H Publishing Group.

Auerbach, S. (2012). Conceptualizing leadership for authentic partnerships: A continuum to inspire practice. In S. Auerbach (Ed.), *School leadership for authentic family and community partnerships: Research perspectives for transforming practice* (pp. 29–51). New York, NY: Routledge.

Barker, J. A. (n.d.). Motivating quotes. Retrieved from http://www.motivatingquotes.com/dreams.htm

Barna, G. (2009). *The power of vision* (updated and revised ed.). Ventura, CA: Regal Books.

Barna Group. (n.d.). About Barna Group. Retrieved from http://www.barna.org/about

Berliner, D. C., & Biddle, B. J. (1995). *The manufactured crisis: Myths, fraud, and the attack on America's public schools*. New York, NY: Perseus Books.

Bernhardt, V. L. (2004). Continuous improvement: It takes more than test scores. *Leadership, 34*(2), 16–19.

Blackaby, H., & Blackaby, R. (2011). *Spiritual leadership: Moving people on to God's agenda*. Nashville, TN: B&H Publishing Group.

Boa, K. (2012). Communicating vision. Retrieved from http://bible.org/seriespage/communicating-vision

Casey, J. M. (2005). Practitioner's guide to creating a shared vision. *Leadership, 35*(1), 26–29.

Collins, J. (2001). *Good to great: Why some companies make the leap... and others don't*. New York, NY: HarperCollins.

Collins, J. C., & Porras, J. I. (1994). *Built to last: Successful habits of visionary companies*. London, UK: Century.

Devos, G., & Bouckenooghe, D. (2009). An exploratory study on principals' conceptions about their role as school leaders. *Leadership and Policy in Schools, 8*(2), 173–196.

Doolittle, G., Sudeck, M., & Rattigan, P. (2008). Creating professional learning communities: The work of professional development schools. *Theory Into Practice, 47*(4), 303–310.

Follett, M. P. (1924). *Creative experience*. New York, NY: Longmans Green.

Goals 2000: Educate America Act (P.L. 103-227). Retrieved from http://www.ncrel.org/sdrs/areas/issues/envrnmnt/stw/sw0goals.htm

Green, R. L. (2010). *The four dimensions of principal leadership: A framework for leading 21st-century schools*. Boston, MA: Allyn & Bacon.

Hallinger, P., & Heck, R. (2002). What do you call people with visions? The role of visions, mission and goals in school leadership and improvement. In K. Leithwood, P. Hallinger, & Colleagues (Eds.), *The handbook of educational leadership and administration* (pp. 9–40). Dordrecht, Netherlands: Kluwer.

Hargreaves, A. (1995). Renewal in the age of paradox. *Educational Leadership, 52*(7), 14–19.

Kantabutra, S. (2010). What do we know about vision. In G. R. Hickman (Ed.), *Leading organizations: Perspectives for a new era* (2nd ed., pp. 258–269). Thousand Oaks, CA: Sage.

Kohn, A. (2011). *Feel-bad education and other contrarian essays on children and schooling*. Boston, MA: Beacon Press.

Kozol, J. (2005). *The shame of the nation: The restoration of apartheid schooling in America*. New York, NY: Crown Publishing Group.

Kouzes, J. M., & Posner, B. Z. (2007). *The leadership challenge* (4th ed.). San Francisco, CA: Jossey-Bass.

Leech, D., & Fulton, C. R. (2008). Faculty perceptions of shared decision making and the principal's leadership behaviors in secondary schools in a large urban district. *Education, 128*(4), 630–644.

Malone, T. (n.d.). Where there is no vision the people perish. Retrieved from http://www.fbbc.com/messages/sermon_no_vision.htm

Marshall, S. P. (2006). *The power to transform: Leadership that brings learning and schooling to life*. San Francisco, CA: Jossey-Bass.

Marzano, R. J., Waters, T., & McNulty, B. A. (2005). *School leadership that works: From research to results*. Alexandria, VA: Association for Supervision and Curriculum Development.

Maxwell, J. C. (1993). *Developing the leader within you*. Nashville, TN: Thomas Nelson Publishers.

McEwan, E. K. (2003a). *Seven steps to effective instructional leadership* (2nd ed.). Thousand Oaks, CA: Corwin Press.

McEwan, E. K. (2003b). *Ten traits of highly effective principals: From good to great performance*. Thousand Oaks, CA: Corwin Press.

Mitchell, E. (2006). Participation in unanimous decision-making: The New England Monthly Meetings of Friends. Retrieved from http://www.philica.com/display_article.php?article_id=14

Neuman, M., & Simmons, W. (2000). Leadership for student learning. *Phi Delta Kappan, 82*(1), 9–12.

No Child Left Behind Act of 2001, Pub. L. No. 107-110, § 115, Stat. 1425 (2002).

Northouse, P. G. (2012). *Introduction to leadership: concepts and practice*. Thousand Oaks, CA: Sage.

Pearce, C. L., & Conger, J. A. (2010). All those years ago. The historical underpinnings of shared leadership. In G. R. Hickman (Ed.) *Leading organizations: Perspectives for a new era* (2nd ed., pp. 167–180). Thousand Oaks, CA: Sage.

Ravitch, D. (2010). *The death and life of the great American school system: How testing and choice are undermining education* (revised and expanded). New York, NY: Basic Books.

Schlechty, P. C. (2009). *Leading for learning: How to transform schools into learning organizations*. San Francisco, CA: Jossey-Bass.

Senge, P. (1994). *The fifth discipline: The art and practice of the learning organization*. New York, NY: Doubleday.

Sergiovanni, T. J. (1992). *Moral leadership: Getting to the heart of school improvement*. San Francisco, CA: Jossey-Bass.

Siccone, F. (2012). *Essential skills for effective school leadership*. New York, NY: Pearson.

Sisson, C. K. (2012a, August 25). Columbus schools begin work on "new vision." *The Dispatch* [online]. Retrieved from http://www.cdispatch.com/news/article.asp?aid=18502

Sisson, C. K. (2012b, September 29). Columbus schools craft vision statements. *The Dispatch* [online]. Retrieved from http://www.cdispatch.com/news/article.asp?aid=19280

Smith, B., & Lucas, T. (2000). A shared vision for schools. In P. Senge, N. Cambron-McCabe, T. Lucas, B. Smith, J. Dutton, & A. Kleiner (Eds.), *Schools that learn: A fifth discipline fieldbook for educators, parents, and everyone who cares about education* (pp. 289–303). New York, NY: Doubleday.

Smith, B., Kleiner, A., Senge, P., Lucas, T., Cambron-McCabe, N., & Dutton, J. (2000). A primer to the five disciplines. In P. Senge, N. Cambron-McCabe, T. Lucas, B. Smith, J. Dutton, & A. Kleiner (Eds.), *Schools that learn: A fifth discipline fieldbook for educators, parents, and everyone who cares about education* (pp. 59–100). New York, NY: Doubleday.

Warren, R. (2002). *The purpose driven life: What on earth am I here for?* Grand Rapids, MI: Zondervan.

Young, P. G. (2004). *You have to go to school—you're the principal!: 101 tips to make it better for your students, your staff, and yourself*. Thousand Oaks, CA: Sage.

Yukl, G. (2010). *Leadership in organizations* (7th ed.). Upper Saddle River, NJ: Pearson.

Chapter 2

Continuous School Improvement

Samuel J. Smith

Suppose one of you wants to build a tower.
Won't you first sit down and estimate the cost to see if you have enough money to complete it?
For if you lay the foundation and are not able to finish it, everyone who sees it will ridicule you,
saying, "This person began to build and wasn't able to finish."
—Jesus Christ (Luke 14:28–30, New International Version)—

OVERVIEW

Building upon the previous chapter's discussion of the importance of a shared vision, this chapter will address the fleshing out of that vision through a cycle of school improvement. It will explain how the school's vision statement—if current, relevant, and understood by stakeholders—is central to all school-improvement initiatives. This chapter will present theories and practical models for data-driven decision making and will outline recommended steps for setting realistic goals, implementing those goals, and assessing the degree to which they have been met.

Objectives

By the end of this chapter, the reader should be able to do the following:

1. Collect and use data to identify goals, assess organizational effectiveness, and promote organizational learning.
2. Develop and implement improvement plan to achieve goals.
3. Promote a climate of continuous improvement.
4. Monitor and evaluate progress and revise plans.

INTRODUCTION

Whether to meet identified benchmarks, to satisfy accreditation standards, or to improve community perceptions of a particular academic institution, administrators often find themselves entangled in the process of school improvement. The stakes can be high. For public schools, punitive accountability measures may result in the loss of federal funds if requirements remain unmet. For private schools, poor performance can turn into a public relations nightmare when word among tuition-paying parents spreads to the community that graduates of College Prep Academy are not as prepared for college as the school had advertised they would be. Stakes can be so high in poorly performing public schools that failure to bring about satisfactory school improvement may result in a turnaround, restart, closure, or transformation—all of which require the replacement of the principal.

Not all school improvements carry such weight. Many are simple incremental changes involving unilateral decisions. These occur frequently and become part of a principal's decision-making routine. More complex changes require the involvement of a leadership team and possibly faculty members and parents in a more systematic shared decision-making model. The higher the stakes and the closer the decision gets to mission-specific issues, the more important it is for administrators to follow a systematic model for school improvement.

BACKGROUND

Historical Background

As long as there have been differing ideas about the purposes and outcomes of education, there have been efforts to change the way in which education has been delivered and the impact it has had on individual students and on society. Until the rise and spread of the American common school movement of the 19th century, however, discussions of school improvement were primarily philosophical arguments by the likes of Plato and Aristotle in ancient Greece, Augustine and Aquinas in the Middle Ages, and Locke and Rousseau during the Enlightenment. Reformation leader Martin Luther proposed a specific plan for common schools in Germany, introducing radical innovations for his day, such as educating the poor, instructing girls, and teaching in the vernacular language instead of in Latin. Luther's ideas, like those of Rousseau and others, found their way into educational practice and policy.

Individual experiments also spawned various types of schools throughout history, many as religious training institutions and others as new models for teaching children—each with its own perspective on how best to educate. One example of an early school reformer was the Swiss educator Johann Pestalozzi, who is credited with improving teacher training and introducing a systematic instructional method implementing the object lesson. Unfortunately, Pestalozzi's poor administrative skills led to the eventual closing of every school he established. Although considered a failure by many of his contemporaries, his proposals impacted schools throughout Europe and the United States through the teachers he had trained and international visitors to his schools (Smith, 2010).

Although various types of reform efforts in the United States brought about tax-funded public schools, multitudinous private schools, and curricular changes within these schools, systematic improvement efforts did not become widely practiced until after the 1957 launch of Soviet satellite *Sputnik*. The concern became not only that the United States might be losing the space race, but also that it might be losing the "brain race" (Urban & Wagoner, 2004). A major reaction to this concern was for President Eisenhower to sign into law the 1958 National Defense Education Act, which provided unprecedented amounts of federal funds for math and science instruction. In the early 1980s, the nation found itself once again concerned about its academic standing among other nations when Japan, Germany, South Korea, and other nations began to surpass the United States in technological advances, automobile production, and academic achievement tests. These circumstances led to what Hoy and Miskel (2013) referred to as four waves of educational reform.

The first wave began when President Reagan appointed the 1983 National Commission on Excellence in Education, whose report *A Nation at Risk* called for states to make drastic reforms in areas such as graduation requirements and length of instructional time. The second wave occurred in the late 1980s when the White House, under President George H. W. Bush's administration, collaborated for the first time ever with the National Governors Association to agree on a set of performance goals. These were later signed into law as the Goals 2000: Educate America Act (1994) by President Clinton, who as governor of Arkansas had been one of the prominent members of the National Governors Association to develop the following eight goals to be accomplished by the year 2000:

© marekuliasz/Shutterstock.com

GOAL 1: All children in America will start school ready to learn.

GOAL 2: The high school graduation rate will increase to at least 90%.

GOAL 3: All students will leave grades 4, 8, and 12 having demonstrated competency over challenging subject matter, including English, mathematics, science, foreign languages, civics and government, economics, the arts, history, and geography, and every school in America will ensure that all students learn to use their minds well, so they may be prepared for responsible citizenship, further learning, and productive employment in our nation's modern economy.

GOAL 4: The United States students will be first in the world in mathematics and science achievement.

GOAL 5: Every adult American will be literate and will possess the knowledge and skills necessary to compete in a global economy and exercise the rights and responsibilities of citizenship.

GOAL 6: Every school in the United States will be free of drugs, violence, and the unauthorized presence of firearms and alcohol and will offer a disciplined environment conducive to learning.

GOAL 7: The nation's teaching force will have access to programs for the continued improvement of their professional skills and the opportunity to acquire the knowledge and skills needed to instruct and prepare all American students for the next century.

GOAL 8: Every school will promote partnerships that will increase parental involvement and participation in promoting the social, emotional, and academic growth of children.

Although incorporating elements of previous reform efforts, the third wave of the 1990s was the most systemic. It focused heavily on comprehensive change throughout school systems and on integration of policy around clear outcomes. The fourth wave is represented by the 2001 No Child Left Behind's emphasis on accountability, excellence, and continuous improvement and the 2009 Race to the Top's focus on competition among the states and rewards for progress and innovation. The reauthorization of Lyndon B. Johnson's 1965 Elementary and Secondary Education Act (ESEA) continued in 2015 as the Every Student Succeeds Act (ESSA) was passed. This law took effect in 2017-2018 and will remain in place until the next reauthorization of ESEA, or a new law is established (Zinskie & Rea, 2016). These waves of reform have required school administrators to implement various types of change, heightening the awareness of the need to acquire effective skills to lead the change process.

THEORETICAL PERSPECTIVES: LEADERSHIP AND CHANGE

Leading Change Through Relational Trust

John Maxwell (2007) is known for popularizing the notion that leadership is influence—nothing more, nothing less. If this can be assumed to be true, what, then, causes one to have sufficient influence on others to lead them through personal or organizational change? Relational trust is a critical component. Christophersen, Elstad, and Turmo (2012) found that "the potential for quality improvement in schools can best be realized by focusing on strengthening human relationships" (p. 12). Change can be intimidating, especially for veteran teachers whose paradigms and practices have been solidified through years of experience. Others—especially novice teachers or those lacking self-efficacy in their own performance—may question the motives of an administrator who introduces an instructional initiative requiring significant change. Their sense of inadequacy may cause them to feel threatened, possibly to the point of fearing that their employment may be in jeopardy.

In order for meaningful change to occur and to be sustained, relational trust is vital. Hoy and Miskel (2013) define relational trust as "a general sense of confidence and dependence among students, teachers, and parents based on social respect, personal regard, role competence, and personal integrity" (p. 314). If a campus climate is devoid of relational trust or if that trust has recently been violated, it will not easily or quickly be cultivated again. The administrator's reputation for productive longevity, professional leadership, organizational management, and personal relationships will serve as brick and mortar to rebuild a climate of trust. It is only in such a climate that genuine change can flourish.

In order for meaningful change to occur and to be sustained, relational trust is vital.

When educational change fails, it is usually because of ineffective leadership. There certainly may be other reasons for the failure, such as incorrect assumptions on which an initiative is based, a misinterpretation of best-practices research, or a flawed implementation plan. Overwhelmingly, however, failure can be attributed to lack of leadership. Gorton and Alston (2009) provide the following list of roles that building-level principals assume who have successfully led their schools through change:

- Believer: is committed to the project.
- Advocate: promotes and defends the project.
- Linker: connects project to other parts of the system.
- Resource Acquirer: allocates tangible and intangible resources.
- Employer: hires and assigns project staff appropriately.
- Leader: supplies initiative, energy, and direction.
- Manager: provides problem-solving assistance and support.
- Delegator: lets others lead as appropriate.
- Supporter: encourages others through the change process.
- Information Source: provides frequent feedback regarding the progress of the change.

When administrators assume these roles, they increase the probability that change will be embraced, implemented, and sustained by stakeholders.

Resistance to Change

Despite a leader's best efforts to cultivate an environment that fosters change, there will always be some degree of resistance. The more significant the instructional change, the more disequilibrium faculty members may experience, which could be complicated by a sense of inadequacy to implement the change or a negative attitude about the new program itself (Green, 2005). Other factors that may potentially bring resistance to change include the following (Lunenburg & Ornstein, 2004):

- Interference with faculty's economic, social, or esteem needs
- Fear of the unknown

- Threat to existing power or influence
- Knowledge or skill obsolescence
- Limited resources

Gorton and Alston (2009) identify seven types of resisters that administrators may face as they attempt to implement change:

- Positive Resisters: convey verbal agreement with the change but take no action to implement it.
- Unique Resisters: believe that the change will be good for others but is unnecessary for themselves.
- Let-Me-Be-Last Resisters: hope the pilot will fail or that the idea will die out before it reaches them.
- Need-More-Time Resisters: verbally support the change but insist that the timing is premature.
- States' Rights Resisters: claim that their resistance is only because local programs would be better than federal ones.
- Cost-Justifying Resisters: stand on the grounds of fiscal responsibility.
- Incremental Change Resisters: insist that the new must not differ much from the existing program and are the most difficult to win over.

Granted, resistance can be healthy, serving as a guard against misdirected change or groupthink. It can also provide accountability to renegade administrators who may lack the experience, training, or maturity to navigate change and to do so at the appropriate time. With this in mind, leaders would be wise to seek counsel before dismissing all types of resistance.

If after prayerful deliberation an administrative team decides that reducing resistance to change is in the school's best interest, there are several approaches to consider. Strategies not recommended involve punitive measures, the ostracizing of resisters, and demeaning those who object. Bullying—commonly observed on the elementary playground—has unfortunately been all too often the method of choice by many a zealous administrator intent on changing the minds of those who would obstruct progress. Less manipulative and much more dignifying strategies are recommended by Lunenburg and Ornstein (2004): participation, communication, support, and rewards. Encouraging resisters to participate in the planning, design, and implementation of the proposed change may offer them a sense of ownership and empowerment. Instead of feeling that the change is something being done to them, they may become invested to the point that they seek to help bring the project to fruition. Communication, both listening to constituents and providing them with data, has shown to be an extremely effective tool in the reduction of resistance. In order to maximize the value of communication, it is important that it be distributed over time and via a variety of media. To expect that information will be communicated one day and that resistance will end the next is exceedingly naïve. It may take not only time but also repeated iterations of the message through research reports, student and faculty testimonials, and best-practice demonstrations before resistance is reduced. Ironically, the very information intended to provide support may be perceived by faculty as just another directive or as administrative propaganda. Faculty will feel sincerely supported to implement change only after they are trained in the required skills, provided the necessary

"What if we don't change at all ... and something magical just happens?"

Communication, both listening to constituents and providing them with data, has shown to be an extremely effective tool in the reduction of resistance.

materials, and positively encouraged throughout the process. Rewards, as well, assist in reducing resistance. When possible, rewards should be tangible, such as salary increases, bonuses, and paid time off. Nontangible rewards, such as recognition and praise, can also be effective.

There are instances when resistance exists but for none of the aforementioned reasons. It may simply be that the timing is not right. All other factors may seem to be ideal, and the initiative may appear to be the perfect solution for the perceived need. Stakeholders may overwhelmingly support administration in the effort, and an abundance of resources may exist to fund the project. Nevertheless, the project could fail because of inopportune timing. Leadership teams must be aware of stressors or other unusual circumstances that could divert attention, efforts, or resources needed for the proposed change. Some examples of stressors may be other special events that are being promoted at the same time, deadlines due at the time of the proposed kickoff event, or emotional strain from tragic events, such as the death of a student or teacher.

Waiting for perfect timing, however, can itself become a detractor to implementing change. To avoid this, Guthrie and Schuermann (2010) recommend the adoption of a cycle of strategic planning. Change then becomes so routine in the campus culture that less effort is exhausted on navigating resistance. Staff will attain a comfort level with the familiar cycle of collecting and evaluating data, identifying needs, developing implementation plans, and revising those plans as they are assessed. Traditional planning cycles have involved setting goals for 3 to 5 years in the future, each year revising the plan and adding another year. That cycle has become less common in recent years because of volatility in the economy, rapid technological advances, and anticipated legislative changes regarding standards and accountability. Nevertheless, a cycle of planning—even if only on an annual basis—can reduce the "bad timing" factor and can embed improvement into the culture.

Shared Decision Making

Teachers understand that for efficiency's sake, unilateral decisions are necessary. Because they make these types of decisions in their classrooms on a regular basis, they accept that administrators will periodically make routine unilateral decisions as well. Such decisions are manifested as instructions, purposes, and parameters for conducting routine duties. Green (2005) distinguishes these types of decisions as "autocratic" and acknowledges that any healthy organization will be led by an individual who is trusted to make autocratic decisions—either because the decisions are routine or because they are so urgent that time does not permit for the participation of others in the decision-making process. The more significant and lasting the impact of a decision is anticipated to be, the more vital it is that others participate in its development.

Although systemic change requires a highly motivated and goal-oriented leader, that leader cannot continue to make singlehanded decisions and expect meaningful change. Alternatives to the autocratic model include site-based management, participatory governance, and shared decision making. Implementing one of these participatory models of decision making increases teacher morale, enthusiasm, and ownership of proposed changes (Hoy & Miskel, 2013). Therefore, administrators should consider organizational structures to ensure that shared decision making is not left to chance but is intentional. One such structure might be a school improvement committee, as recommended by Gorton and Alston (2009) and Guthrie and Schuermann (2010). Membership on the committee should include all top-level policymakers, leaders, and managers and a representative sample of faculty, parents, and other stakeholders. For nonleaders, membership should be voluntary to ensure that only those who sincerely desire to participate are involved.

It is important for the committee to be supported by the rest of the school and not to be perceived as an out-of-touch, behind-the-scenes, exclusive group. To avoid this, meetings should be open to observers and frequent communication should be made available via newsletters, announcements, websites, and emails. Also, stakeholders who are not members of the committee should be surveyed periodically for their input through questionnaires, interviews, and focus groups. They need to be assured that they are supplying meaningful information that the committee will seriously consider in the planning process.

One caution about school improvement committees—especially if the same members remain for a period of time and they develop a high degree of cohesiveness—is that they can become tools for groupthink, rubber-stamp committees, or groups of "yes" people for charismatic leaders. If a committee is allowed to develop into this type of group, it becomes highly probable that the group will begin to make frequent defective decisions. In order to appear efficient to outsiders or to please the leader, members may become less critical of data and may even become careless about evaluating information sources (Hoy & Miskel, 2013). Ironically, a structure intended to create a culture of open-mindedness may result in closed-mindedness and uniformity of thought.

Classifications of Change

Green (2005) classifies change into two categories: first-order change and second-order change. First-order change is continuous, requiring only small modifications that leave the system stable and undisrupted. It improves the efficiency and effectiveness of programs without drastically transforming the behavior of teachers or students. These first-order changes may not require the involvement of a school improvement committee. Conversely, second-order change is discontinuous. Because second-order changes disrupt the system's equilibrium, requiring individuals to perform in fundamentally different ways, a shared decision-making process should be employed. Leaders must determine whether a change is of the first or second order before taking action. Doing so assists leaders in knowing the degree to which stakeholders might be prepared for the change and what groundwork is essential before implementing the change.

Biblical Perspectives

Moses, Joshua, David, Paul, and Jesus all serve as biblical examples of leading others through change. Perhaps the most prominent example, however, is that of Nehemiah, whose account of rebuilding Jerusalem can be found in the first six chapters of the book bearing his name. He prayerfully sought the Lord for a vision and then shared the vision with the king and other influential leaders. Before approaching the Jewish people with it, however, he strategically analyzed the situation in order to have specific details to communicate. He also collaborated with others to acquire necessary resources so that when he finally approached the Jewish people, he did not simply present a problem but also presented a vision for what the future of Jerusalem would be and a preliminary plan for making it happen. Nehemiah and the Jewish remnant developed a detailed plan of action, delegating each task to a specific group of workers. As always occurs when a major enterprise is under way, opposition and distractions ensued. The project itself was questioned by those outside the effort, and those within were distracted by cultural issues. Nehemiah's motives were questioned, but he refused to enter the fray as his personal character was attacked. Throughout, he displayed openness in his approach with others and a commitment to godly principles.

As previously stated, relational trust is a key component in leading others through the change experience. Nehemiah had gained that type of trust with both kings and commoners. The ultimate leadership model for relational trust, however, is that of God the Father leading His children through life transformation. Proverbs 3:5–6 (New International Version) directs the reader to "Trust in the Lord with all your heart and lean not on your own understanding; in all your ways submit to him, and he will make your paths straight." Whatever approach leaders may take to school improvement, they will find more success as they trust the Lord and as they build trust between themselves and the school's stakeholders.

The book of Proverbs is replete with admonitions to consider the counsel of others:

- "Listen to advice and accept discipline, and at the end you will be counted among the wise. Many are the plans in a person's heart, but it is the Lord's purpose that prevails" (Proverbs 19:20–21).
- "Plans fail for lack of counsel, but with many advisers they succeed" (Proverbs 15:22).

The process of receiving advice and counsel should not be confused with majority rule or leadership by democracy. Leaders are cautioned to tread carefully when moving in a direction that is upstream from the majority, but sometimes standing for what is right and true requires it. A clear biblical example can be found in Numbers 13 and 14. Ten of Moses's 12 spies returned from a data-collecting expedition to Canaan with negative

Leaders are cautioned to tread carefully when moving in a direction that is upstream from the majority, but sometimes standing for what is right and true requires it.

reports: "We can't attack those people; they are stronger than we are" (Numbers 13:31b). Later that night, "all the members of the community raised their voices and . . . grumbled against Moses and Aaron" (Numbers14:1–2). The majority was patently against Moses, Aaron, Joshua, and Caleb, yet these leaders were moving in the direction God intended. As harsh as God's decision may have seemed that "not one of them will ever see the land" that He had promised them (Numbers 14:23), it may have been a necessary measure for His purposes to be fulfilled. Today, many educators decry what they perceive as punitive measures when schools are slated for a turnaround, restart, or closure process in which the majority, if not all, of the staff will be dismissed. Might it be that success at that particular school would be impossible if the same personnel were retained?

Above all, wisdom is paramount in decision making and strategic planning. The epistle of James offers the reminder that "if any of you lacks wisdom, you should ask God, who gives generously to all without finding fault, and it will be given to you" (1:5). Later, James distinguishes between the wisdom of heaven and that of earth. The wisdom of heaven is manifested by a good life and deeds done in humility. It is "pure; then peace-loving, considerate, submissive, full of mercy and good fruit, impartial and sincere" (3:17). On the contrary, earthly wisdom is characterized by envy, selfish ambition, boasting, disorder, and a denial of the truth (3:14–16). James specifically addressed those who would assume to make plans for the future, reminding them that they "do not even know what will happen tomorrow. What is your life? You are a mist that appears for a little while and then vanishes. Instead, you ought to say, 'If it is the Lord's will, we will live and do this or that'" (4:14–15).

SCHOOL IMPROVEMENT IN ACTION

Current Issues and Trends in School Improvement

Accreditation Agencies and Government Influence

In private schools, there are few government regulations requiring improvement plans beyond the adherence to building and health codes. Therefore, plans for improvement are typically motivated by internal needs as identified by school boards or leadership teams or as part of the accreditation process. As private schools approach their initial accreditation process, explicit areas for improvement will emerge through the data-collection and analysis process. Goals will be set with deadlines satisfactory for meeting the approval of the outside accreditation team.

The process for accreditation renewal is similar to the initial process. The same types of data are collected and reviewed to ensure an acceptable level of performance has been maintained for renewal to be granted. It is common, however, for accrediting agencies to introduce new standards or to reinterpret existing ones. In those cases, schools may need to improve procedures or programs to meet the new expectations. Some private school accrediting agencies offer a renewal option that focuses strictly on school improvement. Based on identified areas for improvement from the previous accreditation report, schools are required to show how they have addressed the issues since the most recent accreditation cycle.

Like private schools, public school improvement may also be motivated by internal recognition of needs, but often the impetus for improvement plans is sourced in state or federal mandates. In the early 2000s, No Child Left Behind mandates have served as the stimulus behind most improvement plans, with the focus being on meeting the requirements of adequately yearly progress. The federal government offers School

Improvement Grants for states to distribute to local districts "that demonstrate the greatest need for the funds and the strongest commitment to use the funds to provide adequate resources in order to raise substantially the achievement of students in their lowest-performing schools" (U.S. Department of Education, 2012). By 2013, however, a majority of states had been approved for waivers to portions of No Child Left Behind. States were approved based on their proposals to implement alternative accountability systems or teacher evaluation programs, which themselves become different types of improvement plans (Klein, 2012).

One trend resulting from these waivers is that dozens of states have begun setting varying achievement targets based upon race and ethnicity. This has caused a firestorm among those who valued No Child Left Behind's goal that all students would become proficient in basic skills, despite their race, ethnicity, or socioeconomic status. Critics argue that a lower achievement bar for minorities will result in generally lower minority outcomes, whereas supporters see the trend as the only realistic means to school-wide improvement in academic achievement (Richmond, 2012).

Although federal accountability is most likely here to stay, the practical impact may continue to change with new laws, or interpretations thereof. The ESSA, which replaced NCLB, promises to return some influence back to the states, and in turn, school leaders. However, it may take years for schools to realize the true impact of the changes (Young, Winn, & Reedy, 2017).

Economic Challenges

A challenge common to both private and public schools has been the strain of figuratively having to make more bricks with less straw. While demands from governing entities rise, resources to meet these demands diminish (Odden & Picus, 2011). Administrators find themselves needing to be more creative in acquiring resources to fund initiatives and may need to hire personnel devoted strictly to the task of resource procurement. In an era when society is expecting the primary role of administrators to be that of instructional leader, they are feeling more pressure than ever to do what is expected of many university presidents and to "bring home the bacon."

The Kansas City, Missouri, School District was featured in an issue of *Phi Delta Kappan* (Esselman, Lee-Gwin, & Rounds, 2012) as an example of a district with plummeting available funds but with severe improvements needed. Student achievement levels were low and getting lower, with less than a third of elementary students reading on grade level and a majority of schools posting lower than 25% of students proficient on the state assessment. Billions of dollars had been expended on magnet schools, themed schools, and a career-focused high school—none of which accomplished what had been hoped. Radical cuts in programs were necessary, so the new superintendent eliminated all programs deemed inefficient in order to free resources for the targeted purpose of teaching and learning. This ongoing process of "rightsizing" the Kansas City schools has already shown progress in student achievement and continues to look promising.

According to Odden and Picus (2011), "schools can improve learning and teaching using research-based and best practices-based strategies that in many cases don't require more money and in others where more money will help if it's spent strategically" (p. 42). They found the following strategies to be effective in dire situations where improvements were desperately needed but budget restrictions were limited:

- Resist common cost pressures on schools. Avoid small class sizes (except in primary grades, where they are shown to have a positive effect), unnecessary electives, automatic pay increases, and growing benefits packages.
- Develop a more powerful school vision. Use data-based decision making, set ambitious goals regardless of demographics, and adopt new curriculum and textbook materials.
- Identify necessary resources to meet the new school vision.
- Reallocate resources to meet the new vision.

School Improvement in the News

As part of the American Recovery and Reinvestment Act of 2009—commonly known as the "Stimulus Package"—Congress approved $3.5 billion for School Improvement Grants. This being the largest federal investment in history to improve failing schools, it became a target for the media to track what the results would be. Unfortunately, 3years after the investment, more than a third of schools scored worse in reading and math than before receiving the funds (Layton, 2012). What are the implications of these results and of the Kansas City example mentioned earlier? Although funding is certainly required for most improvement initiatives, it most likely is not the most significant factor in the improvement of student achievement.

One recipient of the School Improvement Grant funds was Shawnee High School in Louisville, Kentucky, where Mr. Keith Look assumed the principal role in 2008. He knew stepping into the position that the school was labeled as one of Kentucky's worst because of declining student achievement over a span of decades (Maxwell, 2010). When *Education Week* first featured his situation, it was the summer of 2010 and—as part of the turnaround procedure required by the federal grant—he was in the process of replacing half of his staff. Typically, in the turnaround model of reform, the principal would also have been removed, but Mr. Look was permitted to stay on with the stipulation that he produce "considerable progress" after 1 year of having received the grant. With so much scrutiny on his school, the Kentucky Department of Education deployed three turnaround specialists to assist Mr. Look. In the summer of 2011, *Education Week* published a follow-up article reporting that attendance was up, suspensions were down, nearly all the teachers were returning the next year, and Mr. Look's contract was being renewed even though it would be months before achievement test results would be available (Klein, 2012). After the second year of the 3-year turnaround process, over half of the students continue to score in the lowest category of math, called "novice" in Kentucky (Kentucky Department of Education, 2012). Because of the media attention given to Shawnee High School, Mr. Look and his staff will continue to undergo the nation's scrutiny as they receive federal School Improvement Grant funds for their 3rd year in the program. Unless significant gains are reported, critics will continue to claim that the resources spent on the program may not be justified.

Federal school reform initiatives have had little, if any, direct impact on private schools. On the state level, however, several states' private schools have been granted an option to participate in voucher programs whereby students in public schools deemed as "failing" may use state funds to attend private schools. Each state administers its programs differently and holds distinct criteria for students and schools to participate. Therefore, state courts have handed down varying rulings on whether these programs pass muster regarding constitutionality. States experimenting with such voucher programs remain unsure of the permanency of their programs as they inevitably are tried through the judicial system. For example, a Louisiana judge ruled in November 2012 that its state's voucher program was unconstitutional because it diverted public tax dollars to religiously affiliated private schools (Plasse, 2012). Florida, on the other hand, has had a voucher program since 2001 that in 2012 provided scholarships for over 40,000 students to attend religious schools (Weber, 2012). It is funded by corporations that are permitted by law to contribute a portion of their state taxes to organizations approved to distribute the Florida Tax Credit Scholarships. Although the organizations distributing the scholarships are private, the chief criticism of the program is that it allows corporations to divert tax dollars that would otherwise go into the state's coffers, reducing available funds for public schools and other state services.

Best Practices in School Improvement

School improvement initiatives are being driven increasingly by centralized governments and less by local entities. State departments of education—often in response to federal mandates—collect data, analyze them, and set time frames for specific improvements to be implemented and results to be realized. As Gorton and Alston (2009) traced the history of school change efforts in the United States, they suggested that "significant and lasting improvement can seldom be prescribed, mandated, or directed by agencies or individuals outside the school" (p. 134). Therefore, leadership for bringing about meaningful change must come from the same level where the change is needed. In most cases, that would be at the school-site level. Building-level administrators can choose a passive approach by simply responding to mandates or become proactive by developing a site-based routine of evaluation and improvement. If properly implemented, a proactive approach will promote a culture of improvement.

leadership for bringing about meaningful change must come from the same level where the change is needed.

Data Collection and Analysis

A common mistake for building-level administrators is to base their decisions on a variety of unreliable sources: intuition, tradition, anecdotes, prejudices, and single-shot observations. This type of decision making results in a concentration on operational issues and on putting out proverbial fires. A more preferred approach is to make data-based decisions. Guthrie and Schuermann (2010) define data-based decision making as "the reliance for analyses and decisions upon systematically and reliably collected information regarding multiple performance and status characteristics of school operation" (p. 264). Administrators have, however, become so inundated with data that expressions such as "information overload" and "drowning in data" have commonly been used to communicate their frustration. Because there is such an influx of data, administrators should work to filter, categorize, and sift through information until it is simplified.

© Ellagrin/Shutterstock.com

Although student achievement data will by far be the most important and mission-specific information collected and analyzed, there are many other types of data also important to developing goals. These can be categorized as data about students, parents, personnel, and fiscal matters. Following is a list of the types of data that should be collected for each category:

- Students: academic achievement, attendance, extracurricular participation, socioeconomic status, gender, race, ethnicity, college and career success
- Parents: participation, attendance at functions, values, perception of school satisfaction
- Personnel: teacher characteristics, attendance, professional development, performance evaluations
- Fiscal Matters: personnel salaries, textbooks, supplies, instructional materials, library holdings, supplemental programs, technology

External and internal environments. Two additional categories of supporting data may be necessary depending on the type of decision being made. Guthrie and Schuermann (2010) identify these categories as external and internal environments. The purpose of collecting data from external environments is to make decisions relating to parent and community perceptions, communication with stakeholders, and public relations. Means of collecting data from external environments might be questionnaires, surveys, interviews, and focus groups. The questions asked would relate to stakeholders' perceptions about the school's services, organizational structure, student success, and—for private schools—tuition costs. Analyzing information from external environments will assist in deciding strategically how to change public perception about the school, usually by disseminating previously unavailable information or by disseminating it in a different manner. It may be that perception can only be changed by actual revisions in procedures, programs, services, or personnel. For instance, it is possible that an individual in a highly visible support staff position is poorly representing the organization but that it has not come to the attention of administration how seriously it is damaging the school's reputation until the analysis of the data from external environments. The second category of supporting data, internal environments, is helpful when decisions are significant and require a substantial monetary commitment. Examples of such decisions might involve a change in salary, benefits, facilities, technology, and any number of other costly improvements.

Comparisons. Data from internal environments are used for comparative purposes. Historical, horizontal, and similar comparisons are made to the present conditions.

Historical comparison. The first comparison is a historical comparison of present conditions to past conditions in the same school. Recent data from the school targeted for improvement are collected and compared historically to past data. For example, if the improvement in question is regarding salary, it would be reasonable to ask the following: What has been the percentage of salary increase each year? Have increases been consistent over the years? How do salary increases for faculty compare to those for support staff?

Horizontal comparison. Second, a horizontal comparison is conducted by comparing recent data from the target school to data from other schools. It is helpful to collect information from other schools that are comparable to the target school in location, size, demographics, and socioeconomic status of the community. As helpful, if not more so, is information from benchmark institutions. These are institutions viewed as models that have already achieved a measure of success to which the targeted school aspires to reach at some point. In the example of salary decisions, an awareness of similar schools assists in knowing how competitive present salaries are with those paid in schools in the same type of market and helps to set salaries for the upcoming budget year. An awareness of benchmark schools assists in setting long-range goals of what salaries should be in future years.

Similar comparison. The third comparison is a similar comparison. In this step, information is collected from organizations or businesses that are similar in some aspects to the target school but are not providing the same services. For example, a school might compare the wages of its office staff, custodians, and cafeteria workers to those of comparable positions at a nearby hospital. A Christian school might compare what it pays its chief administrator to what another Christian ministry of a similar size and budget might pay its chief administrator. Analyzing the results of historical, horizontal, and similar comparisons will assist in making more informed decisions about crucial matters, such as the revision of a salary scale.

Assessment team. So much data must be collected and analyzed in order to prepare an accreditation report or a school improvement plan that the task should not be left to one individual alone. Even if it is part of the job description of a curriculum director or assessment coordinator, there should be a team that assists in the task. Not only will the team ease the workload of filtering through the data, but it will also bring a much-needed measure of accountability so that the decisions and goals set are more reliable and valid. A team of no more than four or five members meeting monthly will minimize the likelihood of individual bias. An individual charged with collecting and evaluating data and then setting organizational goals may be tempted to interpret the data in ways that support the individual's pet projects or personal agenda. A team, however, might ensure that sufficient amounts of data are collected and that they are compared and analyzed thoroughly enough to make valid decisions.

Developing Goals to Carry Out the Mission

If the vision or mission statement of a school is current, relevant, and embraced by its stakeholders, it may serve as an instrument to drive school improvement. The data collected and analyzed should answer the question "To what degree is the mission being accomplished?" Then the goals set should align with the mission statement. Following are some sample mission statements:

- *The mission of ABC School is to provide an appropriate educational program and learning environment that will effectively meet the educational needs of its students and citizens and help its students accomplish educational goals that are significant and transferable.*
- *The mission of City School District is to provide the teaching and learning environments that will ensure, with the support of the students, parents, and community, that all students, upon graduation, will have the academic and social skills and strategies to be successful lifelong learners.*
- *County School is a diverse community of learners that strives for excellence; values individuality; fosters a passion for learning; promotes the balanced development of mind, body, and character; encourages service; and instills a respect for others.*
- *The purpose of Belief Academy is to be a school where Jesus is Lord and students are led to develop spiritually, academically, socially, physically, and in service to others.*

To illustrate how a mission statement should drive a school's goals, it could be argued that there are eight elements of Belief Academy's mission statement that should be evaluated regularly. The first is:

The purpose of Belief Academy is to be a school . . .

It may seem obvious that the institution is a school, and some may believe that this aspect of the mission need not be addressed at all. This element, however, is vital and must be questioned periodically because there are indeed specific functions that distinguish schools from other types of institutions. Is the school's primary focus to that end, or are resources expended unnecessarily for purposes that another institution can and should be doing more effectively? For instance, some Christian schools may be more like a church than a school. They may pride themselves so much in being like a family that their focus is to that end. Although they may be like a church or like a family and may even perform some of the same functions, schools cannot replace these other institutions. Periodically, school leaders—both public and private—must evaluate the degree to which resources are being used for nonschool purposes. Is it possible that the school is offering a service that is better provided by another institution to which families may be referred?

The second element is:

. . . where Jesus is Lord . . .

Often school mission statements include ambiguous terms that need to be defined. For example, the public school mission statements listed previously use terms such as "successful lifelong learners," "passion for learning," and "balanced development." It is important for stakeholders, especially faculty members, to know what is meant by these terms; otherwise, they lose all meaning. In the case of the Christian school, constituents need an explanation of what it means to be a school "where Jesus is Lord." Without clarity, every member of the school community may have a slightly different understanding and may not be carrying out the mission statement as intended. Evaluating and improving upon an undefined element of a school vision is impossible and, over time, that element of the mission statement may become simply a slogan that is paid lip service only.

The third element is:

. . . and students are led . . .

A particular high school that had this phrase in its mission statement began to assess the degree to which students were intentionally "led." After observation and contemplation, the leadership team decided that the process of leadership and mentoring of students to become leaders themselves was left far too much to chance and needed to be more systematically intentional throughout the school. Student leaders were identified in various programs. They were paired with adults and older students who became their mentors. Even parents leaders were identified and were assigned as mentors to individual students. When the school evaluated this aspect of the mission statement, identified areas for improvement, and set intentional goals to address how students were led, the culture of the school began to reflect what was intended in the mission.

The fourth through eighth elements are:

. . .to develop spiritually,

academically,

socially,

physically,

and in service to others.

In this example, the school assessed the degree to which students were achieving in each of the five aspects of student development. An improvement plan was then developed to address weaknesses in each area. In addition, survey questions on the annual parent and faculty questionnaires were aligned to all eight elements of the mission statement to help ensure that the school would remain true to its stated purpose.

Goal theory and decision-making models. The following subsections address two decision-making models commonly used in goal theory: the classical decision-making model and the satisficing decision-making model.

Classical decision-making model. Although many goal theorists consider it to be an outmoded framework, the classical model for decision making is still commonly taught in principal preparation programs. Assumptions of the classical model are that decision making is rational and sequential and that the best possible option may be selected from among all possible alternatives (Hoy & Miskel, 2013). The sequential steps in the classical model include the following:

1. Identify the problem.
2. Establish goals to address the problem.
3. List all possible alternatives to achieve the goals.
4. Evaluate the consequences of each alternative.
5. Select the best possible alternative that will optimize results.
6. Implement the decision.
7. Evaluate the decision.

Lunenburg and Ornstein (2004) present a summary of criticisms of the classical model. They indicate that the model's primary weakness is its naïve assumption that decision makers have access to comprehensive information and can always select the optimal course of action. Decision makers rarely, if ever, have access to complete and perfect data relating to any given problem. Unknowns will always exist; therefore, it is impossible to generate a truly comprehensive list of alternatives. Even if it were possible, limitations and other complexities inhibit leaders from always selecting the optimal alternative. Frequently, time and cost constraints cause leaders to select the most practical or most feasible option rather than the ideal.

Another weakness of the classical model is that complex decisions—rather than being made in a sequential step-by-step fashion—are virtually always made recursively. The door of collecting information never shuts in the process, and the list of alternatives may multiply at any given moment. What may seem optimal when one set of factors is accentuated may be far from it through the lens of a different set. Because of these limitations, educational leaders usually choose the satisficing decision-making model, described next.

Satisficing decision-making model. Contrary to the classical model, satisficing is based on the assumption that decision making is an ongoing, complex process in which there are no final solutions to problems that continually emerge and evolve. The term *satisficing* is used for this model because of the acknowledgment that it is a satisfactory solution being sought and that it is based on a reasonable range of options. This model recognizes that leaders must narrow their attention to the most relevant factors and that the filter for deciding what is most relevant is value laden. The administrator's personal values will influence which options are perceived as most relevant, as will the institution's core values (Hoy & Miskel, 2013).

Types of goals: elimination, preservation, avoidance, and achievement goals. After evaluating mounds of data, administrators must answer a variety of questions before beginning to set and work toward specific goals. One of those questions is "What activity, program, or time-consuming task might be eliminated to make room for the new goal?" Reeves (2009) refers to this weed-pulling practice as setting elimination goals and conveys the story of a principal who received a standing ovation in a faculty meeting after asking this question. As noted earlier, educators are often asked to do more with less, just as the Egyptian pharaoh stopped providing straw for the Hebrew slaves but yet required them to make the same number of bricks (Exodus 5). There comes a point of diminishing returns when administrators ignore the fatigue their faculties experience from the never-ending introduction of new programs. It may consequently garner a great deal of favor toward the administrator and of motivation for the new cause if at least one or two time-consumers are eliminated. If found to be too difficult, the task of setting elimination goals might be made easier if preservation goals are set first. Answering "What do we already have that we want to preserve?" will narrow what remains so that it becomes easier to answer "What do we have that we want to eliminate?"

In addition to preservation and elimination goals, Gorton and Alston (2009) recognize two others: avoidance goals and achievement goals. Avoidance goals are decided by asking "What don't we have that we want to ensure that we don't get?" whereas achievement goals ask "What do we want that we don't have?" Most goals, by the nature of school improvement itself, are achievement oriented. However, it is important to remember that improvement and change do not occur only by adding new procedures. More is not always better; it is oftentimes simply more.

Setting effective goals. Because focusing on too many goals at once can be overly taxing and can diminish results, school improvement plans should include no more than three to five goals. If carefully crafted, these goals can be effective at targeting change. One popular model for writing meaningful goals is to make them SMART. A SMART goal is one that includes the following characteristics(Guthrie & Schuermann, 2010):

- Specific: focused and clearly stated, not vague or general
- Measurable: tangible and quantifiable outcomes
- Achievable: realistic, attainable
- Research based: directly linked to patterns in data
- Time sensitive: a definite date for the goal to be completed

Some administrators, if permitted to do so, may dismiss the goal-setting route altogether because of how cumbersome and tedious it appears. Seeing the process as unnecessary altogether, they elect a route that is less formal in hopes that everyone will jump on board with their agenda. This mistake ironically may make their desired changes all the more challenging to implement. Hoy and Miskel (2013) point out that well-developed goals make school change much easier because they increase attention and effort on the targeted change and strengthen persistence so that faculty are less likely to abandon the project. Of course, this is based on the assumption that the faculty will embrace the said goal. If they indeed embrace it, goals that are challenging and specific will result in much higher levels of performance than those that are too easily attained or vague.

Implementation Plans

In the business arena, over 70% of strategic plans are never implemented (Reeves, 2009)—hours upon hours of time wasted to develop goals just to see them sit on a shelf! The biblical principle of stewardship demands that leaders not waste their own or others' time in such a reckless manner. One effort to avoid such recklessness is to develop plans and accountability procedures for implementation. To outline one specific pattern for every implementation plan is impossible because individual plans depend on the goals to be implemented. Appendix A of this chapter, however, provides an Improvement Plan Template that includes standard elements. A successful plan will address each of the following areas on the template in sufficient detail: (a) carefully crafted SMART goal; (b) actions, strategies, and interventions; (c) timeline; (d) estimated costs, funding sources, and resources; (e) person(s) responsible; (f) procedures for monitoring evaluation; and (g) evidence that the goal was met.

Most accrediting agencies, school boards, state departments of education, and federal grant programs require a great measure of detail in strategic plans. Schools in Freeport, Illinois, however, experimented with a much more abbreviated Plan-on-a-Page, which resulted in significant improvement during the 5 years the district used this model (Reeves, 2009). The one-page plans were easily distributed to all district personnel, who were encouraged to keep them readily available for quick reference. The elements of the Plan-on-a-Page included four key areas: (a) student performance, (b) human resources, (c) partnerships, and (d) equity. See Appendix B for a sample.

Formative Feedback and Summative Evaluation

Whether lengthy or brief, a plan is useless unless it leaps from the page into action. A plan for both formative feedback throughout implementation and summative evaluation at the end will increase the likelihood of successful attainment. Formative feedback is imperative early in the implementation phase. It provides an opportunity to diagnose specific strategies and to make corrections along the way. It also should be an opportunity to celebrate victories at various junctures. Finding something to celebrate early in the cycle of implementation will motivate faculty and encourage them to persevere. Celebrations are also occasions to reinforce specific strategies that are determined to be effective along the way.

Summative evaluation is the moment of truth. It is the official comparison of the data collected before goal setting and the data collected after implementation. If the plan was to change student behavior, how does student behavior compare before and after implementation? If the plan was to improve teacher morale, how does teacher morale compare before and after? Summative evaluation is the time to judge whether or not the plan worked and what to do next. If the plan is deemed effective, it most likely will continue as needed. As exasperating as it may be to decide the plan did not work, such a decision is a moment to reflect, reevaluate, and take the opportunity to attempt a different approach that might make the intended impact. For an example of a systematic model for data collection, analysis, goal setting, implementation, and evaluation, see Appendix C.

CONCLUSION

Countless factors will affect the path school improvement takes in the future: the economy, the renewal of federal education acts, state and local reform efforts, and others. This fluctuation makes it all the more important for educators to view school improvement not as an event but as a cycle, an integral component of campus culture. Educators must own the process and not view it as a dreaded mandate from above. Yes, governing bodies will continue to do what is in their nature—to mandate what is politically expedient. Educators in the trenches, however, must persist in doing what they are called to do, to "serve wholeheartedly, as if [they] were serving the Lord, not people" (Ephesians 6:7), setting goals not because they are mandated to do so but because it is in the best interest of the students God has placed in their care. As educators work to advocate for change in their schools and in regulatory legislation, they must appeal to what Abraham Lincoln called the "better angels of our nature"—improving schools out of a moral imperative rather than an out of an obligatory duty to an external authority.

Discussion Questions

1. How do current trends in U.S. educational reform compare to previous reform movements regarding the impetus behind the movements, the expected outcomes, and the measures of accountability applied?

2. To what degree is it possible to bring about effective change without a high degree of relational trust? What limitations in change efforts might be anticipated when relational trust is lacking?

3. What types of resistance to change have you experienced in schools where you have taught? How was the resistance managed, and do you believe it was handled correctly?

4. For what types of decisions might shared decision making be most effective? For what types of decisions might shared decision making be inappropriate?

5. Do you prefer the classical decision-making model or the satisficing model? Why?

Activities for Enrichment

1. For each of the roles Gorton and Alston (2009) list for principals as they guide the process of change, rate your present principal on a scale from 1 to 5, with 1 being the weakest and 5 being the strongest. Consider what the principal might do to increase the weakest ratings. Either rate yourself on the same roles or ask a colleague you trust to rate you. Discuss with that colleague what you might do to improve in the weak areas.
2. Provide examples for each of the following types of goals and justify how each would improve the school: preservation, elimination, avoidance, and achievement.
3. Evaluate the goals in a school improvement plan from the school where you presently teach or from one that you find online. To what degree do the goals follow Guthrie and Schuermann's (2010) SMART guidelines?

APPENDIX A

Implementation Template

Goal:					
Actions, Strategies, and Interventions	**Timeline**	**Estimated Costs, Funding Sources, and Resources**	**Person(s) Responsible**	***Means of Evaluation***	
				Procedures for Monitoring	**Evidence of Successful Completion** ***What will serve as this evidence?***

APPENDIX B

FREEPORT SCHOOL DISTRICT PLAN ON A PAGE 2007-2008

In partnership with students, family and community, we prepare every student for the world of today and tomorrow through excellence in education.

VISION	GOALS AND MEASURES	ACTION PLANS
STUDENT PERFORMANCE Every student is performing at or above grade level, engaged in his or her learning, and contributing positively to the community.	• By 2010, all students in grades 3-8 will meet or exceed the ILS as measured by ISAT; by June 2008, 87% of the students will meet or exceed the Reading ILS and 92% will meet or exceed the Math ILS on ISAT. • By June 2014, all students in grade 11 will meet or exceed the ILS as measured by PSAE; by June 2008, 78% students will meet or exceed the Reading ILS and 63% students will meet or exceed the Math ILS. • For each of the next 4 years, FSD will move at least 10% of students from "meets" to "exceeds" on the State exams. • By June 2010, all grade 8 students will successfully complete Algebra I or a higher level math course. By June 2008, 80% of grade 7 students will be prepared to successfully complete Algebra I or a higher level math course during the 2008-2009 school year.	▪ By Aug. 31, 2007, each school will identify students, below grade level on State exams and/or local assessments, to receive additional support to move students to grade level. ▪ By June 2007, administration will review and improve its process for academic acceleration in student learning, using data/feedback/ strategies process, at the District, building, and student levels. The data will be reviewed on a monthly basis, using Literacy First reading assessments (K-6), local reading assessments (K-12), and local math assessment (K-12) to develop student level strategies for improvement in both reading and math. This process will be implemented at the start of the 2007-2008 school year.
EQUITY Every person is treated fairly promoting dignity and mutual respect. The diverse talents of all staff and students are fully appreciated and developed.	• By June 2010, close the achievement gap in grades 3-8, with a greater %age of all groups in the "meets" and " exceeds" categories each year. By June 2008, 81% of African American students in grades 3-8 will meet or exceed reading ILS and 85% "meet" or "exceed" math ILS. • By June 2014, close the achievement gap for grades 9-12. By June 2008, 63% of African American high school students will meet or exceed reading and math ILS. • By Sept. 2010, enrollment in high academic courses will mirror the District's ethnic make-up, while low income student group will increase annually 5%age points. • By June 2008, African American representation in extra-curricular activities will meet MOU compliance ranges at elementary through high school, and 70% of FJHS and FHS African American students will participate in at least one extra-curricular or "school connecting" activity. • By June 2010, provide a positive learning environment as measured by 100% of staff indicating that they believe schools are safe/secure and atmosphere is conducive for learning. By June 2008, decrease suspensions and conduct referrals by 10%.	• Communicate "it's okay to be smart" message through AVID, Efficacy, student groups, parent meetings, mentoring, etc. • Enroll all grade 6 students who meet/exceed math standards or pass the Orleans math test in Pre-algebra or Algebra I. • Provide staff development in area of cultural diversity. • Counselors and other stakeholders aggressively recruit minorities and low income students for higher level courses. • Aggressively recruit minorities for extra-curricular activities and develop recruitment plans for activities with limited to no diversity. • Continue faithful implementation of Second Step. • Implement PBIS and ICLE Intervention Pyramid as part of the FHS Freshman Plan.
PARTNERSHIPS Student, family and community partnerships contribute to the success of every student.	**Student Partnerships** • By June 2008, every student will have a set of personal academic goals that are regularly reviewed and updated at least 4 times/year by students, teachers and parents. • By June 2008, there will be an increase of 10 % of students reporting a safe/caring school environment as measured by survey data. **Parent-Family Partnerships** • By June, 2010, 90% of District families will have participated in a research-based parent partnership program focused on student success; by June 2008, at least 10% of District families will have participated in a research-based parent partnership program. • By June 2010, at least 90% of parents will express satisfaction with FSD 145 as measured by a District survey. **Community Partnerships:** • By June 2008, every school will have at least two community partnerships that demonstrate a positive contribution to the physical, social, emotional, and academic growth of students. **Overall:** • By June 2008, increase public awareness of FSD 145 performance beyond 2007 levels. • By June 2010, at least 90% of a valid community sample will be satisfied with FSD 145.	• Implement a plan at each school to set personal student goals by September 1, 2007. • Establish and maintain a student-focus group at each school to 'listen to' and 'learn from' students. • Implement programs to recognize student success. • Establish and implement an approach to engage each family in the review and support of their student's goals and plan. • Implement research-based programs to increase parent participation in support of student success. • Implement strategies to gather input from parents regarding their level of satisfaction. • Support each school's efforts to establish effective community partnerships to serve students. • Work with community partners to recruit, train and sustain an increased number of student mentors. • Establish and implement a comprehensive strategy to enhance school district communications. • Survey a cross-section of community members regarding satisfaction with district programs and services.
HUMAN RESOURCES Our diverse faculty and staff enthusiastically implement best practices and are recognized and valued for our results.	• By August 2010, teaching staff demographics will mirror the Illinois teaching demographics as identified by the State Report Card. • By 2010, the level of African American administrators in the District will have been maintained or increased. • By June 2010, 100% of staff will indicate that they are recognized and valued for district results in student performance, as measured by the annual staff survey. • By June 2010, at least 90% of a valid staff sample will indicate they are satisfied with their work	• Modify Retention and Recruitment Plan to aggressively increase the number of African American teachers and keep a motivated and highly qualified staff. • Support "Educators for Tomorrow" by providing incentives and encouragement for students, staff, and community members to pursue careers in education. • Evaluate, modify, and aggressively improve the impact of the Staff Recognition Program. • Each school and support service department will analyze its staff survey results and develop conclusions, recommendations, and changes to accelerate improvement. • Provide quality staff development activities for all staff.

Adopted: February 21, 2007

APPENDIX C

Program and Learning Assessment Cycle for Excellence

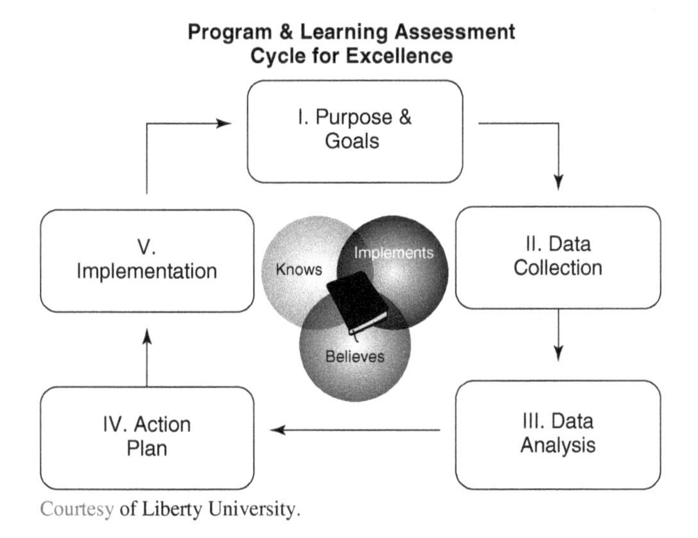

Courtesy of Liberty University.

The above framework is a model of systematic program improvement adopted by Liberty University's School of Education in 2007. PLACE involves specific events, such as an annual Assessment Day and a faculty retreat for data analysis. The five cyclical elements of PLACE are scheduled into the academic calendar. The cycle of improvement revolves around the conceptual framework, which identifies specific proficiencies all students should know, implement, and believe. Used by permission.

REFERENCES

Christophersen, K., Elstad, E., & Turmo, A. (2012). Investigating school-wide antecedents of good practice dissemination from individual subject projects. *Research in Education, 87*(1), 1–14. doi: 10.7227/RIE.87.1.1

Esselman, M., Lee-Gwin, R., & Rounds, M. (2012). Rightsizing a school district. *Phi Delta Kappan, 93*(6), 56–61.

Goals 2000: Education America Act, Pub. L. No. 103-227, § 5801, 108 Stat. 125 (1994).

Gorton, R. A., & Alston, J. A. (2009). *School leadership and administration: Important concepts, case studies, and simulations* (9th ed.). Boston, MA: McGraw Hill.

Green, R. L. (2005). *Practicing the art of leadership: A problem-based approach to implementing the ISLLC standards* (2nd ed.). Upper Saddle River, NJ: Pearson.

Guthrie, J. W., & Schuermann, P. J. (2010). *Successful school leadership: Planning, politics, performance, and power.* Boston, MA: Allyn & Bacon.

Hoy, W. K., & Miskel, C. G. (2013). *Educational administration: Theory, research, and practice.* Boston, MA: McGraw-Hill.

Kentucky Department of Education. (2012). Kentucky school report card. Retrieved from http://applications.education.ky.gov/src/Profile.aspx

Klein, A. (2012, November 7). Respite on educational issues unlikely for election winners. *Education Week, 32*(11), 1–23.

Layton, L. (2012, November 19). School improvement grants produce mixed results. *The Washington Post.* Retrieved from http://www.washingtonpost.com/local/education/school-improvement-grants-produce-mixed-results/2012/11/19/5af52c8a-3292-11e2-bfd5-e202b6d7b501_story.html

Lunenburg, F. C., & Ornstein, A. C. (2004). *Educational administration: Concepts and practices.* Belmont, CA: Wadsworth.

Maxwell, J. C. (2007). *The 21 irrefutable laws of leadership: Follow them and people will follow you.* Nashville, TN: Thomas Nelson.

Maxwell, L. A. (2010, June 16). Tough task of school improvement begins. *Education Week, 29*(35), 1–20.

Odden, A., & Picus, L. O. (2011). Improving teaching when budgets are tight. *Phi Delta Kappan, 93*(1), 42–48.

Plasse, W. (2012). Louisiana school voucher program ruled unconstitutional. *Examiner.com.* Retrieved from http://www.examiner.com/article/louisiana-school-voucher-program-ruled-unconstitutional

Reeves, D. B. (2009). *Leading change in your school: How to conquer myths, build commitment, and get results.* Alexandria, VA: ASCD.

Richmond, E. (2012, November 19). Should schools set different goals for students of different races. *The Atlantic.* Retrieved from http://www.theatlantic.com/national/archive/2012/11/should-schools-set-different-goals-for-students-of-different-races/265411/

Smith, S. J. (2010). Pestalozzianism. In T. C. Hunt, J. C. Carper, T. J. Lasley, & C. D. Raisch (Eds.), *Encyclopedia of educational reform and dissent* (pp. 697–699). Thousand Oaks, CA: Sage Publications.

Urban, W. J., & Wagoner, J. L. (2004). *American education: A history.* Boston, MA: McGraw Hill.

U.S. Department of Education. (2012). School improvement grants. Retrieved from http://www2.ed.gov/programs/sif/index.html

Weber, D. (2012, November 24). Florida already funnels millions in tax dollars to religious schools. Orlando Sentinel. Retrieved from http://articles.orlandosentinel.com/2012-11-24/features/os-tax-credit-religious-schools-20121124_1_religious-schools-private-schools-schools-at-taxpayer-expense

Young, M., Winn, K., & Reedy, M. (2017, December, 1). The Every Student Succeeds Act: Strengthening the Focus on Educational Leadership. *Educational Administration Quarterly.* Volume: 53 issue: 5.

Zinskie, C. & Rea D. (2016, Fall). The Every Student Succeeds Act (ESSA): What It Means for Educators of Students at Risk. *National Youth-At-Risk Journal.* Volume 2, Issue 1.

Chapter 3

Creating an Environment Conducive to Learning

Bunnie Claxton

The authority by which the Christian leader leads is not power but love, not force but example, not coercion but reasoned persuasion. Leaders have power, but power is safe only in the hands of those who humble themselves to serve.

—John Stott—

OVERVIEW

A learning environment that is conducive to learning begins with leadership. Though teachers are leaders in the classroom, they are dependent on administration to lead them in a direction that encourages successful classroom experiences for students. Administrators assume the responsibility of creating a school-wide atmosphere that is conducive to learning for all students. This begins with designing and maintaining a healthy school culture with high expectations for faculty and students. Administrators must provide for the academic, social, emotional, and physical needs of all learners via the faculty. This requires effective administrators to utilize current research and data to ensure all students are provided with every possible opportunity to succeed. Additionally, leaders must promote positive relationships within and beyond the school boundaries while safeguarding culturally responsible instruction and training that affirms student identities. This chapter will focus on the critical aspect of leadership that requires administrators to create a school-wide-environment that is conducive to maximizing student learning for the success of every learner.

Objectives

By the end of this chapter, the reader should be able to do the following:

1. Explain how to create and maintain a healthy school environment that is safe and meets the academic, social, emotional, and physical needs of all learners.
2. Devise a logical plan to provide for positive student engagement via social supports, extracurricular activities, accommodations and services to meet the needs of each individual student.

3. Promote positive relationships that value and support the academic, social and emotional well-being of each individual student.
4. Describe a plan that maximizes culturally sensitive learning for all students.

INTRODUCTION

Creating a learning environment that is conducive to learning is one of the most important responsibilities of a school administrator, and it is one that has the potential to effect the success or failure of a multitude of students. Though there are numerous books and seminars about leadership available and an endless number of opinions about what makes an effective leader, this chapter seeks to impart leadership wisdom from the perspective of the One perfect leader, Jesus Christ. This chapter seeks to unite the biblical wisdom from Christ with the practical knowledge of man to detail important lessons about cultivating an environment that is conducive to learning. "According to Scripture, virtually everything that truly qualifies a person for leadership is directly related to character. It's not about style, status, personal charisma, clout, or worldly measurements of success. Integrity is the main issue that makes the difference between a good leader and a bad one" (MacArthur, 2004). Creating an environment that is conducive to learning begins with integrity and incorporates biblical and practical principles.

The Bible says:

> But Jesus called them to him and said, "You know that the rulers of the Gentiles lord it over them, and their great one's exercise authority over them. It shall not be so among you. But whoever would be great among you must be your servant, and whoever would be first among you must be your slave, even as the Son of Man came not to be served but to serve, and to give his life as a ransom for many"
> Matthew 20: 25–28

Keeping this in mind as you read through this chapter, determine that you will serve those that you lead, rather than approaching leadership with the attitude that your faculty are there to follow your rules and abide by your personal guidelines. Be an imitator of Christ as you lead the flock entrusted to you and they will follow your lead willingly. The true measure of an effective leader is faithful followers.

SERVING THOSE YOU LEAD

Administrators are tasked with creating a culture that is conducive the learning. This is no small task, and it can certainly seem overwhelming. So how should administrators begin the process of creating an environment that is conducive to learning? In order to merge biblical and practice principles, it is important to start with Jesus as our example. Shortly before Jesus was to die on the cross, he spoke to His disciples and said, *"I have given you an example, that you also should do just as I have done to you. Truly, truly, I say to you, a servant is not greater than his master, nor is a messenger greater than the one who sent him"* (John 13:15–16). At the time of this statement, Jesus had just finished washing His disciples' feet. He set a perfect example for us to follow. Jesus, the King of Kings, and the leader of the disciples, took on the role of a lowly servant and washed the feet of those He was trying to influence with His leadership skills. He humbled Himself and did the job of those who should have been serving Him. As a Christian educator, are you willing to do the same? Clearly, we are not referring to you washing the feet of your faculty and staff, but are you willing to do the tasks that you are asking them to do? Is your attitude that the faculty and staff are employed to serve you, or do you

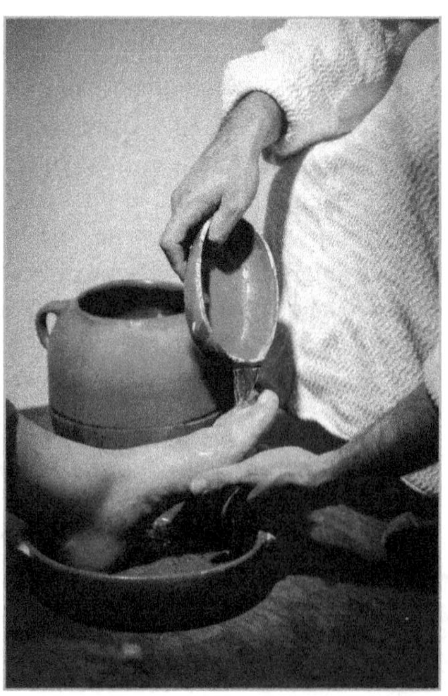

have the heart of a servant like Christ? Mike Huckabee, a prominent Christian leader and former United States presidential candidate said, "I've always believed that leaders don't ask others to do what they're unwilling to do." Would your faculty and staff say this about you? Are you willing to stand in the rain with an umbrella in the carpool line and open doors for students to greet them at school? Are you willing to serve in a lunchroom full of noisy teenagers to assist with lunchroom duty in the place of one of your teachers? Do you assist with standardized testing, or do you hide out in your office to complete your "important" work? These are all questions to consider, as events such as these help to define you as a leader to your students, teachers, and the community, whether you are aware of it or not. Their perception of you as a leader impacts their performance in more ways than you may realize. Throughout this chapter, we will discuss ways that you, as a school leader, can intentionally lead your faculty and staff to maximize student learning and success.

A SHARED VISION

No matter which type of school you work in, urban, suburban, inner-city, rural etc., one of the most critical elements of your leadership is to think comprehensively about the members of your school and community. You need every member to share in and support the vision and mission of the school in order to maximize learning for every student. Where there is a lack of shared vision, there is disagreement, controversy, and complaining. All three of these drain emotional, financial, and time resources. Collins and Porras (1996) define vision as consisting of a core ideology and an envisioned future where the core values are the guiding principles. One of the most effective ways to secure the support of the school and community members, in regard to the school's vision, is by building strong relationships with all members of the school and community, and not just a select few "favorite" teachers or community members. Effective leaders work on building relationships with all members. Think of the school and community as your team and you are the captain. You are all working together toward the common goal of creating an environment that is conducive to learning so that all students can be successful. Building your team so that all members share a common vision serves as the foundation of creating an environment that is conducive to learning. When a school's vision, mission, and goals are widely embraced, leaders are more likely to see an increase in student achievement (Spiro, 2013; Timar & Chyu, 2010).

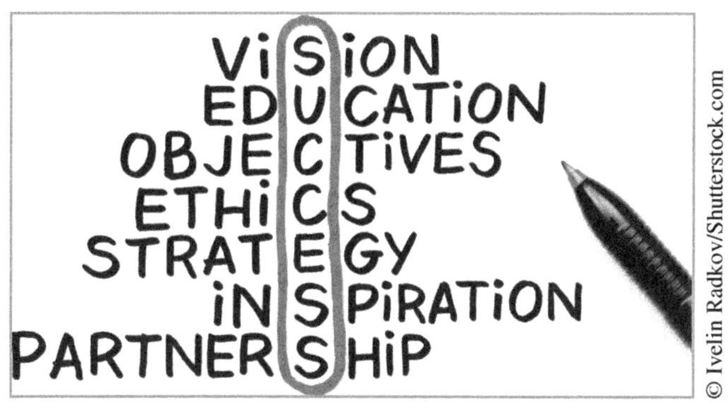

In a study by Berg (2015), one of the key findings was that when personal goals and a company's vision align, there is felt a "sense of the greater purpose, there is a deep, almost spiritual, commitment to making the world a better place and helping the organization contribute to that" (p. 1). In education, this can be seen from several perspectives. For example, from the perspective of an administrator, you receive directives from those who oversee you (e.g. Board of Directors, Superintendent). How do you feel when you are told that you will implement a certain policy, such as teacher attendance, for the teachers in your school without any prior discussions? You are simply told, "you will do this." This attendance policy may be the best policy for your school or it may not. The problem is not necessarily the policy, it is that you were never given the opportunity to warm up to the idea, offer valuable input, or to secure buy-in for the vision. This is an example of neglecting to secure buy-in, which does not easily allow others to share in the same vision.

Another example may be seen from the perspective of the teacher. If you want to adopt a new mathematics curriculum for your school and you give the directive that teachers will adopt a specific curriculum without soliciting their feedback, you will have neglected two very important elements to a shared vision. First, you will be missing some very important information that could reveal that the curriculum you chose on your own may not be the best suited for the students. Teachers are on the frontlines with the students and their input is critical to making a wise decision regarding curriculum adoption. Just like the administrator was denied the opportunity to offer valuable input regarding the teacher attendance policy, these teachers would have been denied this same opportunity. Second, dictating denies the opportunity for buy-in and thus negates the opportunity to share a vision. Again, as an administrator and leader in the field of education, it is important to view your faculty and staff as your team and you need to consistently work on building your team through valuing and prioritizing relationships. At times, you will need to give directives without teacher input. That is simply part of leadership. However, in all decisions you should consider how teacher buy-in will be impacted. To revisit the perfect leadership model we have in Jesus, He encouraged respectful behavior by modeling how a leader can gain buy-in to share a common vision. His incredible example of service shows us that by humbling ourselves to serve our teachers and staff, we build relationships and those relationships are foundational to sharing a common vision. The disciples were impacted so much by Jesus' leadership that they literally gave up everything to follow Him. Philippians 4:9 says, "*What you have learned and received and heard and seen in me—practice these things, and the God of peace will be with you.*" As a Christian leader, remember to lead your school and community by example just as Christ did for us.

Dictating denies the opportunity for buy-in and thus negates the opportunity to share a vision.

CREATING AN EMOTIONALLY AND PHYSICALLY SAFE ENVIRONMENT

School Violence. Creating an environment that is safe emotionally and physically is of utmost importance for producing an environment that is conducive to learning. You are leading the teachers that lead students. The students are counting on the teachers to keep them safe and the teachers and staff are counting on you to do the same for them. Research supports the importance of leaders creating and maintaining an environment that is safe and healthy to encourage student learning (Robinson, Lloyd, & Rowe, 2008; Lenhardt, Graham, & Farrell, 2018).

Creating an environment where learning is the norm requires that students, faculty, and staff feel safe. As an administrator, you are responsible for ensuring the safety of everyone in your school. When considering the number of school schoolings in recent times, variables to consider when devising a plan for school safety include threat assessments, prevention programs, and mental health services. Threats to school safety can originate within the school or may be initiated outside of the school locality. Either way, all aspects of safety must be covered. The intent of this chapter is to help you, as the leader of a learning environment, to cultivate a culture of learning. Faculty or students who are afraid will have their ability to perform stifled and this will negatively impact student achievement (Rossen & Cowan, 2014).

"Targeted violence is a term developed by the U.S. Secret Service to refer to any violent incident where a known or knowable attacker selects a particular target prior to a violent attack, where the victim or target is a classmate, teacher, or school building" (Vossekuil, Fein, Reddy, Borum, & Modzeleski, 2002). That school violence is problematic is not a question. The question is, "what can administrators do to prevent school violence and protect the people in their school?" Though this discussion is far more than could be covered here, there are a few strategies suggested in recent research to consider.

"The National Association of Secondary School Principals (NASSP), in collaboration with five other educational organizations, released a position paper entitled "A Framework for Safe and Successful Schools" with a joint recommendation for improved school safety and access to mental health services for students (Lenhardt et al., 2018, p. 5–6). According to the framework, the purpose of the paper was to:

> . . . provide a common set of recommendations for policies and practices that create and sustain safe, supportive learning environments. The goal was, and is, to reinforce the interdisciplinary,

collaborative, and cohesive approach required to improve school climate, implement multitiered systems of support, advance positive discipline practices, and increase access to the mental and behavioral health services necessary to meet the needs of all children and youth. (p. 1)

Though the intend of this chapter is not to fully explore school violence, this is a topic that is foundational to the physical and emotional well-being of your faculty, staff, and students and to cultivating a culture conducive to learning. For more information on this topic, please review to framework in detail.

ACADEMICS: SETTING THE STANDARD USING DATA

Setting the academic standard for your school may be approached from a variety of angles. For example, it stands to reason that academic standards should be set "high," but what does that mean, and how does an administrator achieve "high-standards?" For one school, that may mean improved test scores, for a special education classroom, it may mean that students succeed at functional skills, and for another school, it may mean that all students learn to read. Success and standards are not the same for all schools because the successes and failures of all schools vary greatly. For the purposes of this chapter, we will focus on decision-making practices that will help you and your teachers, in your unique situations, to set and achieve high-standards based on the needs of your school.

The first step to setting the standard at your school is to define what that means in your unique situation. Revisiting the beginning of this chapter, it is recommended that you take a team approach, utilizing your faculty as your greatest asset. Gather the team and host several open discussions about the strengths and weaknesses of student performance. Think of this as a needs-assessment for learning. You want to define the need and then set the priority for making improvements.

One of the most important aspects of setting academic standards, for you as a leader, is to begin by modeling the way you want academic achievement to be approached. Remember that Christ modeled for us what He wanted us to mimic. Do this with your faculty. When you begin the process of setting standards or changing standards, do it grounded in data-based decision making. For the purposes of this chapter, data-based decision making is defined as: information that is systematically collected and organized to represent some aspects of schools with regard to school development or instructional purposes (Lia & Schildkamp, 2013). For the most part, teachers and administrators tend to make decisions based on experience, intuition, or observation. Though this may be fine in many situations, setting standards, improving achievement, and cultivating an environment conducive to learning are far too important to approach without investigating what the current research has to say.

One idea suggested by Schildkamp et al., (2016) is to make use us what they call "data teams." This professional development program, called "the data team procedure," was developed to support teachers in their efforts to use data effectively in the classroom. It is not enough just to have the latest data. There must be a logical way for leaders and teachers to utilize the information in a way that is practical and that is most likely to yield positive results as measured by student achievement. These "data teams" consist of about four to six teachers and one or two school leaders, who work together to use data to solve educational problems within the school (Schildkamp et al., 2016). The main responsibility of the data team is on professional development focused on the use of data for improved student achievement, rather than on teacher experience, opinion, or intuition. Using data teams to teach teachers how to use data is a practical way to improve the use of data to make decisions in your school.

SOCIAL IMPLICATIONS AND EXPECTATIONS

As a leader in education, the social context of your school is extremely important. Just as faculty and students need to feel safe, they also need to feel socially accepted. This can be extremely difficult in a world where many people seem to have developed stronger "relationships" online than they are have developed in person. This trend is not limited to the younger generation. Many adults seem to feel safer in online relationships with people that they have never actually met. Teachers and students alike may find it easier to hide behind a cell phone and pretend to have hundreds or thousands of friends, when the reality is that it may be stretch to actually have a handful of real friends. Researchers have focused on how using a cell-phone while with a friend during face-to-face interaction impacts the quality of the relationship and communication (Vanden Abeele, Antheunis, & Schouten, 2016) and relational outcomes (McDaniel & Coyne, 2016). Research reveals that many people find themselves oscillating between trying to be emotionally and relationally in the present while having a face-to-face friend, while also trying to maintain an online presence to fulfill the expectation to remain instantly available to those communicating on the phone. It is a challenge to fulfill both roles and most people fail at one while only minimally attending to the other. How many times have you been in the middle of a sentence only to have the person you are talking to totally ignore you to answer a text or look on social media? This behavior is so prominent that the term "phubbing" was created and refers to being snubbed by someone using their cell phone when in your company (Roberts & David, 2016). How many times have we all done this and experienced this? As an administrator, how will you handle the use of cell phones and how will you encourage social interactions? You are responsible for both the teachers and the students and both have an innate need to feel cared for, accepted, and socially relevant. It is hard for people to feel accepted when being snubbed and, as an administrator it is hard to monitor. You may even think that it is not your job to monitor. To some degree, that may be true, but if this behavior is having a negative impact of students and faculty building relationships, it may be time to put some proactive measures into place such as limiting or disallowing cell phone use at certain times (e.g. during recess, art, music, clubs, etc). Perhaps this goes back to integrity and teaching students how to treat one another in social situations.

SOCIAL SUPPORTS

Building a Sense of Community for Faculty. Team building may help with building relationships as well as increase student achievement. Teachers need to feel a sense of friendship, yet many, if not most, teachers work in isolation. When teachers work together for a common purpose, a sense of comradery and self-relevance may develop. Dik, Byren, and Steger (2013) stated that "along with love, play, and community, work at its best offers a core context for construction of self and contributing to society in ways heartfelt, personally meaningful and socially relevant" (p. 17). To build these relationships and increase academic achievement, consider instituting learning communities in your school. According to McLaughlin and Talbert (2006), there are three general suppositions about ways to change school culture to include learning communities:

- A teacher community of practice develops through joint work on instruction, usually starting with a focus on one facet of instruction—subject content, students, or assessment of student learning
- Teacher learning in a community depends upon how well the joint work is designed and guided, or the extent to which an effective learning environment is created for the teachers
- Teacher learning community development, spread, and sustenance depends upon proactive administrator support and broad teacher leadership.

Incorporating learning communities in the school is about increasing student achievement and building relationships. It is also about changing the culture of the school to one that promotes a sense of excellence that is to be achieved as a team. Administrators must convey their expectations for the teachers work and also ensure that the teachers have enough time, knowledge, and resources to work in these learning communities together. This cannot be one more assignment for teachers that they do not have the time or resources to complete. As the administrator, it is your job to set them up for success. Building teacher learning communities may promote social acceptance and increase student achievement at the same time; promoting a win-win situation.

Building a Sense of Community for Students. Feeling accepted and needed is something that is a universal need. Research reveals that students who feel rejected experience high rates of anxiety and report a lower degree of feeling a sense of well-being in the classroom (Levpuscek, 2012). Just like faculty, students need to feel a sense of purpose and acceptance. Though a cell phone may serve that purpose at times, to some degree, a cell phone may also be very destructive in that it does not provide a friend when at the lunchroom table, on the playground, or while in the gym class. Also, cell phones may tend to leave students feeling undervalued when a picture posted on social media does not receive enough "likes." It is sad to think that something like that can

Promoting collaboration, rather than competition, encourages students to build relationships.

have such a negative impact on students, but it certainly can. So, what can you do to promote a sense of social relevance for the students in your school?

Just as with teachers, students need to experience common goals and common ground. Promoting collaboration rather than competition encourages students to build relationships. After school clubs are one way to get students to share common interests, which may help build relationships. Some schools support "club day" once a month. This is a time when students are able to choose a club of interest to participate in during the school day. This can be a great way to support students in building friendships since it provides them with the opportunity to socialize. It is important that these clubs not just be seen as a time for the teachers to take a "break." Rather, these clubs should be seen as an opportunity to intentionally engage students in face to face interactions and relationship building activities. There is potential here to support students socially and emotionally which may improve the overall learning environment.

STUDENTS WITH EXCEPTIONALITIES

Creating an environment conducive for learning is not just about the school as a whole, it is about the parts of the school that make up the whole. If you have not experienced it already, you will find that there are many different groups of students within the school that need support in order to learn most effectively and all of these groups have different needs. Even within each group, there are a lot of different individual student needs. The challenge, which has been a challenge for decades, is how to meet the need of each and every student. This is where your leadership comes in to play. Building and supporting your faculty "team" is a key element of supporting the individual learner. Teachers in the special education classroom and inclusive classroom need to know that you support them as they try to teach students with special needs.

Creating an environment conducive for learning is not just about the school as a whole, it is about the parts of the school that make up the whole.

Typically, students who have a diagnosed disability have an individualized education plan (IEP). These plans are written by a team including the special education teacher, the general education classroom teacher(s), administrator, the parents, counselor, and/or service provider, and sometimes the student. Though the special education teacher is typically the main author, the IEP is a collaborative effort with the purpose of maximizing the educational opportunity for the student with special needs. I wrote a book called, *Planning, Writing, and Implementing IEP's: A Christian Approach*, to elaborate on the IEP process. One of the main points in the book is that IEPs do not, and should not, be perceived as a battle between the members of the IEP team. Every member of the team has unique and valuable information to contribute to the student's education and all members must input must be valued. As an administrator, I would encourage you to read the book, and to have any teachers involved in the IEP process to read it as well. The importance of intentionally promoting an inclusive attitude and building relationships cannot be overstated if IEP meetings in your building are going to be peaceful and productive. Parents need to know that they are valued. The general education teacher needs to feel needed. The special education teacher needs to be appreciated and heard. All members have needs and all members are important. If you want to create an environment that is conducive to learning for the student with special needs, a great place to start is with the IEP.

Some IEP plans cover academic and functional skills. Functional skills may include cooking, learning to ride a public bus, washing laundry, paying bills, getting dressed, personal hygiene, and more. Some may include social skills. For many students, social skills are learned naturally by observing others. For others, this is absolutely not the case. When Temple Grandin, who is autistic, was in school, she said that she was ". . . just like an animal that had no instincts to guide me; I just had to learn by trial and error. I was always observing, trying to work out every social interaction . . . I wanted to participate, but I did not know how" (Grandin, 2006, p. 153). For students who are challenged socially, school can be a very isolated and lonely place, and to spend 12 years in that type of atmosphere can have devastating effects. Temple was blessed to have teachers who supported her, and she graduated and went on to earn a PH.D in animal science. She invented restraint systems to keep animals calm and she invented a center-track restraint system that is used to handle almost half of all cattle in the United States. She has also designed livestock facilities in Canada, New Zealand, and Europe. She is a world renown author and speaker. She is an incredible example of a student with special needs that achieved more than most people thought she ever would. She is why you need to fully support your teachers who teach students with special needs. With your support, there is no limit to the contributions they may make to society.

SCHOOL-COMMUNITY RELATIONSHIPS

As the administrator in a school, you are responsible to monitor programs in the school for compliance, guide program improvement, support faculty and staff, and elicit community support and involvement in education. There isn't a checklist of responsibilities for administrators that one can simply check off to determine effectiveness. If such a checklist did exist, it would be painstakingly long, and it may cause potential administrator candidates to run far, far away. There are never enough hours in the day to accomplish the multitude of tasks necessary, so it is imperative that you learn to prioritize. Look at the big picture first and work your way down into the details, but only go as far into the details as you need to in order to be effective. When you think about the big picture, make sure you include the community in your vision.

In a study conducted in 24 school districts including 407 schools by Epstein, Galindo and Sheldon (2011), it was determined that, despite diverse populations, schools in this study were able to

> . . . establish basic program structures and increase outreach to all families if their districts provided direct assistance on partnerships, if their principals supported family and community involvement, and if school teams rated district assistance as helpful at the school level. These interactions and exchanges take time, however, but it appears that—in time—district and school leaders learn new skills and gather ideas from each other and turn that information into actions to improve their school programs. (pp. 485–486)

Support seems to be a key theme that runs through the lens of success. When students are supported by teachers they achieve more. When teachers are supported by administrators, they are able to help their students achieve more. When administrators are supported by their district, student achievement increases. This reminds me of Proverbs 11:14 which says, "For lack of guidance a nation falls, but victory is won through many advisors. Success is not achieved in isolation of one another, rather it is achieved when members of the school and community are able to work in harmony with one another.

So, what would it look like for an administrator to be supported by a district? This could start with policy at the district level to help guide administrators in their endeavor to establish strong relationships with the community. Having a policy to establish expectations and parameters gives administrators an idea of what their goals should be in regard to community relationships. However, having a policy is not enough, as that does not equip administrators to be successful. Fitzgerald and Quinones (2018) "argue for strategic professional development and mentoring for in-service principals and preparing aspiring principals to work in and with community" (p. 17).

Not all administrators fully understand the benefit of community relationships and the advantages that may be afforded the school (and students) by establishing such associations. Building authentic relationships and partnerships with the community members and businesses has the potential to allow for open discussions where both parties learn from one another, where disagreements are discussed in a non-threatening atmosphere with the genuine interest of the students prioritized. When open discussions are welcomed, school leaders and community members learn from one another and are more likely to establish a trusting relationship where both parties are able to support learning.

© Rawpixel.com/Shutterstock.com

Administrators may support and value the idea of building community relationships but may not possess the skills or knowledge necessary to do so, which is why principal training programs need to prepare aspiring leaders and why districts need to support administrators with professional development designed to inform and train administrators on how to establish effective community partnerships (Fitzgerald & Quinones, 2018). New principals report having few opportunities in their preparation programs to learn the skills necessary to build and maintain cooperative partnerships, especially with parents from low-income communities (Miller & Martin, 2015). Since administrators are tasked with student achievement, it is important to establish, maintain, and nurture relationships that will support this endeavor. Building a two-way bridge between the school and the community takes skill and intentionality, but when these bridges are effectively established, student achievement is likely to flourish.

CULTURALLY SENSITIVE LEARNING

With the passage of the Every Student Succeeds Act (2015), standards have been established for culturally sensitive and culturally responsive teaching and reflection practices. These standards have been established to eliminate the achievement gap between English language learners (ELL) and their non-English learner peers. As of the 2015 school year, over 5 million ELL students attended school in the United States (NCES, 2018). Student who are identified as ELLs are eligible to participate in educational opportunities to help them achieve English proficiency. Many teachers are not certified or educated to teach academic subjects other than the one they are credentialed for via a bachelors, masters, or doctorate degree. Teaching English as a Second Language or Bilingual Education requires certification that encompass teaching second language acquisition skills and meeting the educational needs of ELLs (TESOL International Association, 2018). As an administrator, you may consider professional development as a means of supporting the general population of teachers, however, fully educating these students is likely to require a teacher specialized in this area.

© Monkey Business Images/Shutterstock.com

ELLs are only one group of students to consider culturally. In many, if not most, schools in the United States, there are a wide variety of languages, cultures, ethnicities, nationalities, and socioeconomic backgrounds represented. Modeling inclusive and culturally sensitive behavior requires being intentional. Teachers and students need to see you welcoming different cultural perspectives and practices. Additionally, teachers need to be equipped with culturally sensitive curriculum. Again, professional development in both pedagogy and instructional design may help teachers create a classroom that is more culturally sensitive and thus more likely to be conducive to learning for all learners without excluding anyone based on diversity.

CONCLUSION

Creating an environment that is conducive to learning should be one of your top priorities as an administrator since that is how student achievement takes place. In order to create an environment where students are able to learn, there must be a shared vision and a sense of working together for a common goal. Students, faculty, and staff must feel safe and supported, which means that there academic, social, emotional, and physical needs are provided for. Administrators need a logical plan to promote positive engagement through social supports, extracurricular activities, accommodations, and services so that all learners have their needs met, including those with exceptionalities and diversities. As an administrator, you are tasked with building relationships with students, faculty, staff, parents, and the community. The Lord set a beautiful example of servant leadership in the Bible when he washed the disciple's feet. Another important part of scripture that lends itself to administrative leadership is from 1 Peter 5:1–5, which says:

So I exhort the elders among you, as a fellow elder and a witness of the sufferings of Christ, as well as a partaker in the glory that is going to be revealed: shepherd the flock of God that is among you, exercising oversight, not under compulsion, but willingly, as God would have you; not for shameful gain, but eagerly; not domineering over those in your charge, but being examples to the flock. And when the chief Shepherd appears, you will receive the unfading crown of glory.

This goes back to the beginning of the chapter when we discussed the establishment of a shared vision. Leaders who are able to share their vison and gain the support and participation of students, faculty, staff, parents, and the community are well on their way to establishing an environment that is conducive to learning.

Discussion Questions

1. In this chapter, multiple scriptures were given about leadership. Choose one of the main topics in this chapter and locate a verse or story from the Bible that fully represents or speaks to leadership on this topic.

2. What are three ways that you can share your school's vision with your faculty to gain their buy-in? Why is this important?

3. Describe a plan for ensuring the emotional and physical safety of your faculty, staff, and students.

4. How will you specifically encourage teachers to use data to make decisions in their classrooms? Create a three-year-plan for establishing a culture of data-driven decision-making in your school.

5. Devise a plan for building relationships with the community. Include parents and businesses.

6. Detail specific steps you will take, as an administrator, to support students with exceptionalities and diversities.

Activities for Enrichment

Creating a Safe School Environment: Host a school and community forum to openly discuss school safety. Based on community feedback and faculty and staff contributions, devise a plan to either improve an existing school safety plan or to create one if a current plan does not exist.

Setting the Standard: Host several open discussions with your faculty about the strengths and weaknesses of student performance. With the input of all stakeholders, devise a needs-assessment for learning. Based on the needs-assessment, prioritize the steps necessary to creating an environment conducive to learning and an action plan to succeed. Remember that this needs to be a shared vision and faculty buy-in is a critical component of this plan.

Professional Development: Many of the ideas in this chapter may be further developed through professional development. Choose one of the sections and develop a PowerPoint presentation for faculty development.

REFERENCES

Berg, J. L. (2015). The role of personal purpose and personal goals in symbiotic visions. *Frontiers of Psychology. 6*, 1–13. doi:10.3389/fpsyg.2015.00443

Collins, J. C. & Porras, J. I., (1996). Building your company's vision. *Harvard Business Review. 74*(5) 65–77.

Dik, B. J., Byrne, Z. S., & Steger, M. F. (eds.). (2013). *Purpose and meaning in the workplace*. Washington, DC: The American Psychological Association. doi: 10.1037/14183-000

Epstein, J. L., Galindo, C. L., & Sheldon, S. B.(2011). Levels of leadership: Effects of district and school leaders on the quality of school programs of family and community involvement. *Educational Administration Quarterly, 47*(3), 462–495.

ESSA (2015). *Every Student Succeeds Act of 2015*, Pub. L. No. 114-95 § 114 Stat. 1177.

Farrell, C. C. (2015). Designing school systems to encourage data use and instructional improvement: A comparison of school districts and charter management organizations. *Educational Administration Quarterly, 51*(3), 438–471. doi:10.1177/0013161X14539806

Fitzgerald, A. M., & Quiñones, S. (2018) Working in and with community: Leading for partnerships in a community school, leadership and policy in schools, 1–22. doi:10.1080/15700763.2018.1453938

Grandin, T. (2006). *Thinking in pictures: My life with autism.* New York: Vintage Books

Lenhardt, A. M. C., Graham, L. W., & Farrell, M. L. (2018). A framework for school safety and risk management: Results from a study of 18 targeted school shooters. *The Educational Forum, 82*(1), 3–20. doi:10.1080/00131725 .2018.1381792

Levpuscek, M. P. (2012). Social anxiety, social acceptance and academic self-perception in high school students. Drustveba Istrazivanja, 21(2), 405+

Lai, M. K., & Schildkamp, K. (2013). Data-based decision making: An overview. In K. Schildkamp, M. K. Lai, & L. Earl (Eds.), Data-based decision making in education: challenges and opportunities (pp. 9–21). Dordrecht: Springer.

MacArthur, J. (2004, Oct. 15.). *Grace to You Newsletter.*

McDaniel, B. T., & Coyne, S. M. (2016). "Technoference": The interference of technology in couple relationships and implications for women's personal and relational well-being. *Psychology of Popular Media Culture*, 5(1), 85–98. doi:10.1037/ppm0000065

McLaughlin, M. W., & Talbert, J. E. (2006). *Building school-based teacher learning communities : Professional strategies to improve student achievement.* New York: Teachers College Press.

Miller, C. M., & Martin, B. N. (2015). Principal preparedness for leading in demographically changing schools: Where is the social justice training? *Educational Management Administration & Leadership, 43*(1), 129–151. doi:10.1177/1741143213513185

National Center for Education Statistics. *English language learners in public schools.* Retrieved from: https://nces.ed.gov/programs/coe/indicator_cgf.asp

Roberts, J. A., & David, M. E. (2016). My life has become a major distraction from my cell phone: Partner phubbing and relationship satisfaction among romantic partners. *Computers in Human Behavior*, 54, 134–141. doi:10.1016/j.chb.2015.07.058

Robinson, V. M. J., Lloyd, C. A., & Rowe, K. J.(2008). The impact of leadership on student outcomes: An analysis of the differential effects of leadership types. *Educational Administration Quarterly, 44*(5), 635–674. doi:10.1177/0013161x08321509

Rossen, E., & Cowan, K. C. (2014). Improving mental health in schools. *Phi Delta Kappan, 96*(4), 8–13.

Schildkamp, K., Poortman, C. L., & Handelzalts, A. (2016). Data teams for school improvement. *School Effectiveness and School Improvement, 27*(2), 228–254. doi:10.1080/09243453.2015.1056192

Spiro, J. D. (2013). Effective principals in action. *Phi Delta Kappan, 94*(8), 27–31. doi:10.1177/003172171309400807

Teaching English to speakers of Other Languages (TESOL). International Association (2018). Retrived from: https://www.tesol.org

Timar, T. B., & Chyu, K. K. (2010). State strategies to improve low-performing schools: California's high-priority schools grant program. *Teachers College Record, 112*(7), 1897–1936.

Vanden Abeele, M. M. P., Antheunis, M. L., & Schouten, A. P. (2016). The effect of mobile messaging during a conversation on impression formation and interaction quality. *Computers in Human Behavior*, 62, 562–569. doi:10.1016/j.chb.2016.04.005

Vossekuil, B., Fein, R. A., Reddy, M., Borum, R., & Modzeleski, W. (2002). *The final report and findings of the Safe School Initiative: Implications for the prevention of school attacks in the United States*. Washington, DC: U.S. Secret Service, U.S. Department of Education.

ADDITIONAL RESOURCES

Data Teams:

Schildkamp, K., Poortman, C. L., & Handelzalts, A. (2016). Data teams for school improvement. *School Effectiveness and School Improvement, 27*(2), 228–254. doi:10.1080/09243453.2015.1056192

Individual Education Plans:

Read the book by Dr. Bunnie Claxton: *Planning, Writing, and Implementing IEPs: A Christian Approach*. Dubuque: IA, Kendall Hunt

School Safety:

Supplemental School Safety Framework Guidance_Briefing.pdf

The Safety of the School Environment Using the Framework. Retrieved from: https://www.nasponline.org/resources-and-publications/resources/school-safety-and-crisis/a-framework-for-safe-and-successful-schools

Students with Autism:

Read the book by Dr. Temple Grandin, *Talking in Pictures: My Life with Autism.* New York, NY, Vintage Books

Teacher Learning Communities:

Read the book by McLaughlin and Talbert (2006). *Building School-based Teacher Learning Communities : Professional Strategies to Improve Student Achievement.* New York: Teachers College Press.

Chapter 4

Leading Curriculum Development

Mark A. Angle

Curriculum development is the essential function of school leadership. Whether the role is carried out by a principal, an assistant principal for curriculum, a team leader, a department head, or by leading classroom teachers, the curriculum defines all other roles in a school.

—Jon Wiles (2009, p. 2)—

OVERVIEW

This chapter will provide a brief history of curriculum development in the United States. The reader will be provided with a practical approach to leading curriculum development at the school level, including some common mistakes to avoid. The chapter will conclude with questions and activities that school teams can use to engage in the process of curriculum development.

Objectives

By the end of this chapter, the reader should be able to do the following:

1. Develop and plan curricular goals.
2. Create and communicate a rigorous academic program.
3. Put systems in place to monitor progress.
4. Collect and analyze pertinent data.
5. Foster a climate of accountability for student success.

INTRODUCTION

Curriculum development is "an ongoing process that asks teachers and administrators to think, act, and meet differently to improve their students' learning" (Hale, 2008, p. 8). Curriculum is the content of what is taught both intentionally and unintentionally—the hidden curriculum—through the actions of and by the choices made in terms of what gets included in or excluded from the courses and content that are ultimately delivered to the students. Curriculum is local and global, being driven by both the classroom teacher who plans and delivers lessons and by grade-level or subject teams, school committees, local boards of education, state boards of education, and, more recently, by national collaborations leading to a common set of standards now adopted by a majority of states within the United States. Curriculum is both static and fluid. Some goals, such as learning to read, remain unchanged over the years, whereas others are in a continuous process of revision and flux as students, parents, society, and new technologies demand changes to match the expectations of the 21st-century learner and global citizen.

BACKGROUND

Historical Background

John 1:1 states, "In the beginning was the Word . . ." (King James Version) and this is quite literally true when one considers the history of curriculum in the United States. Not only was the Bible used as a textbook, but also the major purpose of schools was to "teach children to read the Scriptures and notices of civil affairs" (Ornstein & Hunkins, 1988, p. 52). It is understandable that during the Colonial Period (1642–1776), reading was the most important subject followed by writing and spelling. According to Ornstein and Hunkins, colonial schools emphasized religious faith, basic skills, rote memorization, absolute values, and memorization, including memorization of Holy Scripture and the Lord's Prayer.

During the National Period (1776–1850), curriculum evolved as America gained her independence. The concepts of life, liberty, and equality, which were being promoted in the foundational documents of our nation—the Declaration of Independence and the Bill of Rights—were mirrored in the curriculum, where schools developed a new mission for education: an educated citizenry that had the capacity to perpetuate a free, democratic government. In 1816, Thomas Jefferson said to Charles Yancey, "If a nation expects to be ignorant and free in a state of civilization, it expects what never was and never will be" (Lipscomb & Bergh, 1903–04, p. 384). It was Jefferson who believed it was the responsibility of the state to cultivate an educated citizenry and who advocated a plan for the education of all citizens, not just the upper classes.

During the 19th century, American curriculum was influenced by European theorists such as Pestalozzi, who believed that curriculum should be developmentally appropriate for the learner; Froebel, whose "child's garden"—known today as kindergarten—was based on organized play and self-development; Herbart, who advocated that the main purpose of education should be to develop moral character—a throwback to Puritan schools; and Spencer, whose ideas were rooted in the theories of Charles Darwin and focused on practical and utilitarian education for the increasingly industrialized society. As articulated by Ornstein and Hunkins (1988), as America expanded westward, so too the curriculum expanded, adding subjects such as geography, history, science, foreign languages, and fine arts.

By the early 20th century, curriculum development began to be viewed as a field in itself and over time included the ideas of specialists, teachers, and learners. The "science" of curriculum was born when Waples and Tyler (1930), who at the time were colleagues at The Ohio State University, outlined in their book *Research Methods and Teachers' Problems: A Manual for Systematic Studies of Classroom Procedure* the major elements in curriculum and instruction:

1. Defining objectives, organizing content, and adopting materials
2. Selecting learning experiences and diagnosing learners
3. Managing students
4. Outlining techniques of instruction and evaluation

To a great extent, these remain the guiding principles of curriculum development theory.

After the 1983 publication of *A Nation at Risk: The Imperative for Educational Reform* (U.S. National Commission on Excellence in Education, 1983), individual states began to take more control over curriculum development by creating and mandating statewide curriculum standards. This report contributed to the sense that U.S. schools were failing and made 38 recommendations for improving schools across five major categories: content, standards and expectations, time, teaching, and leadership and fiscal support. Although numerous recommendations were not implemented broadly, such as 7-hour school days and 220-day school years, the "standards and expectations" component did garner wide appeal. By 1998, 38 states had drafted academic standards in core subjects (English, math, science, and social studies) and 34 states used standards-based assessments of math and English (Angle, 2002). Yet, in that same year, *A Nation Still at Risk: An Education Manifesto* (The Center for Educational Reform, 1998) stated, "America's educational system is [still] failing far too many people" (p. 2). To address the crisis, the authors of the 1998 *Manifesto* proposed that the central issues for education reform had to do with excellence for all children, high standards for all teachers and schools, and the effectiveness of the system as a whole. They suggested a vast transfer of power from producers to consumers, providing every family the opportunity to choose where its children attended school. To improve schools, the signatories revealed two main renewal strategies, working in tandem: (1) standards, assessments, and accountability; and (2) pluralism, competition, and choice. They defined standards, assessments, and accountability as every student, school, and district being expected to meet high standards of learning; parents being fully informed about the progress of their child and their child's school; and district and state officials rewarding success and having the obligation to intervene in cases of failure (Angle, 2002).

© Rawpixel.com/Shutterstock.com

The focus on state standards and assessment accelerated when in 2001 *No Child Left Behind* (NCLB) became national law and set into place a high-stakes testing component tied to the content standards. NCLB required all states to develop assessments in basic subjects and to administer those assessments to all students at select grade levels in order to receive federal funding. Although standards were set by each state, NCLB expanded the federal role in education through annual testing, annual academic progress requirements, annual report cards, and requirements for teachers to be "highly qualified." For the first time, scores were provided by "subgroups," including traditionally underserved groups of students such as low-income students, students with disabilities, students who spoke English as a second language, and students of major racial and ethnic subgroups. This revealed that some schools were doing well as a whole, but poorly with certain groups of learners. This analysis and disaggregation of data led to a new emphasis on success at the student level, rather than at the school level. The requirement was that all students would reach mastery by 2014. This requirement, however, raised concerns that teachers were too often "teaching to the test." In addition, complaints that the law was underfunded resulted in increasing calls for reform.

In 2009, *Race to the Top* attempted to address the concerns that standardized testing failed to capture higher-level thinking by outlining new systems of evaluation. RTTT provided states with much needed supplemental funding, but also brought with it controversial requirements such as the adoption of Common Core Standards. The U.S. Department of Education also created provision for states to seek waivers from NCLB, provided that the states had an approved plan to raise standards, improve accountability, and implement reforms that improve teacher effectiveness. Both NCLB and RTTT seemed to indicate a trend toward increasing federal influence in curricula matters.

More recently, NCLB and RTT gave way to the Every Student Succeeds Act signed into law in 2015. Although it often takes years to realize the effects of changes in federal education law, ESSA was touted as legislation that will return much of the federal influence that had accumulated over the years, back to the states.

Biblical Perspectives

Whether by design or accident, the personal beliefs, values, and worldview of the curriculum developers will influence what gets included or excluded from the content, what and how content attainment is evaluated, and the theoretical framework from which the curriculum is founded. For example, whether one believes in absolute truth or relative truth will dramatically alter the curriculum. Christianity is built on the premise that truth is absolute; thus, curriculum developed for a Christian school will more likely be built on this foundational belief. Modern culture, however, accepts the belief that truth is relative, something that is created rather than discovered. Those who subscribe to this philosophy will develop curriculum from a different perspective given their belief that truth can change and is a matter of the individual's perspective. Zukeran (n.d.), in an article titled "Truth: Absolute or Relative," presented the following biblical framework for understanding and defining truth:

Whether by design or accident, the personal beliefs, values, and worldview of the curriculum developers will influence what gets included or excluded from the content, what and how content attainment is evaluated, and the theoretical framework from which the curriculum is founded.

Truth is revealed by God. In the first and second chapter of the Book of Romans, Paul stated that God has revealed Himself through creation and human conscience. Further, 2 Timothy 3:16 states, "All scripture is given by inspiration of God, and is profitable for doctrine, for reproof, for correction, for instruction in righteousness." Truth finds its source in God, who is personal and moral.

Objective truth exists and is knowable. God's truth is objective because truth is rooted in the nature of God. God is the source of truth and His truths are true no matter what the beliefs or attitudes of a given culture.

Biblical truth is absolute. God is the author of absolute truth because God is eternal and His character does not change.

Truth is universal. God's truth applies to all people and all cultures because He rules over all creation (Philippians 2:6).

Truth is eternal. Isaiah 40:8 states, "The grass withereth, the flower fadeth: but the word of our God shall stand for ever." Although the application of truth may change, truth itself endures forever.

Truth is exclusive. God states in Isaiah 43:10, ". . . before me there was no God formed, neither shall there be after me."

Truth is coherent. God's nature is to teach what is coherent and logical; therefore, truth statements will not contradict one another.

Truth is comprehensive. God's truth is not fragmented but fits together in a consistent and unified whole with His creation.

If curriculum developers subscribe to Zukeran's biblical framework for understanding truth as articulated in the preceding description, it is obvious to see how the finished curriculum product will vary from the product developed by those who believe instead in relative truth. The discussion of absolute truth versus relative truth is one part of the larger concept of worldview. Everyone has a worldview, but according to the Barna Group (2009), only 4% of Americans identify as having a biblical worldview, defined as believing in the following:

- Absolute moral truth exists.
- The Bible is totally accurate in all principles it teaches.

- Satan is considered to be a real being or force, not merely symbolic.
- People cannot earn their way into heaven by trying to be good or do good works.
- Jesus Christ lived a sinless life on earth.
- God is the all-knowing, all-powerful Creator of the world Who still rules the universe today.

Tackett (n.d.) stated that someone with a biblical worldview "believes his primary reason for existence is to love and serve God." He also argued that developing and adhering to a biblical worldview is important because by diligently learning, applying, and trusting God's truths in every area of their lives, Christians can begin to develop a deep and comprehensive faith that will stand against the unrelenting tide of the culture's nonbiblical ideas. He claimed that if Christians capture and embrace more of God's worldview and trust it with unwavering faith, they will begin to make the right decisions and form the appropriate responses to questions on abortion, same-sex marriage, cloning, stem-cell research, and even media choices.

The task of curriculum development in Christian schools has grown exponentially, if—in addition to content—developers believe that the role of a Christian school education is to promulgate Christian values and beliefs and to help learners develop a biblical worldview. Developers of curriculum in Christian schools must find ways not only to teach these concepts through content, but must also ensure these foundational beliefs are embedded in meaningful ways that can be modeled for learners through curriculum, instruction, and assessment practices.

Developers of curriculum in Christian schools must find ways not only to teach these concepts through content, but must also ensure these foundational beliefs are embedded in meaningful ways that can be modeled for learners through curriculum, instruction, and assessment practices.

CURRICULUM DEVELOPMENT IN ACTION

Leading the Development Cycle

Curriculum is the foundation on which all other aspects of the school are built. Because principals can only indirectly impact student achievement—after all, principals are not in the classrooms providing instruction—it is essential that principals be directly involved in all aspects of the school where the potential to impact student achievement is possible. Curriculum is one of these areas. It is imperative for the principal to take a leadership role in this process. Doing so enables the principal make more informed evaluations of the curriculum itself and of the teachers who are charged with delivering it to the students.

Core Beliefs

Whether in a public or private school setting, before beginning this process the principal must examine the biases that will be brought to the task. The principal needs to consider educational philosophy and leadership style. Perhaps not overtly, but the philosophy and leadership style of the principal will impact the development of the curriculum—both the intentional curriculum and the hidden curriculum.

The task of curriculum development is not one that the principal can or should do alone. Including lead teachers, central office staff, parents, and students is a necessary and critical part of the process. Like the principal, the core development team needs also to examine its philosophy of education and curriculum. In the activities section of this chapter, the reader will find suggestions for leading a discussion and activities that will assist the team in examining its core beliefs. Not everyone on the team will have the same philosophy, nor should they. Diversity among the core development team can lead to a richer and deeper curriculum.

Audience

Once the team has examined beliefs and biases, the next task is to understand the audience for whom the curriculum is going to be delivered. This requires a deep disaggregation of the data for the school. Who are the learners? The team needs to know the demographic composition of not only the school, but also the community, as the community helps set expectations for what learners should know and be able to do after graduating.

What challenges do the learners face? How can the curriculum be presented in a way that maximizes opportunities for learners to overcome common challenges? What background knowledge is lacking? How can the curriculum spiral, or repeat the same content at different times, each time at a higher level of difficulty and in greater depth, to build background knowledge that learners need to be successful? Not only do the team members need to know as much as possible about the learners, but they also must know the demographics of their learners' parents and caregivers. These stakeholders need to understand the rationale for and be able to support the implementation of the curriculum. This is why it is important to include a diverse representation of parents on the development team. Finally, the core development team has a duty to know the characteristics and needs of the community. What skills do business leaders perceive as essential? What do these leaders believe is currently lacking? When complete, the curriculum should first and foremost serve the needs of the learners. The curriculum, however, must also strive to meet the needs of the parents and community.

Mission, Vision, Values, Goals

Curriculum development should begin with a clear understanding of the mission, vision, values, and goals of the organization. If these items have not been revised in some time, they should be reviewed and revised as necessary before curriculum development begins. The mission, vision, and values should not be so theoretical or complex that they are not easily understood. All school employees, students, and parents should be able to articulate the basic tenants of these important statements and they should be embedded in everything the school does. The core development team should regularly ask, "How does this content support our mission, vision, and values?" If the question cannot easily be answered, perhaps that content should not be part of the curriculum. In public schools, the team must ensure the mission, vision, and values at the school level are consistent with and can be appropriately layered on the mission, vision, and values of the school district. In independent private schools, the team must ensure the mission, vision, and values are consistent with the beliefs of the governing board and parents, whose tuition payments and support are necessary for the ongoing success of the school.

Standards

All schools—public and private—must begin the process of creating curriculum with the standards for what students will know and be able to do. As articulated earlier in this chapter, for many public schools, the starting point will be the standards established by that state. For private schools, national standards from reputable professional organizations, such as the National Council for Teachers of Mathematics, should be consulted. For all schools, no one set of standards should serve as the only source of guidance for articulating what students should know and be able to do. Those in Christian schools will need to be aware of the worldview that is presented in the content of these standards and make modifications when necessary to ensure that the standards meet the mission of the school in preparing learners to develop a biblical worldview. All schools should use available standards as a starting point for developing their own. However, all schools should also add standards where needed to ensure alignment with the audience, core belief, mission, vision, values, and goals of the organization.

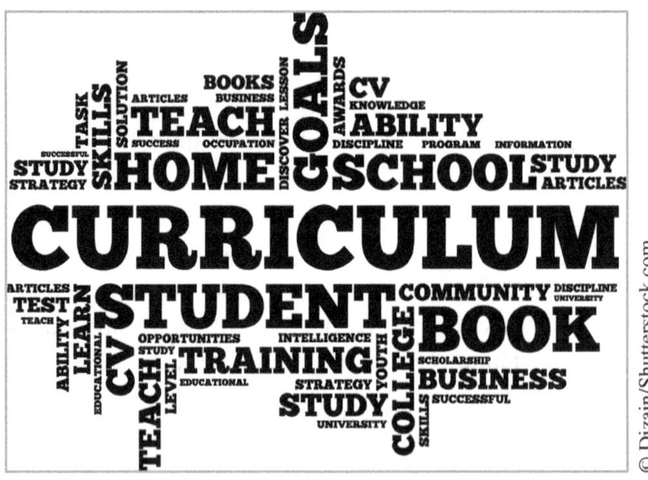

© Dizain/Shutterstock.com

Scope and Sequence

The scope and sequence will serve as the road map that displays the plan for covering all the standards for each grade level within one school year. This is the process of beginning with the end in mind so as to ensure that when the school year comes to a close, all of the required standards have been taught. The scope and sequence is not a day-by-day document; rather, it is a big-picture glance of the timeline for delivering the curriculum. Considerable thought must be given to developmental appropriateness and skills that build on one another to ensure the content is presented in the most logical and appropriate manner and that learners have the greatest opportunity to have access to the necessary background knowledge they will need to learn new content when it is presented. Opportunities must also be included for spiraling of the curriculum. That is, the opportunity must be available to go back to previously taught content and review what has been learned so that it remains available and usable by students.

Pacing Guide

Once the scope and sequence is completed, the pacing guide can be created. A pacing guide is a more detailed curriculum map that shows in greater detail the specific standards that are going to be taught each grading period, weekly, and even daily. This detailed guide brings the standards into greater focus and provides more specificity for delivering the curriculum. Think of it as taking a cross-country road map and developing it into daily itineraries for the trip. If enough time and energy have been devoted to ensuring the scope and sequence is appropriately aligned, the creation of the pacing guide will go more smoothly. It can be expected, however, that changes to the scope and sequence will need to occur during this time of creating the more detailed, daily guide. During this process, both the scope and sequence and the pacing guide should be considered fluid documents that are being revised and improved as additional thought is given to the process and content of delivering the curriculum standards. Moreover, both documents should be constantly reviewed and revised even after they move from draft to final version. This is necessary because thinking about delivering content is different from actually doing so. As teachers work with learners, realizations that content sequence, timing, number of days devoted to a specific standard, and other aspects do not work as well in reality as they worked on paper. Thus, it is essential to have in place a reporting process whereby those teachers who are actually delivering the content to learners have nonthreatening ways to let the developers know what is working well and what needs to be changed so the curriculum can be in a process of continuous improvement.

Objective Maps

Objective maps provide unit lesson plans that individual teachers can use as resources to develop their daily lesson plans. These maps help ensure the content is being delivered to learners in the correct order and at the right pace. Objective maps should be available as a guide to assist teachers but must not be used to the extent that individual teacher judgment and creativity are jeopardized. Teachers should have enough flexibility on a daily basis to deliver the content in the ways they know are most meaningful for their learners; they should also be held accountable for student learning. The best way to ensure this occurs is through effective use of benchmark assessments.

Benchmark Assessments

Benchmark assessments provide a tool for teachers and students to measure what has been taught and learned. Additionally, intentional benchmark assessments can provide important practice in the format of state assessments. They can also inform plans for remediation, ensuring all students are ready for the high-stakes assessments that are typically administered at the end of the school year. Benchmark assessments should be used to identify the areas in which the school and classroom instruction need to improve. When implemented correctly, they not only help students and teachers, but they also reveal problems within the curriculum design that can be addressed in ongoing revisions and improvements, leading to a cycle of continuous school improvement. Benchmark assessments should be given at the end of each grading period. The best benchmark assessments are created by groups of teachers, but if time constraints are a problem, they can be created at the central office level. Because the format of the benchmark assessment mirrors the format of state assessments, the student gains experience with the test-taking strategies that are necessary for high-stakes accountability. Although the benchmark assessment is useful for students for this reason, the real value of benchmark assessments is in using the data to inform instruction and to improve the curriculum. Benchmark assessments must follow best practices for creating effective assessments and must measure content at varying levels of thinking. A question-by-question analysis should be completed after each assessment and used in the following ways: classroom level, grade level or subject area, and school level.

- **Classroom level:** The teacher must determine which students have mastered what content and which students need additional instruction in specific skills and standards. This should happen as soon after testing is completed as possible, and teachers must reteach content in small groups or to the class in the areas that are of concern revealed by the assessments results.
- **Grade level or subject area:** Teacher teams, by grade level or subject area, must compare the results of their class to the group as a whole. Teachers have a responsibility to identify what they are teaching well and the areas in which their students are struggling. In the best situations, teachers will group students across classrooms so that reteaching is done by the teacher who had the best results with that particular content.
- **School level:** Benchmark assessment presents a key opportunity to improve the curriculum. If many students across several teachers did poorly on a particular standard, the curriculum developers need to ask several critical questions:

    1. Was the content presented at the right time?
    2. Was enough time provided in the pacing guide for students to master the content?
    3. Did students have the necessary background knowledge?
    4. Did teachers have the necessary resources to teach the standard?
    5. Were the questions reliable and valid?

Used effectively, benchmark assessments will improve student success immediately through remediation of nonmastered content and will also improve their future success by ensuring they are comfortable with test-taking skills and the format of end-of-year high-stakes tests. Benchmark assessments will improve instruction as teachers analyze what they taught well and what they need to teach differently to ensure attainment by all learners. They will improve collaboration as teachers learn their colleagues' strengths and develop innovative ways of delivering content based on the strengths of each team member. Additionally, they will improve the curriculum as refinements are made with regard to content, pacing, and resources available for students and teachers.

Implementing and Evaluating the Curriculum

Effective use of benchmark assessments is one method of evaluating the curriculum. Additional mechanisms, however, must also be in place to ensure each teacher delivers the required curriculum so that all learners within the school have an equal opportunity for success.

Supervising and Coaching Teachers

As suggested earlier in this chapter, the principal must be actively involved in the curriculum development process from start to finish. This is critical so that when principals supervise teachers, they are aware of the following:

- What content teachers should be delivering (standards)
- At what time of year (scope and sequence)
- How much time teachers should have devoted in their lesson plans to delivering the standards (pacing guide)
- Kinds of activities that are suggested for teachers to use for delivering the standards (objective maps)

More often now than in the past, principals are viewed as instructional leaders or academic coaches who help their teachers improve their teaching effectiveness. Although this is a time-consuming process, especially given the many management pieces that principals must also handle, there is no better way for the principal to impact student achievement than through effective supervision and providing meaningful feedback that encourages teachers to improve their instruction so that student achievement improves.

Evaluating Instruction Versus Evaluating Curriculum

Principals and supervisors must remember the difference between evaluating instruction versus evaluating the curriculum. In some cases, student achievement will be less than desired not because of issues with the curriculum, but instead because of the inability of the teacher effectively to deliver the curriculum to the learners. This is where principal as academic coach comes into play. The principal can provide feedback to help teachers improve their pedagogy, can model lesson delivery, and can require the observation of other teachers.

Common Mistakes

Lack of Alignment Among Standards, Instruction, and Assessment

One common mistake made by curriculum developers is a lack of alignment between the identified content standards, daily instruction, and benchmark assessment. Sometimes this happens because these three pieces are created in vacuums. This is why it is essential that the curriculum development team include teachers who are going to be responsible for delivering the instruction. When teachers are intimately familiar with the standards and the rationale for including those standards in the curriculum, they are more likely to ensure they are taught to mastery. Conversely, the curriculum development team must be involved in the assessment process. Minimally, the team must review benchmark assessments prior to administration to ensure they match standards. The team will help ensure not only that the correct standards are included on the assessment but also that they are weighted appropriately based on the percentage of time devoted to each standard in the pacing guide. Only when there is a seamless integration between standards, instruction, and assessment will the curriculum be most viable.

Lack of Horizontal and Vertical Articulation

The lack of horizontal and vertical articulation can be a major barrier in the success of the school as a whole. Horizontal articulation refers to the idea that teachers at common grade levels are delivering the same content at the same time. Critics will often suggest that this takes the creativity out of teaching. Horizontal articulation does not suggest that individual teachers not use their own professional judgment or creativity within their classrooms. Rather, it is an acknowledgement that every child in the school should have the same curricular experience regardless of the teacher to whom they happen to be assigned. The best way that principals can ensure horizontal articulation occurs is to give grade-level teachers common planning time and require that they team-plan at least once each week. Another important way to achieve horizontal articulation is for the principal to find ways to send teachers to observe in the classrooms of their grade-level colleagues several times each year. This not only helps with horizontal articulation but also serves as a professional development tool as teachers learn and grow from watching their colleagues teach and manage their own classrooms.

Vertical articulation refers to the delivery of the curriculum across grade levels. This is more difficult to attain than horizontal articulation for the same reason that it is difficult to achieve alignment of standards, instruction, and assessment. Often, the curriculum has been developed grade by grade or subject by subject in vacuums, with no one looking at the bigger picture. Principals rightly want all teachers to be experts in their grade-level or subject content, but teachers must also know how their piece of the puzzle fits into the total educational experience for the learner. Ultimately, learners must be provided with a seamless program from start to finish if they are going to be able to meet their full potential. Vertical articulation can best be achieved when principals find ways to allow teams of grade-level or subject-specific teachers to go as teams to observe other classrooms throughout the school. For example, all the third-grade teachers go together to observe the teachers in all the other grade levels in the school. Like horizontal visits, vertical visits provide a professional development activity and offer teachers an opportunity to see firsthand how their content fits into the content of the grade levels immediately before and after their own and then into the bigger picture. Too often educators are guilty of seeing school through the lens of the teacher. Learners would be better served and better prepared for their futures if educators forced themselves to see the curriculum—from beginning to end—through their eyes. Vertical visits help create this opportunity.

Misuse of Data

Data from benchmark assessments should be used to inform instruction and evaluate the curriculum, not as high-stakes tests for students. Teachers should analyze benchmark data immediately after the assessment is given and determine what they need to reteach. Small groups should be formed for remediating specific deficient skills. Creative principals will find ways to provide instruction in these flexible groups before school, during the school day, or after school immediately after the benchmark assessment is completed because they understand that some skills are prerequisites for mastery of skills to be taught in the next grading period.

Another way benchmark data should be used is to evaluate and improve the curriculum itself. Curriculum developers must determine if adequate time or resources were devoted to the skills on which many students were deficient and then make adjustments to the pacing guide and objective maps to correct these issues.

CONCLUSION

Wiles (2009) said it best: "Curriculum development is the essential function of school leadership. Whether the role is carried out by a principal, an assistant principal for curriculum, a team leader, a department head, or by leading classroom teachers, the curriculum defines all other roles in a school" (p. 2).

This chapter has provided a brief history of curriculum development in the United States and given the reader a detailed, practical approach to leading curriculum development at the school level. Similarities and differences in the process between public, private, and Christian schools have been delineated, but it is apparent that the process is more similar than different. Specific strategies have been given not only for development of the curriculum but also for evaluating it in terms of teacher delivery of the content, student attainment of the content, and the quality of the curriculum itself.

Discussion Questions

1. Which group of stakeholders (teacher, learner, society, government, church, and family) appears to have had the most influential voice in the development of curriculum standards? Which stakeholder group may appear to have been left out of the development of standards? What evidence leads to your conclusion?

2. Consider the unique characteristics of a scope and sequence for one particular cluster group (PK–2, 3–5, 6–8, or 9–12). How is the process for that cluster group similar to or different from those for the other cluster groups?

3. How important is it for grade-level teachers or content-area teachers to collaborate when creating the scope and sequence?

4. Is there value in collaborating across grade levels (for example, K–2 teachers working together) or across subject areas (math and science teachers working together)? Why or why not?

5. Reflect on your own experiences as a learner and teacher. How often was the learning environment interrupted by announcements, fire drills, school assemblies, and other distractions? How do these interruptions play a role in the development of an effective and realistic curriculum, scope and sequence, and detailed semester pacing guide? How might the curriculum developer help maximize time for teaching and learning?

6. What are some of the standardized tests given in your school or other surrounding schools? To what degree are these tests accurately aligned with curriculum and instruction?

7. What are some of the programs, action plans, intervention plans, and so forth that are being implemented (or that you feel should be implemented) to improve learning?

Activities for Enrichment

1. Use your favorite search engine to search for "education philosophy survey." Use one of the available online tools to determine with which philosophy you most align: essentialism, perennialism, progressivism, social reconstructivism, or existentialism.
2. Use your favorite search engine to search for "leadership style survey." Use one of the available online tools to determine your preferred leadership style: authoritarian, participative, or delegative.
3. Consider how your worldview impacts your belief and opinions about curriculum development. Think about your beliefs regarding the roles of the teacher, learner, society, government, church, and family in the development of the curriculum.
4. Select one stakeholder group (teacher, learner, society, government, church, and family) and consider the degree to which that particular group should influence decisions about the development of curriculum. Have you seen examples of when the involvement, or lack thereof, from this particular group has helped or hindered curriculum development?
5. Articulate a demographic description, mission statement, vision, values, and goals for a school. Be sure that your demographic description includes the size of the student body, the demographics of the community, the school facilities, the structure of the school program, and the extracurricular offerings.
6. Research the national, state, and other published standards (such as Bennett or Hirsch) for a grade cluster/subject area of interest to you (e.g., grades 3–5 math).
7. Conduct an in-depth analysis of the standards from several different sources for one specific grade level or subject area. Consider the similarities and differences. Think about the strengths and weaknesses of each set of standards. Also, consider how you might combine the sets by taking the best from each to produce an ideal curriculum.
8. Configure a sample scope and sequence that articulates when and for how long certain content or skills will be taught.
9. Create a detailed pacing guide that includes standards to be taught daily for an entire semester. Include pre- and posttest assessments, school holidays, and some "flexible time" within your guide.
10. Practice creating objective maps for standards that would be covered during a grading period. Remember to include time for pre- and posttest assessments.
11. Design a benchmark assessment to measure a set of standards that might be taught during a specific grading period. The questions should measure attainment of the content and should mirror your state's standardized assessments in format and style.
12. Imagine that you have just been asked to be the chair of a committee tasked with creating a new curriculum for a content area at your school. Because of high attrition, most of the teachers with whom you will be working have less than 5 years of teaching experience and have never participated in a curriculum development process. Consider how you would go about leading this committee toward the goal of creating a viable curriculum.

REFERENCES

Angle, M. A. (2002). *Does music matter? Using school-wide student participation in elective music program to predict variability in student achievement.* Unpublished doctoral dissertation, University of Virginia, Charlottesville.

The Barna Group. (2009, March 06). Barna survey examines changes in worldview among Christians over the past 13 years. Retrieved from http://www.barna.org/barna-update/article/21-transformation/252-barna-survey-examines-changes-in-worldview-among-christians-over-the-past-13-years

The Center for Education Reform. (1998). *A nation still at risk: An education manifesto.* Washington, DC: Author.

Hale, J. A. (2008). *A guide to curriculum mapping: Planning, implementing, and sustaining the process.* Thousand Oaks, CA: Corwin Press.

Lipscomb, A., & Bergh, A. (1903–04). *The writings of Thomas Jefferson* (ME ed., Vol. 14). Washington DC: Thomas Jefferson Memorial Association of the United States.

No Child Left Behind (NCLB) Act of 2001, Pub. L. No. 107–110, § 115, Stat. 1425 (2002).

Ornstein, C. O., & Hunkins, F. P. (1988). *Curriculum foundations, principles, and issues.* Englewood Cliffs, NJ: Prentice Hall.

S. 844—112th Congress: Race to the Top Act of 2011. (2011). Retrieved from http://www.govtrack.us/congress/bills/112/s844

Tackett, D. (n.d.). What's a Christian worldview? Retrieved from http://www.focusonthefamily.com/faith/christian_worldview/whats_a_christian_worldview.aspx

U.S. National Commission on Excellence in Education. (1983). *A nation at risk: The imperative for educational reform: a report to the nation and the Secretary of Education, United States Department of Education.* Washington, DC: Author.

Waples, D., & Tyler, R. (1930). *Research methods and teachers' problems: A manual for systematic studies of classroom procedure.* New York, NY: MacMillan.

Wiles, J. (2009). *Leading curriculum development.* Thousand Oaks, CA: Corwin Press.

Zukeran, P. (n.d.). Truth: Absolute or relative. Retrieved from http://www.evidenceandanswers.org/articles/truth.pdf

Chapter 5

Developing the Faculty

Russell L. Claxton

What nobler employment, or more valuable to the state, than that of the person who instructs the next generation.
—Cicero, Roman statesman—

OVERVIEW

There is no greater investment of time and resources than that devoted to the continuous development and improvement of a school's faculty. Great instruction is not something that is achieved. It is not a destination or pedagogical plateau at which teachers eventually arrive and settle in for the duration of their careers. Great instruction is something that is continually honed, refined, and built upon. Such a process relies heavily on the principal to support it, align it, and create a culture in which improving instruction is a norm, not an activity relegated to a day or two designated during summer break. This chapter will briefly discuss the progression and perception of professional development through the past century and then focus on the practical aspects of developing productive, ongoing training for teachers.

Objectives

By the end of this chapter, the reader should be able to do the following:

1. Identify the professional development needs of a school and staff.
2. Involve faculty in the identification of professional development needs and the development of a quality instructional program.
3. Maximize time spent on quality instruction.
4. Promote the use of technology to support teaching and learning.
5. Monitor and evaluate the effectiveness of the instructional program.

INTRODUCTION

The importance of faculty professional development is one of the pivotal points for any school or district. Not only does it help shape the culture of the school, but it also sets its course. Structured, focused, and methodic faculty development can be the driving force for positive change or continued growth and achievement within a school. Conversely, a haphazard cascade of training without clear goals and a strategic plan may do more harm than no training at all. Such random professional development is comparable to a rudderless boat drifting along a river—better to stay tied to the dock than flounder, beating and bobbing along without purposeful navigation. However, a well-developed and needs-based plan can impact a faculty's growth immeasurably.

BACKGROUND

Historical Background

Considering the historical progression of professional development is worthwhile, especially to analyze shifting trends that occurred decade by decade within the U.S. education system. The driving force behind much of the professional development in the past four decades has been the result of national or state legislative initiatives. This legislation typically has impacted teachers in the form of new training to align with educational policies or philosophies en vogue at the time. In the most basic view, most professional development is geared toward the implementation of a new curriculum or the delivery of the curriculum. More times than not, it is more about a curricular change rather than a pedagogical change.

© Dusit/Shutterstock.com

Possibly the first professional development activity that most closely resembles our current concept of teacher training occurred in the early 1920s in the Denver School District. Jesse Newlon, a progressive administrator, convinced the Denver School Board to pay teachers a stipend to collaborate outside of the classroom to create a new curriculum. Although the teachers were not being trained themselves in a new curriculum or instructional strategies, this was the first recorded instance of teachers being compensated outside of the classroom to be a part of a wholesale change that would take place within their school.

The 1930s were highlighted by the Eight-Year Study (also known as the Thirty-School Study) led by the Progressive Education Association. During this time, teachers were tasked with analyzing their current core curriculum and modifying it to integrate subject matter to promote greater post–high school success. Continuous staff development, changes in assessment and student guidance, and teacher-created resources were at the center of this movement. This was one of the earliest large-scale reforms attempted through professional development. Coincidentally, the results of the Eight-Year Plan were negligible. Later studies showed little or no difference in student achievement between groups of students attending progressive schools and those attending traditional schools (Aikin, 1942).

During the 1940s and the first half of the 1950s, most professional development revolved around vocational training and the tracking of students for local economic and job force needs. Although the movement was a national one in general, the curricular focus and teacher development were adapted at the local level. During the Cold War era, the 1957 launch of the Soviet *Sputnik* satellite spurred an American reaction to the progressive-era dominance in education. Critics blamed the nation's lag in the Space Race on John Dewey's student-centered approach, which they perceived as lacking intellectualism—a "dumbing down" of U.S.

education. The 1960s, therefore, saw a renewed rigor in academic standards, and thus a renewed interest in training teachers to implement a more didactic pedagogy that produced college-bound students proficient in science and math. The charge was led by the National Science Foundation, and institutes for teacher professional development were created to train teachers in implementing a more rigorous curriculum and instructional techniques during the summer months. At this point, teacher professional development on the whole was a macro movement. Although common today, individual site-driven training specialized for particular school needs was rare during the post-*Sputnik* era.

The 1970s and 1980s may be categorized as the research-to-reform era. Countless studies were conducted over these two decades in order to assess the current state of practice and achievement. Results of such studies led to an explosion of reform manifested in new curriculum and ultimately new teacher development. The *Nation at Risk* report published in 1983 by President Ronald Reagan's National Commission on Excellence in Education exemplifies a research-driven reform. It should be noted, however, that most the commission's research focused on comparisons of the United States with other nations in the areas of the economy, gross national product, crime, teenage pregnancy, student academic performance, and so forth. It did not evaluate the effectiveness of any particular curriculum or instructional methodology.

A surge in constructivist theory and methodology occurred in the 1990s. Colleges of teacher education were dominated by constructivist professors who convincingly persuaded future educators that constructivism was the philosophy upon which instructional practice should be grounded. Reform efforts initiated from the grassroots of the profession and from the halls of universities were increasingly targeting the learning process itself and how the student experiences that process. Constructivists raged against the simultaneous reform movement originated by legislatures. They perceived the standards-driven, regimented instructional approach as too conformist and suffocating to student learning and creativity. As constructivists encouraged professional development that was more about pedagogy than about curriculum, a huge debate raged between the two camps. The constructivist camp regarded teaching as more of a student-centered art and was represented by the likes of Theodore Sizer (1994). The opposing camp—made up of philosophical essentialists and perennialists—viewed teaching as a knowledge-based science and was given voice by a number of traditionalists, one of the most prominent being E. D. Hirsch (1988), who wrote *Cultural Literacy: What Every American Needs to Know*. Among educationists, constructivist philosophy prevailed, and constructivist instructional strategies became the focus in professional training. One of the most noticeable shifts, however, was that local districts took on the main role of decision making in professional development, and it was becoming more common for individual schools to design their own professional development programs. During this time, principal-led professional development was widely becoming accepted as the norm, and the role of the principal was evolving into one of an instructional leader, rather than just a building manager.

The 2000s experienced an unparalleled resurgence in standards-based high-stakes testing and accountability. With the 2001 authorization of No Child Left Behind, teachers encountered top-down curriculum changes to align with standardized assessments that proclaimed greater rigor and more relevance to a student's ability to compete in a global market. "College and career ready" became the catchphrase as the United States looked to up the ante on student achievement. Almost every state undertook a complete curriculum overhaul, which trickled down to teachers in the form of new training in data analysis and formative instructional practices to monitor student progress continually. Although professional development was still a local enterprise and allowed for unique approaches in pedagogy, it was an end-result-oriented movement. Concerning student target achievement, federal and state departments of education basically said, "We don't care how you get there; just get there."

The current state of professional development, by necessity, has become more comprehensive. Although pedagogical training and strategies to meet accountability measures are still prevalent in K12 professional development, strategies to address social and economic issues have become increasingly common. Strategies to improve instruction are often coupled with training regarding school climate, school safety, college and career readiness, teacher leadership, and behavior management just to name a few (Riddell, Jacobson, & Campisi, 2019). Changes in federal legislation from NCLB to ESSA will most likely result in a return to professional development activities customized at the school or district level.

Biblical Perspectives

In his letter to the Corinthian church, the Apostle Paul admonished, "Everything should be done in a fitting and orderly way" (1 Corinthians 14:40, New International Version). As a Creator of order, God designs perfect plans aligned to the ultimate good of man. So too should instructional designs align to the good of students. Central to biblical teaching, the principles of order and forethought do not occur void of intentionality and careful planning. Instructional leaders cannot expect that teachers in their schools will consistently deliver instruction in a fitting and orderly way unless they receive ongoing support and training to do so.

Instructional leaders cannot expect that teachers in their schools will consistently deliver instruction in a fitting and orderly way unless they receive ongoing support and training to do so.

The mission of the school is underpinned by the strength of its teachers as instructors and their ability to continually improve. This improvement ensues only with support and ongoing training. An example of such support derives from the process of mentoring, which is illustrated throughout the Bible. Moses mentored Joshua; Jesus mentored His disciples; Paul mentored Timothy. Mentoring—or discipleship—is a powerful means of developing in others not only skills but also, and even more important, dispositions. Because attitudes and values are more caught than taught, an intentional mentoring program is a vital aspect of any professional development program.

Another notion exemplified in Scripture is that of modeling. Jesus modeled his ministry and life of sacrifice and service to his disciples, and then he told them, "Very truly I tell you, whoever believes in me will do the works I have been doing, and they will do even greater things than these, because I am going to the Father" (John 14:12). In a society replete with celebrities, athletes, and politicians who often reject the status of role model, people yearn for leaders who are confident enough to point the way. Since the advent of progressive education and constructivist theory, the role of the teacher has been described less as an authority and more as a facilitator, guide, and fellow learner. Similarly, the emphasis in administration is for school leaders to practice collaboration and distributed leadership. Of course, there are sound reasons grounded in research for teachers and administrators periodically to practice such approaches, but they should not completely abandon their responsibility to serve as role models. The Apostle Paul told the Corinthians, "Follow my example, as I follow the example of Christ." If instructional leaders embrace their status as mentor and role model, it will develop a culture of leadership that will carry over to the teacher's relationship with students.

Theoretical Background

Albert Bandura's (1977) social learning theory is commensurate with the biblical principle of modeling as previously described. Unlike B. F. Skinner's (1971) behaviorist framework based on the assumption that new skills are learned by being reinforced through a series of stimuli and responses that are reinforced by rewards, Bandura's notion of modeling promotes the idea that learning occurs when one acquires self-efficacy by seeing another person model a specific behavior. In a mentoring relationship, for instance, a novice teacher may—after observing a veteran teacher—think, "If Mrs. Jacobs can teach her students to write such persuasive essays, certainly I can if I implement the same strategies." Social learning theory assumes that teachers will develop their own instructional skills more effectively through a prolonged relationship with another more experienced teacher than they would by simply attending conferences, reading books, or even receiving incentive pay for increasing their students' achievement test scores. An additional benefit to teachers developing self-efficacy through social learning experiences is that their morale and overall job satisfaction increase (Klassen, Usher, & Bong, 2010).

© Tashatuvango/Shutterstock.com

If one were to ask the faculty at any given school to define and describe professional development, their responses would vary immensely. As public schools became common in the 19th century, requirements to become and remain a teacher were minimal. The focus of teacher qualifications revolved more around personal attributes than academic skills and background. As formal training became increasingly common for teachers prior to their entrance into the field of education, in-service training was still not a priority. In recent decades, professional development has undergone a change not only in title, but in practice. Not only has the nomenclature changed over the years—such as staff development or teacher in-service, professional development has also taken on a variety of forms. For many educators, professional development has taken on a negative connotation. Some teachers may recall in-service experiences that included untold hours of faculty meetings during the few days of planning before students returned from summer break. These sessions often focused on "telling" the faculty about a new procedure, often followed by handouts or emails with further details. This type of isolated professional development neither develops professionals nor improves student achievement.

Professional development in a broad sense refers both to the development of an educator in his or her professional role and to the development of a group of educators toward a common goal (Glatthorn, 1995). In today's climate of educator accountability, it has become increasingly important for school leaders to make the most of their professional development time and resources. Professional development can no longer be a one-time event that occurs during preplanning. Effective professional development must now be an organic process that allows educators to learn, grow, and adjust, sometimes even during the school year.

In today's climate of educator accountability, it has become increasingly important for school leaders to make the most of their professional development time and resources.

A study by Birman, Desimone, Porter, and Garet (2000) delineated the professional development process into three categories: form, duration, and participation. Identifying the form of professional development is to determine the most effective means of communicating and developing skills toward accomplishing a goal. Duration refers to the time requirements of a particular professional development activity. There are instances in which a single session may be sufficient for a professional development activity. At other times, professional development activities may span a period of months or even years to accomplish the desired results. Participation identifies the individuals or groups that will be targeted by a professional development activity. Some professional development initiatives require participation from an entire school district, whereas others may only include an individual teacher. It is important to identify the correct group when planning activities.

Teacher and organizational time is focused to support quality instruction and student learning.

Common Errors

Too often, school leaders look at professional development as something that "just happens." Without an organized plan, professional development can become reactionary. Some of the common errors in planning (or in failing to plan) professional development are often unintentional but can still undermine the goals of the organization. The following subsections describe some of the common errors that school leaders make in planning professional development activities.

Without an organized plan, professional development can become reactionary.

Overly Ambitious

As is the case in many areas of education, ineffectiveness is not always the result of a failure to act but is sometimes the result of overly ambitious agendas. Some professional development programs include too many people, endeavor to accomplish far too much, and attempt to be completed in too short and too fast a time frame. Striving to lead on the cutting edge of school improvement may be detrimental at times. A more prudent approach would be to observe strategies attempted by others and to evaluate their success before committing resources to a similar strategy. Some school leaders, however, pride themselves in being the first to adopt the latest and greatest strategies. Following every fad or trend results in an inability to do anything with consistency and to attain long-term success. Likewise, spreading one topic out over an inordinate amount of time results in a disconnect with the goal. Creating a professional development focus and a set of priorities helps to identify a reasonable number of goals, as well as the most effective strategies for achieving those goals.

Insufficient Resources

Jesus taught His disciples to consider the cost before starting a project—to ensure they had the resources to complete it (Luke 14:28). This is good advice regarding professional development. Improving the quality of a school staff requires resources. These resources may include money, time, relationships, and other opportunity costs. As most schools are becoming increasingly budget conscious, it becomes increasingly important to use limited professional development funds wisely. It may be beneficial to send a group of teachers to an out-of-state conference, but are the benefits of this trip worth the expense and sacrifice of other budget items? Expensive conferences, guest speakers, canned programs—all can potentially be big-ticket items. Before allocating school dollars on professional development expenditures, school leaders should consider if other, more cost-effective options are available. Furthermore, when a commitment is made to a professional development activity, it is important to consider the long-term financial requirements needed to continue the activity to completion.

For both public and private schools, the U.S. Department of Education makes Title I and Title II funds available for qualifying schools. These funds may be used for conference registrations and other types of training opportunities. To qualify for Title I or II grants, a school or district must report an assessment of professional development needs. The report must include an explanation of how the professional development activities will contribute to accomplishing specific academic achievement goals and how the training will directly benefit teachers. Private schools interested in receiving Title I or II funds are encouraged to contact their local public school district office and request information from the director of federal grant programs.

Lack of Buy-in

No matter what decision a school leader makes, some faculty will support it, and others will be in opposition. Although there are few decisions a school leader makes that are enthusiastically supported unanimously by the faculty, there is a greater likelihood that professional development will be well received if the purpose and process of the activity are understood and if faculty can clearly see a benefit. Ideas that may require additional time and effort from teachers will be met with much less resistance when their advantages, especially to student learning, are obvious.

School leaders must at times promote unpopular initiatives. For example, it may be necessary to reallocate resources away from the professional development budget and toward a state or federally mandated initiative. Educators may be faced with the challenge of implementing programs that they do not personally support, which makes rallying support from others difficult. Site-based decision making has been touted as a remedy for lack of buy-in, but even when a leadership team or the majority of faculty vote to implement a specific type of professional development, there most likely will still be a degree of resistance. Nevertheless, support for professional development is likely to be strengthened by including faculty in decisions whenever possible—making sure lines of communication are open and clearly presenting the purpose and benefits of the activity.

Failure to Consider the Past

"Well, that's how we've always done things around here!" "We've tried that many times before, but it just didn't work." Anyone who has served as a school administrator for any length of time has heard these statements. Although such statements are considered counterproductive in most leadership circles, ignoring them may prove to be detrimental. Leaders who refuse to consider the past may be undermining their own authority. For instance, new principals may choose to do things very differently from their predecessors, but there may also be a benefit from knowing what has been successful and unsuccessful in the past. Attempting to implement a program that failed previously is not impossible, but a wise leader would ask important questions, such as why the program failed and what could be done differently to avoid the negative results.

An example of such a scenario occurred when a high school principal sought to start a freshman academy. The proposed academy was the result of a necessity to alleviate school overcrowding in a rapidly growing attendance zone. The faculty was told that the freshmen would be moved out of the main building and into portable classrooms. With little planning and input from teachers, the freshmen were transported to portable classrooms, and the ninth-grade academy was begun. Within months, however, students, parents, and faculty began to express discontent, and by the end of the school year, the freshman academy experiment was deemed a failure. A few years later, the same high school once again began to plan a freshman academy. Unlike the previous time, though, the planning began with informational meetings, surveys, question-and-answer sessions, and input from students, parents, and faculty. The purpose of the freshman academy was clarified and goals for improving student achievement were identified. Faculty members who were interested in working with ninth-grade students were heavily involved in the planning and in the implementation of the academy model. This time, the freshman academy was a success, and effective professional development had paved the way.

Although it may not always be possible to build enthusiasm for all professional development programs, it is important to try. Sometimes support can be developed quickly; at other times, it can be a slow process. However, allowing faculty input in the planning and implementation process often improves professional development results.

Overgeneralized

At some point, everyone's inbox receives a mass email that does not pertain to the recipient. Though it may be perceived as a minor unnecessary annoyance, that experience multiplied many times illustrates the frustration of sitting through hours of irrelevant professional development that seems unrelated to success in one's job. Educators will often make a concerted effort to hone their skills or improve their students' performance, but they may experience frustration if they perceive professional development as unrelated to their effectiveness. For example, developing lesson plans is a skill that is considered important to most educators. To streamline the submission of lesson plans, principals may decide that they want all teachers to submit their lesson plans online. If the majority of the faculty is already submitting online lesson plans, there would be no need to conduct a school-wide professional development session to train teachers how to submit electronic lesson plans. This type of professional development would best be implemented only with teachers who are still developing in this area.

Implications

In order to plan effective professional development in education, it is important to answer core questions regarding the purpose of such programs. First, will it impact student achievement? Research supports the idea that effective professional development impacts student achievement (Yoon, Duncan, Lee, Scarloss, & Shapley, 2007). Some of the other questions that provide a foundation for professional development plans include the following:

- What are the specific needs of the school that can be addressed through professional development?
- What are the achievement goals of the professional development plan?
- Is the activity one we are choosing or one that is required?
- What are the most effective strategies for accomplishing professional development goals?
- What resources are required?
- What resources are available?

Once these foundational questions are answered, a school leader may move forward with a plan that addresses the needs of the school. Involve the faculty, or at least faculty representatives, in the selection of professional development priorities. Although some professional development initiatives may be mandated from outside of the school, discretionary professional development should address the specific needs of each school or district. Classroom teachers can often provide unique and practical insight into the professional development needs of their classrooms and school.

CONCLUSION

Educators cannot be satisfied with the instructional skills developed during their college preparation or the induction program to their first teaching position. The field of education constantly progresses and is such a dynamic profession that it requires flexibility and adaptability from true lifelong learners. With increased expectations of accountability, state and federal legislation, and standards-based instruction, preparing and supporting teachers through change has become a requirement of all school leaders. Effective professional development can have a significant impact on school climate, instructional quality, and student academic achievement, but to maximize that effect, professional development must be a process and not strictly an event. Continuous improvement can become a reality when school leaders inspire teachers to develop a positive mindset regarding new programs, skills, and strategies.

professional development must be a process and not strictly an event.

Giving staff the freedom to fail is another important part of effective professional development. Hearing a concept is only the beginning of developing a skill that may improve instruction. Allowing staff a chance to experiment with strategies learned during professional development activities can improve the chances of effective implementation. Identifying must-haves as opposed to optional aspects of professional development helps teachers to navigate the process of developing new skills.

Discussion Questions

1. What has been the most effective professional development activity in which you have participated, and why? What has been the least effective, and how could it have been improved?

2. What have been some of the most significant changes to the concept of school professional development in recent years?

3. What is the role of the school leader in establishing a professional development program? What aspects of the program might be out of the school leader's control?

4. How might school data be used to drive a professional development program?

5. What are some strategies that promote faculty collaboration to accomplish professional development goals?

Activities for Enrichment

1. Review the professional development plan of a school or district with which you are familiar. Identify activities that appear to have been mandated, and those that are presented as optional. Consider the needs being addressed by the plan and future implications.

2. Conduct an Internet search on professional development programs. Identify current threads or trends. Are any obvious changes in the professional development process addressed?

CASE STUDIES

CASE 1: MATH SCORE

As a second-year principal of an 800-student middle school containing grades 6–8, you are called into the superintendent's office to discuss the recent decline in seventh- and eighth-grade math scores on the state standardized math assessment. You are instructed to develop a plan to improve scores on the next assessment. Several faculty members have informed you that the previous principal had focused on reading scores in prior years because of a similar decline in reading achievement. The reading scores improved substantially after several years of focus and professional development, and you are now expected to make similar improvements in math achievement.

1. What are the first steps of planning an improvement strategy?
2. What are some of the key elements of a professional development plan to improve math instruction?
3. Which faculty members will most likely be involved in the planning of the improvement strategies? Which faculty members will actually be involved in the process once a plan is developed?
4. The superintendent has emphasized that there should not be a decline in reading scores as math improvements are made. How will you address this issue in your plan?

CASE 2: CURRICULUM CHANGES

After several years as a high school assistant principal responsible for curriculum, you felt well qualified as an instructional leader when offered the principal position at the same school. In the fall, after 2 successful years as the principal, you are informed that the state has developed a new and very different curriculum to better align with national standards and that the new curriculum will be implemented the following school year.

1. How will you communicate the anticipated changes to the staff?
2. How will you plan for the implementation of the new curriculum?
3. What timeline considerations need to be addressed when developing a plan?
4. What activities might occur during the summer leading up to implementation of the new curriculum?
5. How do you build support among faculty regarding the new curriculum?

CASE 3: BEHAVIOR MANAGEMENT

As the headmaster in a private K–12 school in an affluent area, you have enjoyed leading a school with very few discipline problems. Over the past year, you have noticed a significant increase in discipline referrals and classroom management issues. There are still many teachers in the school who rarely have a discipline problem, but there seems to be a growing number of teachers sending students to the office or writing discipline referrals on a regular basis. You have decided that some changes need to be made before the problem worsens.

1. What questions should be answered before developing a plan of action?
2. How might this problem be addressed as a professional development issue?
3. Because the problems seem to be more prevalent with some teachers than others, how do you decide how each teacher will be involved in the improvement process?

CASE 4: PROFESSIONAL CONFERENCE

As a school leader, you and your leadership team have identified a significant need to provide professional development in the area of assessment. A district-level administrator has informed you of an outstanding out-of-state conference that will take place this summer. You believe that this conference would be beneficial to any of your staff members who attend, but your professional development funds are limited and the conference is expensive.

1. How do you determine who, if anyone, from your school will attend this conference?
2. How can your professional development funds be maximized in this situation?
3. What are other options that you may want to consider if this conference is determined to be unaffordable?

REFERENCES

Aikin, W. (1942). *The story of the Eight-Year Study*. New York, NY: Harper.

Bandura, A. (1977). *Social learning theory*. Englewood Cliffs, NJ: Prentice Hall.

Birman, B., Desimone, L., Porter, A., & Garet, M. (2000). Designing professional development that works. *Educational Leadership, 57*(8), 28–33.

Glatthorn, A. (1995). Teacher development. In L. Anderson (Ed.), *International encyclopedia of teaching and teacher education* (pp. 31–35). London: Pergamon Press.

Hill, L. P. (1921). *The wings of oppression*. Boston, MA: Stratford.

Hirsch, E. D. (1988). *Cultural literacy: What every American needs to know*. New York, NY: Random House.

Klassen, R., Usher, E., & Bong, M. (2010). Teachers' collective efficacy, job satisfaction, and job stress in cross-cultural context. *Journal of Experimental Education, 78*(4), 464–486.

Pedigo, M. (2003). *Differentiating professional development: The principal's role*. Westerville, OH: National Middle School Association.

Riddell, R., Jacobson, L., & Campisi, J. (2019, January 7). 6 K-12 Trends to Watch in 2019. Retrieved from: https://www.educationdive.com/news/6-k-12-trends-to-watch-in-2019/543915/

Sizer, T. R. (1994). *Horace's compromise: The dilemma of the American high school*. New York, NY: Houghton Mifflin.

Skinner, B. F. (1971). *Beyond freedom and dignity*. Indianapolis, IN: Hackett.

Yoon, K. S., Duncan, T., Lee, S. W., Scarloss, B., & Shapley, K. (2007). *Reviewing the evidence on how teacher professional development affects student achievement* (Issues & Answers Report, REL 2007–No. 033). Washington, DC: U.S. Department of Education, Institute of Education Sciences, National Center for Education Evaluation and Regional Assistance, Regional Educational Laboratory Southwest. Retrieved from http://ies.ed.gov/ncee/edlabs

ADDITIONAL RESOURCE

A portion of the school's professional development resources will most likely go toward requirements handed down from the district, state, or federal level. In situations where the building-level leader has significant autonomy in developing a professional development plan, it may be helpful to use outside resources. There are many websites that provide professional development ideas to address specific needs for support in developing an entire program. One example is the *Learning Forward* website that can be found at the following address: http://www.learningforward.org/standards.

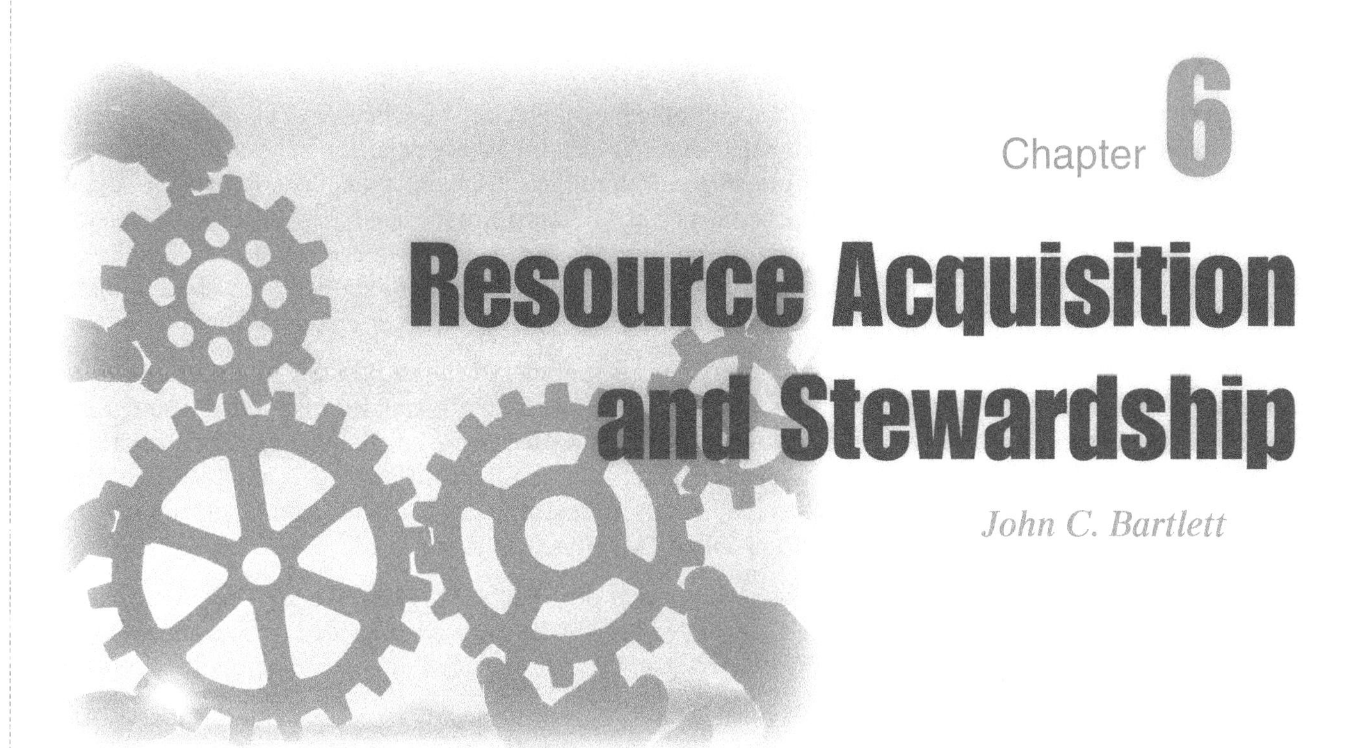

Chapter 6

Resource Acquisition and Stewardship

John C. Bartlett

From everyone who has been given much, much will be demanded;
and from the one who has been entrusted with much, much more will be asked.
—Jesus Christ (Luke 12:48b, New International Version)—

OVERVIEW

Previous chapters have addressed issues of vision casting, data-based decision making, and faculty development. The present chapter will take these and other issues into account as it discusses the acquisition and management of school resources to increase school effectiveness and student achievement. It will explain how schools and school systems acquire resources, use them to drive the mission and vision of the school, and develop relationships to further student achievement. This chapter will present current funding plans for both public and private institutions and will address best practices in garnering community financial support.

Objectives

By the end of this chapter, the reader should be able to do the following:

1. Use data to identify goals and assess organizational effectiveness.
2. Obtain, allocate, align, and efficiently utilize human, fiscal, and technological resources.
3. Prioritize and allocate limited resources.
4. Safeguard the values of democracy, equity, and diversity.

INTRODUCTION

It happens throughout the nation, stories so unbelievable but completely true: People of all socioeconomic levels walk into convenience stores and lay down a couple dollars for lottery tickets. For some, the purchase represents a financial sacrifice. For others, it is a small token of their discretionary budget. Regardless, each purchase is made with the dream of picking the numbers that will transform the buyer's life forever. The paths for many winners, however, do not end in the transformed lives that were anticipated. For instance, Ken Proxmire won a million dollars just to file for bankruptcy within 5 five years, and William Post won $16.2 million to find himself a decade later living on a meager Social Security check of $450 per month (McIntyre, 2012).

Unfortunate stories such as these two are not reserved solely for lottery winners. Vince Young had the world by the horns. The star quarterback for the University of Texas Longhorns, Young led his football team to an unlikely national championship during the 2006 Rose Bowl. Accolades were only eclipsed by the size of his $58 million contract. This story, however, has an equally sad ending. Several media outlets have reported that Young spent thousands of dollars every week on food and drink, and after just 6 years as a professional football player, Young had squandered nearly $30 million dollars (McIntyre, 2012).

The stories go on. In June 2012, Curt Schilling, star pitcher of the 2004 Boston Red Sox World Series, announced that his entire $50 million fortune had evaporated because he invested in a video game company that had filed for bankruptcy. The endless stories of fortunes squandered leave many to ask the simple question: Why?

Examples of such poor stewardship are not unique to athletes, popular-culture icons, or lottery winners. As economic volatility has plagued the United States and its citizens during the recent recession, such squandering of resources has been displayed by a number of school systems. Alex Kellog (2009) reported in the *Wall Street Journal* that Detroit Public Schools was on the verge of declaring bankruptcy, and in February 2012, Governor Rick Snyder signed legislation granting state support for other troubled Michigan school districts in the form of loans and bonds (Michigan, 2012).

No one else in the Bible had more to say about stewardship and handling money than King Solomon as he penned his treatise on wisdom. Solomon made no mistake by stating his advice with direct instruction on priorities: "Wisdom is supreme; therefore get wisdom. Though it cost all you have, get understanding" (Proverbs 4:7, New International Version). This is contradictory to our human nature to seek primarily to acquire wealth; however, Solomon does not leave riches and wealth to the fool: "The plans of the diligent lead to profit as surely as haste leads to poverty" (Proverbs 21:5).

BACKGROUND INFORMATION

School Funding

From the earliest one-room schoolhouses to the modern-day comprehensive high school, the process of acquiring and disbursing resources has consistently been a root of controversy and political differences. The earliest public schools were funded by local townships to educate students with resources provided by resident farmers, parents, and churches. Quite often, the teacher would be paid a small stipend and given room and board through various community members. Over the past several decades, sustained school funding has remained largely a local and state effort, with states providing approximately 50% of funding, local governments providing approximately 40%, and the federal government contributing roughly 10% of overall K–12 education funding (New America Foundation, 2012). In relation to the 2009 recession, federal funding has increased to roughly 20%:

> Federal funding for education had never exceeded 10% of the total until 2009–10. Because of the severe revenue declines in state revenues, ARRA (American Recovery and Reinvestment Act of 2009) provided $100 billion in stimulus funding to states—much of it used for education—and EduJobs provided another $10 billion in funding for 2010–11, all of it focused on filling education funding holes and saving jobs in school districts. The effect of these resources was an increase the federal share of school district funding to approximately 20% of the total in 2010–11. (Picus & Odden, 2011, p. 293)

Total funding for education in the United States—including local, state, and federal dollars—presently exceeds $700 billion, making the United States the world's leader in funding for education. In fact, "More is spent by the United States, in the aggregate, than by hugely populous nations such as China and India. Spending per pupil is higher in the U.S. than in every country except Switzerland" (Guthrie & Ettema, 2012, p. 20).

Although the role of the federal government in education has expanded in recent years, education remains largely a local effort due to the 10th Amendment of the U.S. Constitution, which reads, "The powers not delegated to the United States by the Constitution, nor prohibited by it to the States, are reserved to the States respectively, or to the people," thus giving power to the states over all facets not mentioned in the Constitution. Courts have supported and backed the opinion that educational funding and resource allocation have been the purview of the states. To reinforce this position, the U.S. Supreme Court ruled in *Rodriguez v. San Antonio Independent School District* (1973) that "Education, of course, is not among the rights afforded explicit protection under our Federal Constitution." The Court continued, stating, "nor do we find any basis for saying it is implicitly so protected" (para. 44).

© Rawpixel.com/Shutterstock.com

A brief glimpse of state constitutions reinforces the notion that education is the purview of the individual states and not a function of the federal government. For instance, the Tennessee State Constitution reads, "The State of Tennessee recognizes the inherent value of education and encourages its support. The General Assembly shall provide for the maintenance, support and eligibility standards of a system of free public schools" (Tenn. Const., art. XI, § 12). The New York State Constitution also highlights this point: "The legislature shall provide for the maintenance and support of a system of free common schools, wherein all the children of this state may be educated" (New York Const., art. XI, § 1). The Virginia State Constitution includes a quality clause, "The General Assembly shall provide for a system of free public elementary and secondary schools for all children of school age throughout the Commonwealth, and shall seek to ensure that an educational program of high quality is established and continually maintained" (Va. Const., art. VIII, § 1). To fulfill these responsibilities, states typically rely on income and sales taxes for primary funding of education within the state. In the majority of states, funding is then distributed to individual school districts based on one of the following funding models:

1. *State Operation of Public Schools*: Full state funding is provided to the school systems for complete operation of the schools. An example of this is the state of Hawaii, which essentially has one school district, run by the state, and a single state school board (Brimley, Verstegen, & Garfield, 2012).

2. *Complete State Support*: This is typically done by the state collecting state property tax, state sales tax, and personal property tax and then distributing funds through grants based on a per-pupil basis to the local school systems. In this system, local governments can still augment funding to aid local schools (Brimley, Verstegen, & Garfield, 2012).

3. *Foundation Program or District Power Equalization*: This is accomplished by the state funding school systems on a per-pupil basis expecting the local government to contribute a large sum of money to operate schools. Generally, states distribute funding through a legislatively approved formula. School districts with high concentrations of students with disabilities, English language learners, or high-poverty districts would typically be funded at different levels. The driving philosophy of this funding method is that certain populations of students require more resources to aid them in mastering state standards. Of course, more resources imply the need for more funding (New America Foundation, 2012).

Traditionally, in a foundation program or power equalization program, states have left a large amount of educational financing to local entities such as cities, towns, counties, and parishes. Often, local governments fund education through real property taxes (taxes levied based on the value of land and improvements on the land) levied against the citizens and landowners within the local government's jurisdiction (Brimley, Verstegen, & Garfield, 2012). As McCuddy and Pirie (2007) noted, "Property taxes have traditionally been the primary source of local tax revenue; the resources devoted to education were to a large extent a function of the property tax base in a community" (p. 958).

Biblical Perspective

While Adam and Eve were still in the Garden, the first directive God gave them was that they were to be stewards of the Garden and of the many resources God had provided them.

> So God created man in His own image; He created him in the image of God; He created them male and female. God blessed them, and God said to them, "Be fruitful, multiply, fill the earth, and subdue it. Rule the fish of the sea, the birds of the sky, and every creature that crawls on the earth." God also said, "Look, I have given you every seed-bearing plant on the surface of the entire earth and every tree whose fruit contains seed. This food will be for you, for all the wildlife of the earth, for every bird of the sky, and for every creature that crawls on the earth—everything having the breath of life in it. I have given every green plant for food." (Genesis 1: 27–30, Holman Christian Standard Bible)

This theme of stewardship is found throughout Scripture; Jesus referred to stewardship in Matthew 25:14–30 as He discussed financial stewardship in the parable of the talents. Similarly, in Luke 19, Jesus told of a ruler who gave 10 minas to 10 slaves and then departed on a long trip. Upon his return, the ruler called the slaves in to see what they had done with what they had been given:

> At his return, having received the authority to be king, he summoned those slaves he had given the money to, so he could find out how much they had made in business. The first came forward and said, "Master, your mina has earned 10 more minas." (vv. 15–16)

The second slave returned and was given similar treatment as he also made a profit. The third slave had kept his minas hidden and received starkly different treatment:

> And another came and said, "Master, here is your mina. I have kept it hidden away in a cloth because I was afraid of you, for you're a tough man: you collect what you didn't deposit and reap what you didn't sow." He told him, "I will judge you by what you have said, you evil slave! If you knew I was a tough man, collecting what I didn't deposit and reaping what I didn't sow, why didn't you put my money in the bank? And when I returned, I would have collected it with interest!" So he said to those standing there, "Take the mina away from him and give it to the one who has 10 minas." (vv. 20–24)

Different from the parable of the talents, the parable of the minas has each slave receiving the same amount of resources. Through this and other parables, it is obvious that Christ emphasized resource stewardship and management throughout His earthly ministry. This stewardship is seen after Christ fed the multitudes with five loaves of bread and two fishes. At the end of the miracle of reproduction and blessing, Jesus demanded that the disciples retrieve the left overs so that nothing would be wasted: "When they were full, He told His disciples, 'Collect the leftovers so that nothing is wasted'" (John 6:12). In Drexler's (2007) *Schools as Communities*, he stated the importance of stewardship:

> Resource Management is not merely about managing personnel, planning, and budgeting; it is nothing less than the means by which leaders reflect the image of God in the skillful stewardship of the people, ministry, and resources entrusted to their care for the glory of God and for the good of others. (p. 178)

During His ministry, Jesus also discussed the practice of counting the cost, setting a budget, and proper planning. In Luke 14, Jesus presented the idea that there is a cost to following Him:

> For which of you, wanting to build a tower, doesn't first sit down and calculate the cost to see if he has enough to complete it? Otherwise, after he has laid the foundation and cannot finish it, all the onlookers will begin to make fun of him, saying, "This man started to build and wasn't able to finish." Or what king, going to war against another king, will not first sit down and decide if he is able with 10,000 to oppose the one who comes against him with 20,000? If not, while the other is still far off, he sends a delegation and asks for terms of peace. (vv. 28–32)

Although the context of this scripture is obviously a call to count the cost when following Christ, the fundamental idea of planning and budgeting is relied on to communicate an overarching truth. This idea of strategic planning is not lost on Drexler (2007): "Undergirded by prayer, strategic planning is an essential component of effective leadership" (p. 182).

Ultimately, effective resource management relies on the integrity of the manager.

Ultimately, effective resource management relies on the integrity of the manager. The Christian world is littered with leaders who have struggled with integrity issues—whether financial or personal. The message of Scripture is clear: "Make yourself an example of good works with integrity and dignity in your teaching. Your message is to be sound beyond reproach, so that the opponent will be ashamed, having nothing bad to say about us" (Titus 2:7b–8). Blackaby and Blackaby (2011) discussed the need for leaders to walk with integrity, hand in hand with God: "He [God] asks leaders to walk with Him so intimately that when He reveals His agenda they immediately adjust their lives and their organizations to His will and the results bring glory to God" (p. 47).

Perhaps there is no greater example of resource management in Scripture than that of Joseph, who, being enslaved and imprisoned, yet faithful, found himself placed in charge of all resources in Egypt. Joseph took the following steps:

© alexmillos/Shutterstock.com

1. Surveyed and accounted for the available resources: "Joseph left Pharaoh's presence and traveled throughout the land of Egypt" (Genesis 41:46b).
2. Developed a plan:

   > Let Pharaoh do this: Let him appoint overseers over the land and take a fifth of the harvest of the land of Egypt during the seven years of abundance. Let them gather all the excess food during these good years that are coming. Under Pharaoh's authority, store the grain in the cities, so they may preserve it as food. The food will be a reserve for the land during the seven years of famine that will take place in the land of Egypt. Then the country will not be wiped out by the famine. (Genesis 41: 34–36)

3. Executed the plan:

   > During the seven years of abundance the land produced outstanding harvests. Joseph gathered all the excess food in the land of Egypt during the seven years and put it in the cities. He put the food in every city from the fields around it. So Joseph stored up grain in such abundance—like the sand of the sea—that he stopped measuring it because it was beyond measure. (Genesis 41:47–49)

4. Managed the resources efficiently with little waste:

> Then the seven years of abundance in the land of Egypt came to an end, and the seven years of famine began, just as Joseph had said. There was famine in every country, but throughout the land of Egypt there was food. Extreme hunger came to all the land of Egypt, and the people cried out to Pharaoh for food. Pharaoh told all Egypt, "Go to Joseph and do whatever he tells you." Because the famine had spread across the whole country, Joseph opened up all the storehouses and sold grain to the Egyptians, for the famine was severe in the land of Egypt. Every nation came to Joseph in Egypt to buy grain, for the famine was severe in every land. (Genesis 41:53–57)

5. Made investments to ensure future success:

> Then Joseph said to the people, "Understand today that I have acquired you and your land for Pharaoh. Here is seed for you. Sow it in the land. At harvest, you are to give a fifth of it to Pharaoh, and four-fifths will be yours as seed for the field and as food for yourselves, your households, and your dependents." And they said, "You have saved our lives. We have found favor in our lord's eyes and will be Pharaoh's slaves." So Joseph made it a law, still in effect today in the land of Egypt, that a fifth of the produce belongs to Pharaoh. Only the priests' land does not belong to Pharaoh. (Genesis 41:23–26)

Current Issues and Trends in School Finance

Funding Equity

The amount of income generated from local property taxes is dependent upon the corresponding wealth of individual jurisdictions. Reliance on this method has resulted in disparate funding among school districts, thereby creating an inequitable system of wealthy and poor school districts. Therefore, property values in particular school districts affect their ability to attract and retain teachers as well as to build and maintain facilities:

> Wealthier, property-rich localities have the ability to collect more in property taxes. Having more resources to draw from enables the district to keep tax rates low while still providing adequate funding to their local school districts. Poorer communities with less of a property tax base may have higher tax rates, but still raise less funding to support the local school district. (New America Foundation, 2012, para. 12)

These disparities have resulted in a system of "haves" and "have nots" based on the relative wealth of the school district. In some instances, rural communities have been concerned that their best teachers are often recruited by wealthy suburban districts that are more capable of enticing them with higher salaries. This disparity of teacher salaries essentially creates a "farm team" for wealthier school districts as they cherry pick the best teachers away from poorer districts. "On the whole, regional characteristics and level of student need accounted for much of the variation in expenditures per student between districts in different geographic locales" (Wan et al., 2012, p. iv). This fact has led to a rash of lawsuits since the mid-1970s. In *Rodriguez v. San Antonio Independent School District* (1973), the plaintiff sued the school district in federal court for inequitable funding between schools districts, citing the 14th Amendment and the equal protection clause over the inequitable per-pupil funding among adjacent school districts:

> Parents of students in the Edgewood Independent School District challenged the inequities in Texas's public school funding system. Edgewood was one of seven school districts within the San Antonio area, and its student body was ninety percent Mexican-American and six percent African-American. Given the district's low property values, even after taxing itself at a relatively high rate and receiving supplemental aid from both the state and federal government, Edgewood could spend only $356 per pupil. By way of comparison, another San Antonio school district, the relatively affluent and predominately white Alamo Heights, could tax itself at a rate twenty percent below the rate in Edgewood and still have $594 available per pupil. (Gillespie, 2010, p. 995)

The federal court in this case, however, ruled that school funding was not a federal issue and that the federal courts had little jurisdiction in the matter. The result was a flood of lawsuits in state courts in at least 45 states. The lawsuits typically alleged that the states violated the equal protection clause in that they distributed money for education in an unequal fashion (Tresnowski & Sullivan, 2011).

Funding Adequacy

In the late 1990s, school-funding litigation shifted from a focus on equity to a focus on adequacy. The argument shifted from equal protection clauses in state constitutions to the education clause actually written into the state constitutions requiring states to provide for a public school system. The adequacy argument centered on the idea that per-pupil funding did not sufficiently address the learning needs of high-risk or low-performing students. Kent and Sowards (2009) defined educational adequacy as the following:

> [Educational adequacy] looks at student needs and notes that within districts there may be variations in student needs that require differentials from the equal per-student spending. Among those differences would be a high percentage of low income families or of students who require English as a second language instruction or have special education needs. This standard focuses more on equality of outcomes than on equality of resources. (p. 27)

The premise of educational adequacy would require more resources for students living in poverty, for English language learners, and for students with disabilities because of the additional aid needed to achieve a minimal level of mastery on state standards (Brimley, Verstegen, & Garfield, 2011).

Adequacy plaintiffs have litigated successfully in 25 states (Gillespie, 2010). One of the most notable of such lawsuits is *Rose v. Council for Better Education, Inc.* (1989), where the plaintiffs held that Kentucky was not funding an adequate education. *Rose* was a landmark case not only because of the outcome of the ruling but also because of the definition it provided of an adequate education based on the following seven criteria:

1. Sufficient oral and written communication skills to enable students to function in a complex and rapidly changing civilization.
2. Sufficient knowledge of economic, social, and political systems to enable the student to make informed choices.
3. Sufficient understanding of governmental processes to enable the student to understand the issues that affect his or her community, state, and nation.
4. Sufficient self-knowledge and knowledge of his or her mental and physical wellness.
5. Sufficient grounding in the arts to enable each student to appreciate his or her cultural and historical heritage.
6. Sufficient training or preparation for advanced training in either academic or vocational fields so as to enable each child to choose and pursue life work intelligently.
7. Sufficient levels of academic or vocational skills to enable public school students to compete favorably with their counterparts in surrounding states, in academics or in the job market. (Gillespie, 2010, pp. 1003–1004)

School adequacy litigation in recent years has resulted in funding shifts from local to state governments: "some common conclusions, namely, that such judgments reduce funding inequality between districts by increasing spending in the poorest districts and that they do so by transferring responsibility for education funding from local to state governments" (Berry & Wysong, 2010, p. 63).

Most recently, school adequacy lawsuits have lost momentum: "Since 2009, six of the eleven state courts to issue decisions in adequacy cases have ruled against plaintiffs" (Tresnowski & Sullivan, 2011, para. 4). It is still too early to determine if this is a substantial shift in judicial thinking or simply an unwillingness of the courts to grant relief during a period of economic downturn.

Achievement Gaps

The simple definition of an achievement gap is the disparity of academic performance between any two student groups. Achievement gaps are often identified by politicians and educators alike as an injustice that should be prioritized and remedied. Even when funding is distributed adequately and equitably, achievement gaps may still exist.

Although many would agree that achievement gaps are a problem, the challenge becomes much more complicated when trying to identify a solution. A discussion regarding removing or reducing an achievement gap needs to start with two assumptions. 1. Resources affect student achievement, and 2. Schools must operate with limited resources (financial, human, technological, etc.). These statements often result in discussions about the need to use resources more efficiently, and this may be true. Or some may comment that not all resources affect achievement, which would raise the question, then why use those resources?

So in theory, removing or reducing an achievement gap would mean increasing resources allocated toward the lower achieving group. If a school is working with limited resources, then increasing resources for one group must mean reducing resources somewhere else (even time is a resource). Those making the financial decisions will have to identify priorities for allocation of resources. This is not to suggest that funds should not be diverted from one group or program to meet the needs of a lower performing group, but it is important to point out that achievement gaps cannot be addressed in isolation form other groups or programs in a school. Increasing overall funding can help address these issues, and schools often have to find creative ways to do this, but there is still going to be some limit on the amount of resources available. Reducing achievement gaps may be possible, but will often require making difficult decisions.

Federal Role in Funding

Although the federal role in education has been somewhat limited by the courts, the federal government's role in pre-kindergarten through 12th-grade education has nonetheless increased over the years. According to the National Center for Education Statistics (NCES), in 2008 the federal government provided only 8% of the necessary funding required to operate public schools. State and local governments provided the remaining finances. As noted earlier, that percent has increased in recent years based on increased federal spending. In 2011, boosted by the EduJobs bill in the American Recovery and Reinvestment Act of 2009, the total federal share was approximately 20% of overall K–12 funding.

Although the federal role in education has been somewhat limited by the courts, the federal government's role in pre-kindergarten through 12th-grade education has nonetheless increased over the years.

The current federal role in education financing has its roots in major education reform initiatives dating as far back as the Eisenhower administration. After the Soviet Union launched *Sputnik*, the U.S. Congress passed the National Defense Education Act, which supplied $887 million for loans to students entering math and science and to supply money for the states in order to strengthen math, science, and foreign language initiatives (Knight, 2012). In 1965, Congress passed the Elementary and Secondary Education Act (ESEA), which provided funding to school districts in five different categories:

1. Title I—also known as "Education for Children of Low-Income Families"
2. School Libraries
3. Supplemental Services
4. Research
5. State Departments of Education (Hanna, 2011)

This foray into education funding by the federal government mainly focused on low-income and other underserved students as a part of Lyndon Johnson's war on poverty. As Michelman (2012) explained,

> In 1965, few Americans likely paid more than scant attention to the federal government's increasing role in education decision making. K–12 education was a longstanding state and local responsibility,

> with more than 90 percent of the cost of public school funding being provided by the states and districts. The federal government reserved most of its authority to ensuring that its resources helped disadvantaged children and those with special needs. (para. 1)

In the subsequent 2 years, federal funding for education increased by $2.5 billion, permanently increasing the role of the federal government in education (Hanna, 2005). Over time, ESEA has taken on different forms, with one of the most recent being its 2001 reauthorization, better known as No Child Left Behind, which granted money to the states based on a more stringent accountability system:

> In 2002, President George W. Bush reauthorized ESEA and renamed it the No Child Left Behind Act (NCLB). Suddenly everyone had an interest in the government's expansive new role in education. NCLB required states to conduct annual testing in reading and math for students in grades 3–8 with the tests requiring alignment with state academic standards. (Michelman, 2012, para. 2)

An additional foray into education funding by the federal government was part of the 2009 American Recovery and Reinvestment Act, which added over $4 billion to educational funding to be distributed at the sole discretion of the U.S. Secretary of Education. The disbursement of funds to the states and individual school districts was based on their willingness to reform:

> Funds were awarded not on the basis of formulas or authorized programs, but according to states' willingness to embrace a "reform" agenda set by the Obama Administration. To qualify for grants of up to $700 million, states were required to change their education laws and policies to meet five key conditions. They had to join the Common Core Standards initiative; upgrade data systems; base teacher evaluations at least in part on student test scores; implement the Administration's proposed 'turnaround' models for low-scoring schools; and lift legal limits on the number of charter schools. (Crawford, 2011)

Although the 1965 Elementary and Secondary Education Act was written to be revised and reauthorized by Congress every five years, a lack of bipartisanship kept the 2001 version (NCLB) from being reauthorized for over a decade. Finally, In 2015, Congress approved reauthorization of ESEA and coined it the Every Student Succeeds Act (ESSA). Much of this legislation was scheduled to be implemented in 2017–2018, but the full effects may not be realized for several more years. Although federal education funding can vary from one year to the next, much of the funding in ESSA will be through block grants, giving states more freedom to spend funds as they see fit (Every Student Succeeds Act, 2019).

The federal government currently spends more than $40 billion annually on pre-K through 12th grade education programs. "Through the U.S. Department of Education, the federal government provides more than $40 billion a year on primary and secondary education programs. The two largest programs are No Child Left Behind Title I grants to local school districts and Individuals with Disabilities Education Act (IDEA) Special Education State Grants" (New America Foundation, 2012, para. 6). Other federal spending programs impacting education include the National School Lunch Program administered through the Department of Agriculture, Head Start through the Department of Health and Human Services, Youth Employment and Training Activities, and YouthBuild administered through the Department of Labor. In all, the U.S. Department of Education accounts for less than 3% of the total federal budget (New America Foundation, 2012).

Private School Funding

By virtue of the nature of private schools, access to public funds outside of a voucher or school choice system is limited at best. Therefore, private schools must look to nonpublic funding to pay for teachers, curriculum, buildings, and other expenses. Of course, the range of private school tuition is as broad as the types of private schools. For example, Avenues—The World School in New York City boasts a $39,750-per-year price tag with additional student fees running approximately $2,000 per year (Avenues, 2012). On the opposite end of the spectrum, parents can find church-affiliated schools that may be relatively affordable.

In their study of U.S. private schools, Broughman, Swaim, and Hryczaniuk (2011) found the following:

- In the United States, 33,366 private secondary and elementary schools existed.
- Sixty-eight percent of private schools had a religious orientation; among them, they enrolled 80% of the students in private schools and employed 72% of the teachers employed in private schools.
- Most private schools were located in cities and suburbs of those cities.
- Of private schools, 45% enrolled fewer than 50 students.
- Of private school students, 73% were white, 9% Hispanic, and 9% African American.
- The student–teacher ratio was an average of 11 to 1.
- Sixty-four percent of school graduates attended a 4-year institution after high school graduation. (pp. 2–3)

The nature of private school financing creates a new set of challenges in budgeting and planning. Aside from a handful of private schools, tuition is the primary funding source. Only very few established private schools maintain an extended donor base capable of supporting the needs of the school. While developing a private school budget, administrators and the governing board should consider the financial impact of the following:

> The nature of private school financing creates a new set of challenges in budgeting and planning.

- Transportation: the cost to transport students; in many schools this is the responsibility of the parents and families. In some areas of the country, public school system bussing is available for the students.
- Facilities: the cost to build, clean, and maintain proper school facilities. The current average cost to build a facility, $250 per square foot, fluctuates based on the price of building materials, availability of labor, and the current state of the economy.
- Energy: the cost to sustain proper air temperatures and lighting levels along with other utility costs to run the school.
- Health and safety: the cost to provide proper medical care at the school. Many private schools do not provide full-time nursing because of the expense.
- Instruction: the cost to attract and retain qualified teachers. This also includes the total cost of employment for each individual, which would consist of taxes and benefits.
- Professional development: the cost to provide ongoing in-service training in curriculum development, instructional strategies, campus safety procedures, technology usage, and so forth.
- Food services: the cost to provide cafeteria services. In certain circumstances, private schools can opt into the federal school lunch program provided by the U.S. Department of Agriculture.
- Library services: the cost to provide appropriate media services, including books, instructional technology, periodical subscriptions, and so on.
- Counseling services: the cost to provide the appropriate number of counselors for the included grade levels.
- School leadership and support: the cost to hire and staff the principal and assistant principals.

One of the main challenges facing a private school administrator is that of balancing the demands of parents with the fiscal reality of the school. This challenge manifests itself in projecting staffing levels, as it is the responsibility of the administrator and governing body to determine the appropriate student-to-teacher ratios and to determine the staffing levels the school should sustain based on enrollment. Quite often, this is a source of conflict in projecting student enrollment for an upcoming year.

Athletics is another source of potential struggle for private school administrators. The use of athletics to market the school and to attract students for potential enrollment is a double-edged sword, as the athletic program often is in competition with the larger school for the same dollars. Coaching supplements are often met through athletic fees charged to the student athlete separate from and in addition to the cost of tuition. The initial and ongoing costs of athletic facilities, however, are often absorbed through fundraising and capital outlay by the private school. In many cases, athletics can be very useful to market the school and to attract new students, but to do so requires a commitment to invest adequate monetary and other resources to sustain a well-maintained athletic department.

Nonconventional Funding Sources

The bulk of this chapter has been dedicated to the traditional sources of school funding—taxes and tuition. For the typical school administrator, however, there is a need to find supplemental funding. Sources of such funding often start with the community and parents served by the school. In many public schools, administrators rely heavily on student fees:

> Public schools across the country, struggling with cuts in state funding, rising personnel costs and lower tax revenues, are shifting costs to students and their parents by imposing or boosting fees for everything from enrolling in honors English to riding the bus. . . . Public-school administrators say the fees—some of which are waived for low-income families—allow them to continue to offer specialty classes and activities that would otherwise fall to the budget ax. Some parents support that approach, saying they'd rather pay for honors physics or drama than see those opportunities eliminated altogether. (Simon, 2011, para. 4)

Other ways that school administrators partner with the community to raise supplemental funds involve engaging the parents and communities through parent organizations, school foundations, grant writing, and the establishment of endowments.

A controversial trend has been for schools to acquire additional revenue through the activity of the vendors serving the school. Soft drink companies, for example, have been one of the main vendors to provide both monetary and tangible resources. In exchange for permitting soft drink companies to place machines on campus, schools receive a percentage of total cash sales and possibly other incentives, such as athletic scoreboards. It is not uncommon for large high schools to earn in excess of $15,000 per year from sales of Coca-Cola, Pepsi, or other products. It became increasingly popular in the 1990s for schools desperately in need of additional income to sell "pouring rights" to one particular soda company. This soda company then held exclusive rights to be the sole provider of beverages sold in concession stands, campus stores, and soda dispensing machines. By 2005, nearly half of the nation's elementary schools and 80% of high schools had entered into contractual agreements with soda companies (Philpott, 2012, para. 2). In response to concerns about nutrition and the influence of corporations on children, many states have since passed stringent laws regulating sales of sugary drinks to students in public schools, resulting in a decrease in supplemental income to the schools. In response, schools have begun looking to other places to make up the much-needed revenue. In recent years, some schools have gone so far as to sell advertising space on campus.

Until the development of digital cameras and the technology that made taking and developing pictures cost effective, portrait vendors served as another source of income. Like soft drink companies, portrait vendors typically pay the school a percentage commission. In some instances, portrait vendors guarantee a certain amount of money, with the school receiving a percentage of sales over a designated amount. The development of affordable digital technology has substantially cut commissions, as increasing numbers of schools are choosing to perform the service themselves or to contract with a photographer who will provide more affordable portrait packages to student families.

School Finance in the News

Broken Systems

Earlier school-finance litigation was based primarily on the equal protection clause, which is a state's educational clause guaranteeing an adequate public education to its citizenry. A more recent wave of lawsuits has been based on the "broken system theory." For example, in *Robles-Wong v. State of California* (2010), a coalition of California students and their parents brought litigation against the state alleging the education system guaranteed by the state was broken. Plaintiffs asserted that the current level of funding was not only inadequate but also needed to be overhauled because of the inability of the state to fund schools sufficiently for students to achieve mastery of the content standards (Tang, 2011). The broken system theory is described as follows:

> Unlike the adequacy theory, the "broken system" theory does not ask a court to define a particular quality of education or level of school funding that is promised under the state constitution. Instead, it suggests that state legislatures have a duty, per the text of state constitutions, to provide a "system" of public schools. The theory then argues that the duty to provide a "system" of public schools requires a state to finance its schools in a manner that is rationally calculated to meet the state's academic content standards. (Tresnowski & Sullivan, 2011)

The initial ruling in this case was made in 2011, with Justice Steven A. Brick ruling in favor of the state, noting, "California's constitution doesn't mandate funding levels . . . . [The plaintiffs] failed to demonstrate specific harm a lack of state funding had caused" (Ellson, 2012).

Charter Schools

Although the charter school movement is certainly not new, its popularity and expansion are stretching educational dollars and resources even further. Charter schools are generally funded through an agreement and formula worked out between the state and local school system in which the charter school operates. Generally, a nonprofit board separate from the public school board governs charter schools. Although per-pupil funding is commonly less for students in charter schools, the withdrawal of these students from other schools in the district reduces the amount of per-pupil funding to those schools.

Vouchers

School vouchers represent funds provided to parents to use at a school of their choice, public or private. The vouchers are generally less than the per-pupil expenditure that is spent by the state or local government. In 2011, only nine states had enacted some sort of school voucher program. However, 30 states were considering school voucher legislation during the 2011–2012 legislative sessions (Turner, 2011). In December 2012, a Louisiana judge declared the state's voucher program unconstitutional, as it diverted funds earmarked for public education to private schools. The case is currently being appealed to the state supreme court (Sarlin, 2012).

Practice Implications

Expanded Definition of Resources

Much of this chapter has been dedicated to one type of resource—money. There are, however, at least two additional resources that are deserving of attention and that are as equally important to running an effective school as is money. These two resources are teachers and time.

Teaching positions are generally allotted by the state and by the school system (a) to elementary schools based on students per grade level and (b) to high schools based on total students enrolled. Quite often, the state funding is a base allotment needed to provide a basic level of education. The state appropriations can then be augmented by the local school system to suit the needs of the school and the demands of the community. According to Marzano, Pickering, and Pollock (2001), the impact of the teacher on student achievement is second only to the impact of the home environment; therefore, it is imperative that administrators protect the hiring process to ensure the quality of teachers: "Strategic schools recognize that all else flows from successful hiring, and they employ hiring and assignment practices that link to a vision of what expertise, philosophy, and work schedule would best support the school's need" (Miles & Frank, 2008, p. 25).

Time is another important resource that must always be protected. In the United States, students generally spend 180 school days in the classroom. When mandated testing and other interruptions are factored out, instructional days can be whittled down to 165–170 school days, which equates to between 900 and 1,000 hours of instruction time per school year. There are many intrusions in the life of a school that deteriorate the amount of instructional time available for teachers and students. Activities such as field trips, school picture day, and other school-wide activities are responsible for eating away hours of instructional time each year. Even seemingly brief interruptions, such as intercom announcements during instructional time, consume valuable instructional time.

Resource Alignment

The art of school administration requires an ability to align resources effectively in order to maximize student achievement. It truly becomes a balancing act a principal performs to align school finances with increasing instructional effectiveness of the staff, and organizing a school in such a way as to protect instructional time is the most essential part of overseeing an educational organization. In their work *The Strategic School,* Miles and Frank (2008) dubbed this important work of the principals as the "Big Three." Specifically, strategic schools organize and use resources to accomplish the following "Big Three" tasks:

- Invest in continuously improved teacher quality through hiring, professional development, job structure, and common planning time.
- Create individual attention and personalize learning environments.
- Use student time strategically by emphasizing core academics and literacy. (p. 18)

Best Practices

School Improvement Plans

A school improvement plan (SIP) is developed periodically—sometimes annually—by analyzing data and determining strengths, weaknesses, and goals for improvement. For each goal, a determination is made as to what resources are necessary to accomplish it. For more information on school improvement plans, see Chapter 3.

Auditing

Annual auditing by an outside agency ensures school funds are being handled with integrity. "A comprehensive audit by a qualified agency is the public's best possible assurance of the honest and efficient operation of school fiscal affairs" (Brimley, Verstegen, & Garfield, 2012, p. 315). The annual audit should be in accordance with the state school-auditing manual. It is the responsibility of the school administrator to be familiar with the auditing manual and to ensure compliance with it. Private schools can also hold themselves accountable by conducting an annual financial audit.

Budgeting

The essential tool for an administrator to align financial resources with the school mission and vision is the development of a detailed budget. The detail of the budget will fluctuate depending on the responsibilities of the school administrator, the size and type of school, and the site-based authority of the principal.

Policy Implications

The current state of educational funding in the United States is at the mercy of the health of the economy. In some states and locales where the economy has not been as negatively impacted by the most recent economic downturn, education funding has remained relatively steady. However, in areas of the country that have been particularly hard hit, education funding has struggled to keep pace with fixed-cost increases, such as energy, labor, fuel, and health-care costs. This negative impact on educational funding has been exacerbated by declining land and property values along with lower revenue from decreased sales taxes. As the economy recovers, it will be more important for educators to guard every dollar and resource in order to maximize student achievement.

CONCLUSION

Although the bulk of this chapter has dealt with financial resources and how those resources are allocated, it is important to remember that the other two resources—time and staff—are equally important. The school administrator has been entrusted with the responsibility of ensuring that the resources are in full alignment with the school mission and vision. Equally, the Christian school administrator must be accountable and act with integrity while assigning and using resources.

The school administrator has been entrusted with the responsibility of ensuring that the resources are in full alignment with the school mission and vision.

Discussion Questions

1. How do the steps that Joseph implemented in Genesis relate to the acquisition and stewardship of resources for the school administrator?

2. To what extent does the federal government play a role in funding local education efforts?

3. Compare and contrast funding equity, adequacy, and the "broken systems theory."

4. Discuss the impact of school vouchers and charter schools on school finance in your state.

5. Differentiate between local, state, and federal funding sources and responsibilities.

Activities for Enrichment

1. Review your state's school auditing manual and/or its accounting manual and evaluate your school's procedural compliance.
2. Evaluate the impact that your school's budget has on student achievement. Is there any area that could be changed to drive student achievement?

REFERENCES

Avenues—The World School. (2012). Admissions: Tuition and financial aid. Retrieved from http://www.avenues.org/private-school-tuition

Berry, C., & Wysong, C. (2010). School-finance reform in red and blue. *Education Next, 10*(3). Retrieved from http://educationnext.org/school-finance-reform-in-red-and-blue/

Blackaby, H., & Blackaby, R. (2011). *Spiritual leadership: Moving people on to God's agenda.* Nashville, TN: B & H Publishing Group.

Brimley, Jr., V., Verstegen, D. A., & Garfield, R. R. (2012). *Financing education in a climate of change* (11th ed.). Upper Saddle River, NJ: Pearson Education Inc.

Broughman, S. P., Swaim, N. L., & Hryczaniuk, C. A. (2011). *Characteristics of private schools in the United States: Results from the 2009–10 Private School Universe Survey* (NCES 2011-339). Washington, DC: National Center for Education Statistics, Institute of Education Sciences, U.S. Department of Education.

Crawford, J. (2011). Reauthorization of Elementary and Secondary Education Act. Retrieved from http://www.diversitylearningk12.com/articles/Crawford_ESEA_FAQ.pdf

Drexler, J. L. (2007). *Schools as communities.* Colorado Springs, CO: Purposeful Design Publications.

Ellson, M. (2012, July 11). Appeal filed in state school funding case. *The Alamedan.* Retrieved from http://thealamedan.org/news/appeal-filed-state-school-funding-case

Every Student Succeeds Act (2019). Retrieved from https://ed.sc.gov/newsroom/every-student-succeeds-act-essa/.

Gillespie, L. (2010). The fourth wave of education finance litigation: Pursuing a federal right to an adequate education. *Cornell Law Review, 95.* Retrieved from http://www.lawschool.cornell.edu/research/cornell-law-review/upload/Gillespie-note-final.pdf

Guthrie, J., & Ettema, E. (2012). Public schools and money: Strategies for improving productivity in times of austerity. *Education Next, 12*(4). Retrieved from http://educationnext.org/public-schools-and-money/

Hanna, J. (2011, June 7). The Elementary and Secondary Education Act: 40 years later. *Harvard Graduate School of Education: News Features & Releases.* Retrieved from http://www.gse.harvard.edu/news_events/features/2005/08/esea0819.html

Kellog, A. (2009, July 21). Detroit schools on the brink: Shrinking district heads toward bankruptcy to gain control of its costs. *Wall Street Journal.* Retrieved from http://online.wsj.com/article/SB124813472753066949.html

Kent, C. A., & Sowards, K. (2009). Property taxation and equity in public school finance. *Journal of Property Tax Assessment & Administration, 6*(1), 25–42.

Knight, D. S. (2012). Assessing the cost of instructional coaching. *Journal of Education Finance, 38*(1), 52–80.

Lebherz, L. (2011, September). Education finance litigation: Adequacy v. equity. *Bar Bulletin.* Retrieved from https://www.kcba.org/newsevents/barbulletin/BView.aspx?Month=09&Year=2011&AID=article8.htm

Marzano, R., Pickering, D., & Pollock, J. (2001). *Classroom instruction that works: Research-based strategies for increasing student achievement.* Alexandria, VA: ASCD.

McCuddy, M. K., & Pirie, W. L. (2007). Spirituality, stewardship, and financial decision making: Toward a theory of intertemporal stewardship. *Managerial Finance, 33*(12), 957–969.

McIntyre, B. (2012, Sep. 19). Vince Young has run out of money. *Yahoo! Sports.* Retrieved from http://sports.yahoo.com/blogs/nfl-shutdown-corner/vince-young-run-money-150846064--nfl.html

McNeil, M. (2011, June 20). School finance. *Education Week.* Retrieved from http://www.edweek.org/ew/issues/school-finance/

Michelman, B. (2012). The never-ending story of ESEA reauthorization. *Policy Priorities, 18*(1).

Michigan. (2012, February 7). Snyder signs bills to better position financially troubled school districts, including Detroit Public Schools [Press release]. Retrieved from http://www.michigan.gov/snyder/0,4668,7-277-57577_57657-270873--,00.html

Miles, K. H., & Frank, S. (2008). *The strategic school: Making the most of people, time, and money*. Thousand Oaks, CA: Corwin Press.

Moore, E. H., Bagin, D., & Gallagher, D. R. (2012). *The school and community relations*. Prentice Hall.

New America Foundation. (2012, December 13). School finance: Federal, state, and local K–12 school finance overview. *Background and Analysis*. Retrieved from http://febp.newamerica.net/background-analysis/school-finance

New York Const., art. XI, § 1.

Philpott, T., (2012, August 15). 80 percent of public schools have contracts with Coke or Pepsi. *MotherJones*. Retrieved from http://www.motherjones.com/tom-philpott/2012/08/schools-limit-campus-junk-food-have-lower-obesity-rates

Picus, L. O., & Odden, A. R. (2011). Reinventing school finance: Falling forward. *Peabody Journal of Education, 86*(3), 291–303.

Robles-Wong v. State of California (2010).

Rodriguez v. San Antonio Independent School District, 411 U.S. 1 (1973).

Rose V. Council for Better Education, Inc., 790 S.W.2d 186, 60 Ed. Law Rep. 1289 (Ky. 1989).

Sarlin, B. (2012, December 11). Bobby Jindal defends school voucher program struck down by state court. *Talking Points Memo.* Retrieved from http://tpmdc.talkingpointsmemo.com/2012/12/bobby-jindal-defends-school-voucher-program-struck-down-by-judge.php

Simon, S. (2011, May 25). Public schools charge kids for basics, frills. *Wall Street Journal*. Retrieved from http://online.wsj.com/article/SB10001424052748703864204576313572363698678.html

Tang, A. (2011). Broken systems, broken duties: A new theory for school finance litigation. *Marquette Law Review, 94*. Retrieved from http://scholarship.law.marquette.edu/cgi/viewcontent.cgi?article=5084&context=mulr

Tenn. Const., art. XI, § 12.

Tresnowski, J., & Sullivan, L. (2011). Reading the state school finance litigation tea leaves. *Harvard Law and Policy Review*. Retrieved from http://hlpronline.com/2011/01/reading-the-state-school-finance-litigation-tea-leaves-what-lies-ahead-for-plaintiff-school-children/

Turner, D. (2011, August 2). School vouchers bills "flood" state houses. *CBN News*. Retrieved from http://www.cbn.com/cbnnews/politics/2011/August/School-Voucher-Bills-Flood-State-Houses/

Twight, C. (1994). Origins of federal control over education. *The Freeman*. Retrieved from http://www.fee.org/the_freeman/detail/origins-of-federal-control-over-education#axzz2JoDfeuYS

Va. Const., art. VIII, § 1.

Wan, Y., Norbury, H., Molefe, A. C., Gerdeman, R. D., Meyers, C. V., & Burke, M. (2012). Differences in spending in school districts across geographic locales in Minnesota. (Issues & Answers Report, REL 2012–No. 124). Washington, DC: U.S. Department of Education, Institute of Education Sciences, National Center for Education Evaluation and Regional Assistance, Regional Educational Laboratory Midwest. Retrieved from http://ies.ed.gov/ncee/edlabs/regions/midwest/pdf/REL_2012124.pdf

Chapter 7

Organizational Management and Distributed Leadership

Leldon W. Nichols

The American cultural ideal of the self-made man, of everyone standing on his own feet, is as tragic a picture as the initiative—destroying dependence on a benevolent despot. We all need each other. This type of interdependence is the greatest challenge to the maturity of individual and group functioning.

—Kurt Lewin—

OVERVIEW

Although educational leaders wear multiple hats and play varied roles, this chapter will focus on their role as managers of operational aspects to facilitate the development and maintenance of safe, efficient, and effective learning environments. Within those roles, leaders not only need to develop their own skills, but just as importantly they need to insure that all members of the organization are given an opportunity to develop grow and contribute to the organization. Considerable attention is given to the concept of distributed leadership. As an important resource, distributed leadership can be employed in every level and aspect of educational organizations. Within the chapter are illustrations and principles of leadership from the Bible to help Christian educational leaders integrate a biblical perspective of distributed leadership.

Objectives

By the end of this chapter, the reader should be able to do the following:

1. Evaluate the management and operations systems of the organization.
2. Obtain, allocate, align, and efficiently utilize resources.
3. Develop the capacity of the organization for distributed leadership.

INTRODUCTION

Although principals might prefer spending the bulk of their time being instructional leaders, most of their time is spent on administrative and management duties. Glanz (2006) ranked the actual duties of principals based on a formal study of principals and assistant principals' duties. Performing the duties of instructional leaders ranked 16th, whereas duties of formulating goals, administrative paperwork, parental conferences, school budgeting, student discipline, faculty meetings, lunch duty, emergency arrangements, and school scheduling respectively ranked at the top. Although the duties of operational management are time consuming if not inherently mundane, they are nonetheless important in contributing to the development of safe, efficient, and effective learning environments.

Although principals might prefer spending the bulk of their time being instructional leaders, most of their time is spent on administrative and management duties.

Educational leadership literature makes clear distinctions in the roles of administrators as leaders versus managers. Leaders are generally expected to be risk takers and committed to continuous improvement and change of learning processes, whereas managers are charged with duties related to maintenance of policies and best practices to augment the learning processes (Ubben, Hughes, & Norris, 2011). Ideally, these two roles of educational administrators would be assigned to separate individuals in either a co-principal arrangement or principal and assistant principal structure. The reality is that, in many public and private schools, the principal assumes the duties of both leader and manager. The challenge, then, is to balance these duties while allowing others to be part of the leadership process.

BIBLICAL PERSPECTIVES

Moses, of the Old Testament, invokes a mental image of the heroic leader. Rightly so, because this unlikely character was chosen by God to lead the children of Israel out of Egyptian bondage and back to their Holy Land. He was the quintessential spiritual leader. With the rod in hand, he confronted Pharaoh and called down the plagues of retribution on the Egyptians. At the moment of sure and total destruction of the Israelites, he raised the rod and the waters parted. He went to Mount Sinai and received directly from God the divine policy standards, the Ten Commandments. Yes, he was by all measures an exemplary leader. His role was to lead, and he did so exceptionally. However, the role of Moses as leader changes when the Israelites were denied entrance into the land. For a period of 40 years, they would be sojourners in the wilderness. The culture changed, and the daily-life issues of the Israelites required Moses to play the role of magistrate. The biblical account from Exodus 18 reveals the problem Moses faced as the singular judge. We see how the problem was resolved through practical advice from Jethro, Moses' father in law:

> Moses' father-in-law replied, "What you are doing is not good. You and these people who come to you will only wear yourselves out. The work is too heavy for you; you cannot handle it alone. Listen now to me and I will give you some advice, and may God be with you. You must be the people's representative before God and bring their disputes to him. Teach them his decrees and instructions, and show them the way they are to live and how they are to behave. But select capable men from all the people—men who fear God, trustworthy men who hate dishonest gain—and appoint them as officials over thousands, hundreds, fifties and tens. Have them serve as judges for the people at all times, but have them bring every difficult case to you; the simple cases they can decide themselves. That will make your load lighter, because they will share it with you. If you do this and God so commands, you will be able to stand the strain, and all these people will go home satisfied."
>
> Moses listened to his father-in-law and did everything he said. He chose capable men from all Israel and made them leaders of the people, officials over thousands, hundreds, fifties and tens. (Exodus 18:17–25, New International Version)

Mathew Henry's (n. d.) commentary on this story offers wisdom to all who find themselves in conflicting leadership duties:

> Moses kept to his business from morning to night. Jethro thought it was too much for him to undertake alone; also it would make the administration of justice tiresome to the people. There may be over-doing even in well-doing. Wisdom is profitable to direct, that we may neither content ourselves with less than our duty, nor task ourselves beyond our strength. Jethro advised Moses to a better plan. Great men should not only study to be useful themselves, but contrive to make others useful. (para. 4)

Private and Public School Distinctions

Organizational Structures

Private schools, whether nonprofit parochial or for-profit enterprises, vary greatly in the operational management duties of their principals. This variation is primarily a result of the organizational structure with regard to lines of accountability and responsibility. Some private school principals may be granted a larger degree of autonomy than others who share authority with nonschool personnel in the hierarchy of the proprietary agency's structure. For example, in church-sponsored schools, it is not uncommon for the pastor of the church to assume the responsibility of hiring all school personnel. Additionally, Christian schools often share facilities with a church, thus mitigating the principal's responsibilities for building maintenance. In contrast, because public schools in the United States are agencies of the government and are controlled by centralized districts, the organizational structures are not as varied as their private-sector counterparts. However, the duties, expectations, and responsibilities of building-level public school principals can and do vary—even in the same district. Public charter schools are structured and managed according to the bylaws set by their governing boards. Regarding operational management, the main distinction of charter schools from regular public schools is reduced government funding, thus necessitating entrepreneurial fundraising.

Private schools, whether nonprofit parochial or for-profit enterprises, vary greatly in the operational management duties of their principals.

Professional Licensure

Private schools have considerable latitude as to staff licensure requirements. Depending on the policies of the approving agency under which the private school is chartered, those charged with the hiring of leadership and instructional staff may employ individuals who do not hold state licenses or certificates within their teaching or leadership areas. Under certain provisions, public schools may temporarily employ individuals without a license or certificate. However, considerable time and attention are given to securing certified and licensed school staff in all public schools.

Collective Bargaining

Private and public charter schools are rarely union-affiliated schools. The absence of unions in these schools, however, does not eliminate the managerial responsibilities for careful attention to equitable salaries, benefits, working condition, and the regulations of local, state, and federal governments for all human resource practices.

Current Trends

In the past, differences of duties between public and private school leaders were most evident in the areas of securing human resources and spending authority. That distinction may be fading, however, as noted in the following excerpts from the Wallace Foundation report (Plecki, Alejano, Knapp, & Lochmiller, 2006):

> While district hiring practices often limit the ability of the school principal to screen and select teachers that possess the particular skills needed at the school, there is a trend toward allowing greater school-level decision-making discretion with respect to hiring staff. Some urban districts, like Chicago and Seattle, have adopted hiring processes that allow applicants to apply directly to the school, giving more control to principals and site hiring teams to select candidates. This is particularly advantageous for hard-to-staff schools that suffer from chronic teacher turnover. (p. 21)

The report acknowledges that although the decentralized hiring trend allows the area schools to have closer interaction with potential hires, the following assumptions would apply to each participating school:

- The school has accurately assessed the specific learning needs of the students in the school and the school's existing capacity to meet those needs.
- The school has determined the types of skills needed to be a successful teacher in the specific subject area(s) and context of the unfilled position.
- The school has developed a hiring process that determines not only if candidates possess those skills but also if they can be successful using them given the school context. (Plecki et al., 2006, p. 21)

The report continues with "a related strategy gaining prominence, called school-based funding, [which] deemphasizes the centralization of budgeting and financial administration at the district level and instead relocates it at the school level, empowering individual sites to make funding decisions to affect student learning" (p. 25).

Given the trend toward fiscal decentralization, Plecki et al. (2006) point out the need for specialized leadership training:

> Decentralization also implies that principals and other school leaders have the skills and supports they need to make informed decisions regarding matters of budget and finance. Once again, this kind of budgetary discretion implies a new role for principals and also for district leaders, who shift from making allocation decisions to supporting—as well as monitoring—the decision making of others. These role changes have particular implications for how leaders are prepared initially and how, once in administrative or other leadership roles, their professional knowledge is developed to enable them to handle increasing school-level authority and responsibility for budgets. (p. 26)

Evaluating Operational Resources and Processes

An organization's resources refer to the human, fiscal, and technical assets acquired to carry out the organizational mission. Evaluation of these diverse resources has a common requirement—data. Data include facts and figures from which conclusions may be drawn about the degree to which an organization is effectively maximizing its resources. Because effective decisions rely on the collection and interpretation of valid data, evaluation instruments and practices must provide accurate and meaningful information. Evaluations may need to begin with the consideration of the data-collection processes for each area to be evaluated. If the instruments and methods of evaluation are indeed providing accurate facts, the results must be readily available. Availability of the information means both quick retrieval and ease of interpretation. Principals are far too busy to be spending inordinate amounts of time locating or interpreting data. Creative use of charts, grafts, histograms, or checklists may prove helpful.

The goal of all evaluation is to improve processes. In the field of school administration, it is maintained that the main objective of all processes is to focus on providing a safe, efficient, and effective learning environment. Because the essence of learning suggests change, it is reasonable to assume that all processes in support of learning are themselves also changing and improving. However, to assure that those assumptions are realities, constant attention to evaluation is necessary.

For managing nonhuman resources, numeric values are assigned to money and materials, such as buildings, desks, computers, and so forth. Evaluating how humans effectively and efficiently utilize such things is not as discrete. To aid in understanding the concept of human evaluations, it may be helpful to think of evaluating people as individuals and as members of groups.

In education, it is generally understood that teachers are evaluated individually using both student achievement performance criteria and Individual Development Plans (IDPs). Evaluating support staff individually may involve only use of the IDP or another method, but it is important that everyone be provided the benefit of annual evaluations and regular feedback from the principal. It is also imperative that a record of all evaluations be securely filed.

Strategies for evaluating human resources as members of groups have not been as widely established as they have been for evaluating individuals. Nevertheless, the rationale for having people work collaboratively in groups is the same as that for having them work alone. Whether the work is done by groups or individuals, the expectation is that all work processes within the school should contribute to the improvement of and provisions for a safe, efficient, and effective learning environment. Presented later in this chapter is a model designed to aid in evaluating the effectiveness and processes of distributed leadership in groups.

Distributed Leadership

Historically, leadership literature primarily focused on the attributes of individual leaders. The notion that everything would either rise or fall on leadership was intuitively understood to be the challenge for the individual at the top of the organization. The ideal leader was portrayed as one endowed with exceptional intelligence, stellar character, and irresistible charisma. The following are additional assumptions about leaders:

© Andrii Talanskyi/Shutterstock.com

- Great leaders are rare.
- Effective leaders are aloof from those they lead.
- Successful leaders are born with innate qualities.
- A leader with the "right stuff" can solve problems.
- The best leaders attract loyal followers.

Rather than relying on larger-than-life individuals to provide solutions to challenges, organizations are beginning to understand the value of multiple leaders—particularly leadership emerging from groups that can develop solutions. In the school context, this concept does not diminish the role of the principal. On the contrary, the school principal has been and should continue to be recognized as one of the school's most valued resources. Distributed educational leadership is the development of value-added human resources through work teams or groups to assist principals in their leadership and management objectives.

Day, Gronn, and Salas (2004) provide an exceptional review of the history of distributed leadership in groups. They cite the following quote from C. A. Gibb, which dates back to 1954:

> Leadership is probably best conceived as a group quality, as a set of functions which must be carried out by the group. This concept of distributed leadership is an important one. If there are leadership functions which must be performed in any group, and if these functions may be focused or distributed, then leaders will be identifiable both in terms of the frequency and in terms of the multiplicity or pattern of functions performed. (p. 873)

Kogler Hill (2013) explained that "distributed leadership involves the sharing of influence by team members who step forward when situations warrant providing the leadership necessary and then stepping back to allow others to lead" (p. 289). The concept of multiple leaders and their interaction with followers is key to understanding distributed leadership. Edwin Hollander is credited as being "one of the first people in modern psychology to appreciate the importance of followership and to understand that followers, far from being passive consumers of leadership, have to be enjoined to become active participants in leadership projects" (Haslam, Reicher, & Platow, 2011, Chapter 2). In *The New Psychology of Leadership*, Haslam and colleagues (2011) argued that effective transformational leadership is an in-group phenomenon. In other words, the leader is socially identified by the followers as being one of them. It is thus the followers who empower the leader with such qualities as influence and charisma. Spillane (2006) concurred that "leaders collectively constitute their practice in interaction with followers, and in this way, followers contribute to defining leadership practice" (Chapter 3).

Capacity for Distributed Leadership

Day et al. (2004) described distributed leadership capacity "as an emergent state or a construct that develops over the life of the team; is typically dynamic in nature; and varies as a function of team inputs, processes, and outcomes" (p. 861). Recognized as a formulator of and expert in distributed leadership theory, Spillane (2006) provided the following as necessary elements of distributed leadership:

- Leadership practice is the central and anchoring concern.
- Leadership practice is generated in the interactions of leaders, followers, and their situation; each element is essential for leadership practice.
- The situation both defines leadership practice and is defined through leadership practice. (Chapter 1)

Making reference to tenets of Gestalt theory, Spillane stated,

> From a distributed perspective, simply counting up the actions of leaders will not be sufficient on its own; the whole is more than the sum of the parts. Hence, in a distributed approach, we have to start with the leadership practice, observe it, infer who the leaders are, and begin to explore the interactions among the leaders, followers, and their situation. (Chapter 3)

Similarly, Kurt Lewin (1948) postulated that social behavior (B) is a function (f) of people (P) interacting with others in their environment (E). Lewin, therefore, formulated his theory as B = f(P,E). Current leadership theories reflect Lewin's equation by highlighting the importance of multiple leaders in group contexts. Lewin's equation might well be revised as DL = f(Ls,G) to reflect the current sentiment that distributed leadership (DL) is a function (f) of multiple leaders (Ls) in a group situation or context (G).

Not to be confused with democratic, egalitarian, delegated authority, or shared leadership styles, distributed leadership is an outcome of two or more individuals productively interacting in a group and consequently providing an influence on group outcomes. It is the practice of interpersonal activity that produces distributed leadership. It is not the action or position of a singular person but the practices of two or more individuals in a group that distinguishes distributed leadership from other styles.

Likewise, Spillane (2006) described distributed leadership practice as being "in between" two or more leaders. He employed a metaphor of the two-step dance to describe the in-between concept. Distributed leadership, he emphasized, is like a dance in that it is the interaction of both partners to the music—the contextual situation. He also referred to the collective group, in which distributed leadership is evident as an ensemble of group members improvising as they respond to each other's actions. To further explore the ensemble metaphor, a comparison may be made to jazz music. Mike Pope (personal communication, 2013), a professional jazz bassist, explained an improvisational stratagem called "trading fours." Instrumentalists trade fours

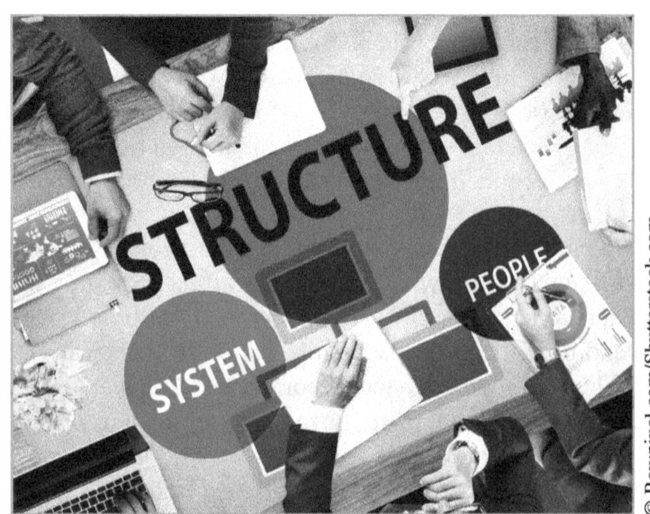

when they spontaneously take turns playing four solo measures at a time, creatively interpreting the music. Further analogies of jazz to leadership practice can be found in the published works of Brian Fraser (2008) and Max DePree (2008).

Human experiences within the context of group phenomena have been observed and reported extensively. Some of those observations are applicable to help understand distributed leadership in a group context. For example, *esprit de corps*, often experienced by military personnel, is the "spirit" of a group that elicits from its members' affective commitment, cognitive engagement, and volitional participation. Also an athletic team, which functions as a unit, is the combined interdependent actions of all members. These observations and the previously mentioned jazz ensemble metaphor should facilitate a deeper comprehension of the ideals of distributed leadership. Although distributed leadership is more than a feeling and is certainly not a game or music, it should be appreciated as a phenomenal outcome of social interaction among multiple leaders in the context of a purpose-driven group.

Validity and Merit of Distributed Leadership

The truism "there is strength in numbers" comes to mind relative to the value of distributed leadership. One might also think fancifully of distributed leadership as the Camelot in the kingdom of leadership practice. The matter of validity is an important consideration. From a biblical worldview perspective, Christian practitioners of leadership should always raise questions about the philosophical roots of theories and their applications in contemporary culture. As Phillips, Brown, and Stonestreet (2008) stated, "Postmodernism has infiltrated many key areas of thought including philosophy, the arts, literature, history, sociology, psychology, inter-cultural studies and increasingly, technology. Its influence, especially in academia, is strong and continues to grow. Therefore, it demands our attention" (p. 49). Although distributed leadership is lacking in both theoretical framework development and empirical research, it embraces a concept of group-engendered leadership identity that could be of concern for Christians. In their book *Making Sense of Your World,* Phillips et al. (2008) offered these insights about personal identity:

The truism "there is strength in numbers" comes to mind relative to the value of distributed leadership.

> From a postmodern perspective, our sense of personal identity is as much a social construct as any other claim about reality. . . . Two key factors reinforce this postmodern view of identity. First, the pluralism of western societies increases our tendency to see ourselves and others as part of groups. This is most clearly seen today in 'identity politics,' or the tendency of many to claim victim status by way of their identification with a particular race, group, or sexual orientation. . . . Second, there is a great fluidity to contemporary life . . . this means that a great amount of flexibility is required of people today. Lines are constantly being drawn and re-drawn, and we are constantly moving in and out of different groups and relationships. (p. 50)

Additionally, Kenneth Gergen (as cited in Phillips et al., 2008) stated, "These relationships pull us in myriad directions, inviting us to play such a variety of roles that the very concept of 'authentic self' with knowable characteristics recedes from view" (pp. 56–58).

While acknowledging philosophical cautions concerning postmodern theory and practice of distributed leadership, administrators should also consider following biblical principles that validate the worth of multiples working together in unity. First, Solomon acknowledged, "Though one may be overpowered, two can defend themselves. A cord of three strands is not quickly broken" (Ecclesiastes 4:12). Drawing attention to the fact that a rope is made strong because of its inter-twisting of three separate strands, this verse has often been referenced as the model of Christian marriage, as husband, wife, and God are united as one. A second biblical illustration of unity in multiples is from Paul's letter to the Ephesians. In this treatise, Paul explained to Gentile believers that God was revealing a mystery. That mystery was the Church of all believers—both Jews and Gentiles. In Ephesians 4:16, using the metaphor of a body with Christ as the head, Paul wrote, "From Him the whole body, joined and held together by every supporting ligament, grows and builds itself up in love, as each part does its work."

Essentials of Distributed Leadership

Three distinct themes emerge from the literature on distributed leadership—so much so that they are clearly the three essentials for understanding the developmental concepts of distributed leadership as well as developing the capacity for practicing distributed leadership.

Training. As indicated earlier, distributed leadership is widely accepted as emerging from the activity between two or more individuals. Scribner, Watson, and Myers (2007) drew attention to discourse, or speech, as the key activity between leaders in groups. They identified two patterns of discourse that emerged from the groups studied: active discourse and passive discourse. Active discourse—being the desired pattern for identifying and solving problems—requires training in the areas of facilitation, interaction, and communication for team members to be optimally productive. Less desirable is passive discourse that relies solely on the conveyance of factual representations and the expressions of feelings. Most training, unfortunately, has traditionally been of the passive nature whereby the training involves leaders presenting facts and their feelings about those facts.

Introducing the concept of distributed leadership should ideally be part of the school's in-service training for all staff. During group formations, the induction or orientation sessions for groups should also include the stated expectations for all group members to engage in the group leadership process. Once the groups are formed and in the process of grappling with the issues charged to the group, opportunities for distributed leadership training will be optimal. The content of the in-process training should include information on how the organization's contextual conditions relate to the group's task. For example, the administrator should reiterate the purpose of the group, clarifying the group's level of autonomy and the degree of administrative support it is to receive. A training session on how change takes place in a complex bureaucratic organization may also help move the group process forward. Training in the use of the dialectic method for reaching consensus would also be appropriate. Continuous training will contribute to and facilitate distributed leadership development.

Developing a culture of distributed leadership in any organization requires strategic training of the organizational leadership. From a social-cultural learning theory perspective, both scaffolding and modeling are important features of training for distributed leadership. Groups in which distributed leadership is fully functioning are so rare, however, that it is conceivable that even experienced leaders and educators may never have observed, evaluated, or participated in a group where multiple leaders are collaboratively interacting in the group processes. This notion underscores the importance of training all future school leaders in the strategies of distributed leadership development.

Trust. Smylie, Mayrowetz, Murphy, and Louis (2007) studied distributed development in six schools for a period of 3 years. Based on their analysis, they concluded that trust is a significant dynamic factor in distributed leadership development. Articulating the theoretical model guiding the study, they posited,

> Trust is only one thread in the thick and complex tapestry that is distributed leadership development. Certainly, there are other environmental, organizational, and interpersonal factors at play in the development of distributed leadership in our focal cases and in the other schools that we studied. (p. 499)

Defining distributed leadership as work, their research theory was framed around the strength of trust:

> If trust is strong, designers may be more likely to develop distributed leadership work that extends to a wider variety of tasks on a wider range of significant subjects than if trust is weak and distrust reigns. If trust is strong, designers may facilitate work that is more challenging and risky, as well as more

> meaningful, significant to the organization, and readily identifiable. Also, if trust is strong, designers may introduce fewer bureaucratic controls and extend greater autonomy to those who assume distributed leadership work. Finally, if trust is strong, designers may be more likely to incorporate processes of collaboration and open bidirectional communication, joint problem solving, full exchange of information, honest assessment, and unbridled feedback. (p. 475)

Time. Singh (2011) presented a comprehensive review of how distributed leadership works in schools. Her thesis was that distributed leadership provides a strategy for teacher-leaders to have a strong and powerful voice in the leadership process. Embedded in her article were several not-too-subtle references to the fact that the development of distributed leadership takes time. Singh wrote,

> Distributed leadership is a gradual process that involves gathering knowledge about the model, examining current practices in the school and district, assessing areas of expertise, building capacity, shifting paradigms, opening dialogue, resolving conflict positively, and putting in time and effort. Working together, districts, school administrators and teachers can move easily toward this model. It can begin with a leadership team and can branch out gradually to other staff members, parents and at higher levels, even students. At first there will be adjustments: but with time, everyone will be accustomed to sharing information, making decisions, solving problems together, being mutually accountable, and growing individually and as a group. (p. 10)

The essential element of time may be the most critical in distributed leadership development in public schools. Intuitively, administrators understand that it indeed takes time for individuals in groups to develop the skills of interpersonal communication in both cohorts and contextual organizational systems. In reality, administrators know that mandates, deadlines, and fix-it-now cultures do not provide much time for the social side of group processes to synchronize. Therefore, the lack of time may prove to be the most detrimental to the development of distributed leadership.

The postmodern culture, as it has evolved in the context of Western civilization, is impatient. This collective impatience may be driven by the demands of those who assume the power of choice. As Phillips et al. (2008) stated, "The productivity of Western civilization has created a culture that is mostly defined by its consumerism. Ours is a culture of unlimited choices, from cereal to philosophies, and the only absolute value is to value everyone's right to choose their own existence, even their own meaning" (p. 88).

Just as cultural and social revolutions have historically impacted school environments and tried the patience of the most dedicated educational leaders, so too will current conditions. From a Christian perspective, the choice is how to respond to the impatient demands of those whom God has called administrators to serve.

Moses knew something about a culture of impatient, demanding people. This is seen as the story of Moses advances from the Genesis account noted earlier. There, Moses displayed one of the most important qualities of a great leader: He listened to and heeded good advice! The unlikely source of a better way to lead was his father-in-law Jethro. Based on Jethro's advice, Moses implemented the plan of multiple judges with good results. Life in the camps was much improved, according to the biblical record. Later, Moses' greatest test was recorded as the people became impatient with him and complained about the lack of food and water:

> Moses and Aaron went from the assembly to the entrance to the tent of meeting and fell facedown, and the glory of the Lord appeared to them. The Lord said to Moses, "Take the staff, and you and your brother Aaron gather the assembly together. Speak to that rock before their eyes and it will pour out its water. You will bring water out of the rock for the community so they and their livestock can drink."
>
> So Moses took the staff from the Lord's presence, just as he commanded him. He and Aaron gathered the assembly together in front of the rock and Moses said to them, "Listen, you rebels, must we bring you water out of this rock?" Then Moses raised his arm and struck the rock twice with his staff. Water gushed out, and the community and their livestock drank.

> But the Lord said to Moses and Aaron, "Because you did not trust in me enough to honor me as holy in the sight of the Israelites, you will not bring this community into the land I give them." (Numbers 20:6–13)

In summary, Moses obviously was fed up with these impatient ingrates. He did, however, do some things right. First, faced with difficult people in a difficult situation and not knowing what to do, he went to God. God told him exactly what to do to provide water for the people. Moses again, like a good leader, listened—but this time not completely. He got his staff, the symbol of his God-given authority, and called the people into assembly. What happens next, though, is critical. Moses had lost his patience with the people, and he wanted to vent his anger toward them. He yelled, "Listen, you rebels, must we bring water out of this rock?!" God did not tell Moses to speak to the people; He was told to speak to the rock and not to the people, but he spoke his mind first. Then, he struck the rock twice. Yes, water came out from the rock, but Moses had made a critical leadership error that literally removed him and Aaron from leadership.

This story has been debated in theological circles for centuries as to important lessons to be learned from Moses' disobedience. From a Christian leadership perspective, five salient lessons emerge:

1. God uses multiple leaders and requires equal accountability.
2. Acute situations can alter the perceptions and expectations of leaders.
3. Impatient and obnoxious people need astute leadership.
4. Where human leadership patience ends, God's grace begins.
5. Although God uses human leaders, He does not share His Glory with them.

In the final analysis of the story, it is plausible to believe it was Moses' reference to "we" in verse 10 that prompted God's rebuke and severe judgment. The King James Version of the text is worded, "And the LORD spake unto Moses and Aaron, Because ye believed me not, to sanctify me in the eyes of the children of Israel, therefore ye shall not bring this congregation into the land which I have given them." The "sanctify me" means that they had not "set God apart" from themselves as being the sole provider of the water. The main point of the lesson is that Christian leaders should never lose patience with those to whom they are called to lead or serve and should humbly give the glory to God for all their successes.

Implementing and Evaluating Distributed Leadership

Built on grounded theoretical frameworks, Figure 7.1 presents a strategic model for distributed leadership (DL) development among members in groups. Blake and Moulton (1964) developed a managerial grid that conceptualized how individuals are either people-oriented or task-oriented leaders. Tuckman (1965), following the notions from earlier sequential stage theories of group development by Bennis and Shepard (1956), suggested the four stages of forming, storming, norming, and performing to describe group development. Drawing inspirational and ideological constructs from these and other theories, the four stages of distributed leadership development illustrated in Figure 7.1 are suggested as a conceptual model that illustrates how the interactivity between group members at different stages of group development contributes to the formation of distributed leadership. The assumption is that all groups using this strategy will be striving for collaboration and shared responsibilities. It is also assumed that the individuals who make up the groups are, in the general definition of the word, leaders who have responsibilities to and/or influence with others in the system. The size of groups can be as few as two and as large as practical for collaborative process and progress. The model can be interpolated and applied to ongoing work groups, process improvement groups, or temporary task groups.

Figure 7.1 depicts the model in a four-stage grid. The x-axis of the grid indicates the four group progressions and expectations stages, and the y-axis lists the four human reactions or expectations of group members at each stage. Of significant importance is to note the placement of the above-mentioned essential elements for distributed leadership: trust, training, and time. Ideally, there would be no limit to the number of times the group would need to meet before emerging to the next stage. Also, it is conceivable that a group

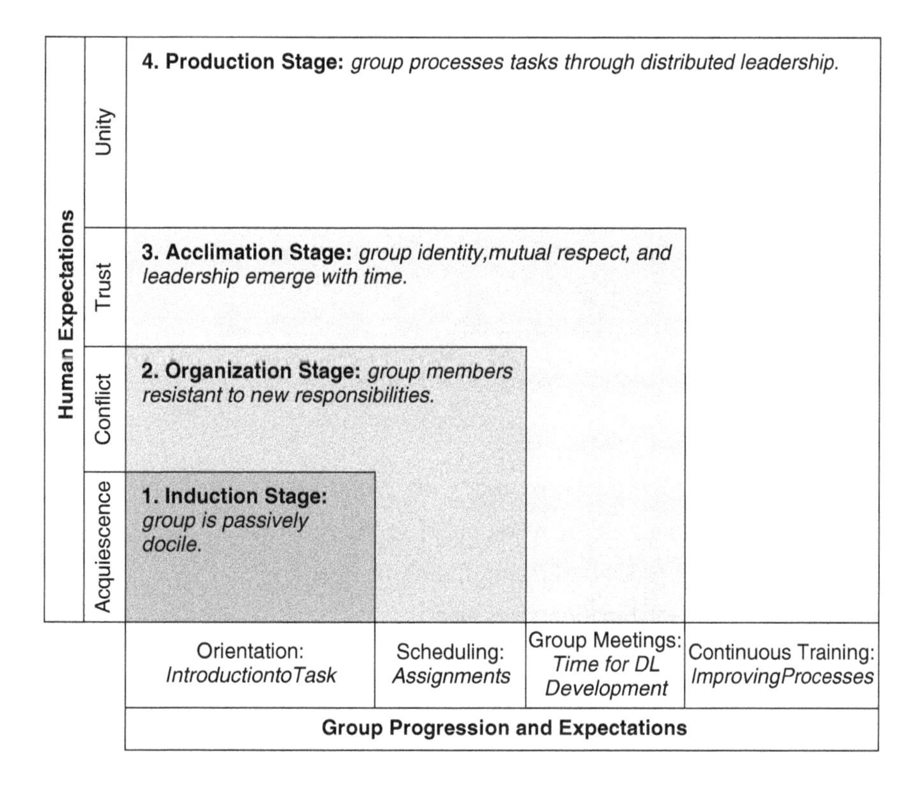

Figure 7.1. ***Leldon W. Nichols's model of four stages of distributed leadership (DL) development.***

may regress to a lower stage in response to repopulation of group personnel and/or changes in tasks. Finally, for a purpose-driven group, stage four is not a point of arrival or process termination. Quite the contrary, stage four is the point at which a group is ready to function as a team with multiple leaders. Furthermore, the words *unity* and *harmony* should not be interpreted as a tranquil balance among leaders. According to Kurt Lewin's (1948) force-field analysis theory, a group or organization would not change or move forward if all opposing forces are in balance. That notion applied to the distributed leadership model would suggest that leaders may be in harmony or unity on the vision or purpose of the group but be in opposition on issues of methods for improvement. Expanding on the application of Lewin's theory in schools, Ubben et al. (2011) stated:

> The productivity of a school staff, the state of the school/community relations program, the success level of the intramural program, among any number of other observable situations are all subject to explanation (and change) by force field analysis. Movement (i.e. change) will take place only when an imbalance is created. An imbalance will occur by eliminating forces, by developing new forces, or by affecting the power of existing forces. The imbalances "unfreeze" the current situation, the situation will change, and a new state of equilibrium will be achieved. (p. 73)

In the four-stage model shown in Figure 7.1, the continuous emergence of new leaders and/or roles should be sufficient to keep the group from debilitating equilibrium stagnation or groupthink syndrome. From a biblical perspective, the Bible reference to "iron sharpening iron as one man sharpens another" (Proverbs 27:17) does not eliminate the possibility of sparks flying in the process. The following questions serve to evaluate a group's progress and process:

Stage 1

_____ A. Were all members in attendance for the induction meeting?

_____ B. How many orientation-type meetings will be necessary?

_____ C. Do all members comprehend the purpose of the group?

Stage 2

_____ A. Are all members enthusiastically engaged during meetings?
_____ B. Are intra-group conflicts being addressed openly in meetings?

Stage 3

_____ A. Do members of the group express optimistic attitudes about processes?
_____ B. Do members show pride in group identity?
_____ C. Is there evidence of progress toward group tasks?
_____ D. Are members assuming leadership roles?

Stage 4

_____ A. Are members working harmoniously in processing group tasks?
_____ B. Are all members contributing to improvements of group processes?
_____ C. Are group objectives being processed through multiple leaders?
_____ D. Is effective distributed leadership clearly evident?

CONCLUSION

The day-to-day operational demands of any educational institution can be daunting. The principal, as the head of the school, is expected to possess versatile leadership skills for the multiple roles inherent in the job. In addition to being the public relations figurehead and the lead change agent for instructional improvement in the school, the principal is charged with the management responsibilities of monitoring and evaluating the human, fiscal, and technical resources. Research reveals that the principal is the key to guiding schools in developing safe, efficient, and effective learning environments for the students, teachers, and staff. The principal is the most valued and indispensable resource of any school. Research also shows that principals who have developed the capacity for distributed leadership in their schools are consistently the most successful in leading their schools toward improvements in instructional and management processes (Louis, Leithwood, Wahlstrom & Anderson, 2010).

The capacity for distributed leadership is both an attribute of the principal and a characteristic of the school culture. Day et al. (2004) pointed out the importance of moderating and guiding a group through outside leadership input. The principal's initial and ongoing mediating input is critical for developing leadership output from a group. Just as there is no phenomenon of perpetual motion in mechanical science, there is no perpetual progress in groups without the occasional input force. Principals who know how to provide that force have the capacity to develop the value-added resource of distributed leaders from within the school. They also understand that in a purpose-driven group, everything rises or falls on distributed leadership.

> The capacity for distributed leadership is both an attribute of the principal and a characteristic of the school culture.

For the Christian, there is also the personal resource of the Holy Spirit who leads and guides the pursuit of truth. The Spirit draws individuals to the wisdom from above, as James stated in his epistle. In James 3:17, he enumerates the following characteristics of godly wisdom: pure, peaceable, gentle, willing to yield, full of mercy, productive without partiality, and without hypocrisy. God asked Job the rhetorical question, "Who puts wisdom in the heart of man?" (Job 38:36). Job knew that it comes from the Father above. It is not an exaggeration to say that the spiritual qualifications for a school principal today are to have the wisdom of Solomon and the patience of Job. God provides what is needed every day by grace and through the ultimate resource of the indwelling Holy Spirit.

Discussion Questions

1. Evaluate any group you are presently associated with using the four stages of group development model in Figure 7.1. Identify the current stage of the group. Are multiple leaders productively interacting? If so, how? If not, why not? How might you apply the four stages model to improve the functionality of the group?

2. After viewing Biola University's YouTube video "Lead Like Jesus," explain how Ken Blanchard's four points are applicable to distributed leadership development. The video is available at this URL address: http://www.youtube.com/watch?v=nGPg7o6JeQo.

3. If you were the principal in the case study "Safety First" (see the following case study), what suggestions would you give to the superintendent regarding the utilization of a distributed leadership strategy for the school's committee on safety?

CASE STUDY: SAFETY FIRST

In the post-Columbine era, school safety became a priority issue for school leaders everywhere. Although there had been school shootings in the past, like the one in 1985 at Goddard Middle School in Goddard, Kansas, where the principal was killed and others seriously injured, Columbine was an unconscionable massacre. The consensus was that something had to be done to assure the safety of children while at school. The following is a fictional case study to represent how some school districts responded to this tragic incident.

Like school superintendents across the nation, Dr. Oschar Helms, superintendent of public schools in Cosmopolitan, took the initiative to make sure that the students in his schools would be safe. He formed a task force made up of school leaders, parents, and others to produce a plan that would assure all that anything like Columbine would not happen in his district on his watch. The newspapers and media were there to cover Dr. Helms's press conference announcing his initiative for safe schools. He passionately and eloquently outlined his master plan for the newly created Task Force for Safe Schools. It did not take long for the local folklore to begin framing Dr. Helms as the hero leader who would indeed save the children from danger. The task force members were mostly well connected and in-the-know people from the Cosmopolitan area. A school board member was on the committee along with one assistant principal and three classroom teachers. Raymon Rod, a successful businessman known for his no-nonsense and take-charge lifestyle, was announced to be the leader of the task force committee.

Fourteen years later, on Monday morning, December 17, 2012, Dr. Paul Love, current superintendent of Cosmopolitan schools, sat at his desk rereading the unthinkable newspaper accounts of the terrible shooting at Sandy Hook Elementary School in Newtown, Connecticut. His heart was moved by the heroic act of Principal Dawn Hochspung, who gave her life in attempting to stop the gunman from killing her kids. He saw her Twitter site from October 17 showing the students lined up outside for the evacuation drill with the caption Principal Hochspung had written, "Safety First at Sandy Hook." His silent prayers were for those families who had lost so much. His "God have mercy" petition was audible. In those reflective minutes, he recalled bits and pieces about a Task Force for Safe Schools that was formed 14 years earlier in Cosmopolitan. In the 3 years he had been superintendent, however, he had not seen any evidence that such a committee ever existed. His support staff had reported "nothing in the files" from any Task Force for Safe Schools initiative. Superintendent Love had been around education long enough to know how typical this situation was. "Many committees are formed with little or no results," he thought to himself. Because of Sandy Hook, he expected some local pressure on him to say or do something about safety in the Cosmopolitan schools.

You have been Principal of Littleton High School for 2 years. Littleton is a stable, middle-class, mixed-race suburb of Cosmopolitan. Your students and staff reflect all the cultural values of the greater community. There are 400 students in your building, which is a 75-year-old structure with an adjacent gym and sports stadium. Your telephone rings, you answer, and Superintendent Love greets you warmly. After pleasantries are exchanged, Dr. Love tells you he is calling all the principals in the school system in the aftermath of the Sandy Hook incident. He says he wants to hear from each principal personally and to assure each one that central office support and intervention are available if needed. He suggests that at the next principals meeting, "we should share some ideas about how to improve security in the area schools." He states that he would like for any discussion to be broad in scope to include all safety issues, such as environmental safety, safety related to natural disasters, and even food and nutritional safety in addition to personal security. You listen with great interest as he suggests forming building-level safety committees at each school to help improve the unique safety and security issues for respective schools. He asked if you have some knowledge of the distributed leadership model, to which you positively reply. He thinks distributed leadership might also need to be discussed as the right model for safety committees. He brings the call to a close with "Be thinking about it. Who should be on a committee like that at your school? Should they be short-term or ongoing committees? How could we support, monitor, and evaluate the success of such a group?" With that, the conversation ends and your planning for the next principals meeting begins.

REFERENCES

Bennis, W. G., & Shepard, H. A. (1956). A theory of group development. *Human Relations*, *9*, 415–437.

Blake, R. R., & Mouton, J. S. (1964). *The managerial grid.* Houston, TX: Gulf.

Day, D. V., Gronn, P., & Salas, E. (2004). Leadership capacity in teams. *The Leadership Quarterly, 15*(6), 857–880. doi:10.1016/j.leaqua.2004.09.001

DePree, M. (2008). *Leadership jazz.* New York, NY: Doubleday.

Fraser, B. (2008). *Jazz think.* Victoria, B.C.: Trafford.

Glanz, J. (2006). *What every principal should know about operational leadership.* Thousand Oaks, CA: Corwin Press.

Haslam, S. A., Reicher, S., & Platow, M. (2011). *The new psychology of leadership.* New York, NY: Psychology Press.

Henry, M. (n.d.) *Matthew Henry's concise commentary.* Retrieved from http://www.ccel.org/ccel/henry/mhcc

Kogler Hill, S. E. (2013). Team leadership. In P. G. Northouse (Ed.), *Leadership, theory and practice.* Los Angeles, CA: Sage.

Lewin, K. (1948). *Resolving social conflict.* New York, NY: Harper & Row.

Louis, K. S., Leithwood, K., Wahlstrom, K. L., & Anderson, S. E. (2010). *Learning from leadership: Investigating the links to improved student learning.* New York, NY: The Wallace Foundation. Retrieved from http://www.wallacefoundation.org/knowledge-center/school-leadership/key-research/Pages/Investigating-the-Links-to-Improved-Student-Learning.aspx

Phillips, G. W., Brown, W. E., & Stonestreet, J. (2008). *Making sense of your world.* Salem, WI: Sheffield Publishing.

Plecki, M. L., Alejano, C. R., Knapp, M. S., & Lochmiller, C. R. (2006). Allocating resources and creating incentives to improve teaching and learning. Retrieved from http://www.wallacefoundation.org/knowledge-center/school-leadership/key-research/Documents/2-Allocating-Resources-and-Creating.pdf

Scribner, J., Sawyer, R., Watson, S. T., & Myers, V. L. (2007). Teacher teams and distributed leadership: A study of group discourse and collaboration. *Educational Administration Quarterly, 43*(1), 67–100. doi: 10.1177/0013161X06293631

Singh, K. (2011). Teacher leadership: Making your voice count. *Kappa Delta Pi Record, 48*(1), 6–10.

Spillane, J. P. (2006). *Distributed leadership.* San Francisco, CA: Jossey-Bass.

Smylie, M. A., Mayrowetz, D., Murphy, J., & Louis, K. (2007). Trust and the development of distributed leadership. *Journal of School Leadership, 17*(4), 469–503.

Tuckman, B. W. (1965). Developmental sequence in small groups. *Psychological Bulletin, 63*, 384–399.

Ubben, G. C., Hughes, L. W., Norris, C. J. (2011). *The principal: Creative leadership for excellence in schools.* Upper Saddle River, NJ: Pearson.

Wallace Foundation. (2009). *The SAM Project: Making time for principals to be instructional leaders.* New York: Wallace Foundation. Retrieved from http://www.wallacefoundation.org/Pages/SAM.aspx

Chapter 8

Proactive Measures for School Safety

Russell L. Claxton

Children can't learn if they're worried about their safety.
—Laura Bush—

OVERVIEW

School should be a safe place for students to learn and interact, but far too often there are reports of instances in which students end up in harm's way. From natural disasters to school violence, a crisis can occur at any time, without warning, and in unlikely locations. Although there is no way to prepare for every possible emergency that could occur on a school campus, having a comprehensive emergency plan can help avoid, or prepare for, some of the most common crisis situations. A well-thought-out plan can also provide general guidance for unusual situations that cannot be anticipated. This chapter will address key components that should be considered when preparing and communicating emergency preparedness plans to a school community. The chapter will also address types of school emergencies and common scenarios for which school leaders should be prepared.

Objectives

By the end of this chapter, the reader should be able to:

1. Identify key components of a school emergency preparedness plan.
2. Discuss school preparation regarding inclement weather and natural disasters.
3. Address common medical emergencies.
4. Identify school facility issues that affect school safety.
5. Plan for interaction with outside organizations regarding school safety.

INTRODUCTION

Although one of the most difficult aspects of leading a school, safety is of utmost importance. Therefore, providing students with a safe learning environment should be a top priority for the school leader. The difficulty lies in preparing for situations that are often unpredictable, unforeseen, and unprecedented. Whether it is a natural disaster or a human act of violence, educators must learn from past experiences to help protect current and future students from harm. Still, there is no way to be totally prepared for all potential scenarios regarding school safety.

providing students with a safe learning environment should be a top priority for the school leader.

This chapter will discuss the basics of evaluating, preparing, and implementing emergency preparedness plans and procedures. It is important for all school leaders to have a written plan in place and to communicate that plan to all stakeholders. Although there is no one school emergency plan that would fit all schools, there are common elements that should be addressed in most schools. School leaders should develop plans that specifically address common school-wide and individual emergencies, while also addressing general, potential emergency categories. These plans should address issues of both school safety, which is the prevention of unsafe situations, and crisis management, which includes how to respond to a crisis once it occurs.

BACKGROUND

In recent years, there has been no shortage of school crises reported in the news. From tornadoes to school shootings, a regular school day can quickly turn into a school crisis without warning. Whether school emergencies have actually increased or whether the awareness simply is amplified due to instantaneous electronic media, society increasingly demands that school leaders ensure that schools are safe for their children. Indeed, school leaders should do everything within their power to create a safe school environment. Christian administrators are held to an even higher level of accountability in caring for those for whom they have been entrusted. The Bible tells us to value others above ourselves (Philippians 2:3). A biblical worldview adds to the professional standard of promoting a safe school environment, the standard of caring for students as if they were our own.

Historical Perspective

One of the most notable school tragedies was the Columbine shooting in 1999. This incident sent a shock wave across the country and left school leaders and communities asking how such instances could be prevented in the future. In the decade that followed, school systems scrambled to develop policies and guidelines to help prevent another school calamity. Parents and community members became increasingly sensitive to any comments, even rumors, of threats from students. Unfortunately, these precautions have not prevented such random acts of violence from recurring in schools.

School leaders can hope they will never experience a school crisis of the magnitude of a shooting, but most will experience at least some crisis situations. It is difficult to identify trends in school safety, as information often contains political bias. Some individuals insist that schools are becoming increasingly unsafe. Others, however, argue that school safety is actually improving per capita but that increased media coverage makes schools appear to be unsafe. Either way, the issue of school safety has been brought to the forefront.

Theoretical Perspective

From a theoretical perspective, Maslow's hierarchy of needs supports the importance of school safety. Once students have their basic physical needs met, the next most important area of need is safety (Koltko-Rivera, 2006). When students feel like their environment is unsafe or that their personal safety is being threatened, they can become distracted and lose academic focus. Schools that are identified as being unsafe are often also categorized as low achieving. Although poverty and other factors may contribute significantly to low achievement in schools, ongoing occurrences of violence or other criminal activity can

When students feel like their environment is unsafe or that their personal safety is being threatened, they can become distracted and lose academic focus.

significantly hinder student achievement. Isolated yet serious incidents, such as a natural disaster, can have a negative residual effect on student achievement long after the incidents have occurred.

Biblical Perspectives

When a tragedy occurs, especially one that involves children, the question often arises: "Why would God allow this to happen?" Although difficult to answer, this question is addressed by at least two biblical truths that apply to issues of safety. One truth is that, since the first sin was committed in the Garden of Eden, sin and the consequences that go along with it have been present in our world. All of humankind has experienced the results of sin. Although attempts to blame tragedies on specific groups or even on specific sins are often unfounded, there is some truth that the harm faced on earth is directly or indirectly related to the brokenness brought about by the presence of sin. Romans 8:21 describes the state of mankind as a "bondage of corruption" (King James Version). This is not to say that suffering is a direct result of an individual's own sin—only that pain, suffering, and evil exist in the world because of sin. In the Old Testament, for example, wrath came upon the "whole community of Israel" because of the sin of one man, Achan (Joshua 22:20).

The second truth is that God can, and in fact is the only One who can, truly protect from harm. Troubles present in society and specifically in schools today are certainly not new. The Bible states, "In those times there was no peace to him who went out or to him who came in, for many disturbances afflicted all the inhabitants of the lands" (2 Chronicles 15:5). Although it is difficult to answer the question of why bad things happen to good people, the Bible clearly indicates that His people can experience His blessings in regard to protection. There are many biblical passages that can provide comfort in a society where safety cannot be guaranteed outside of God's protection. Proverbs 1:33 states, "Whoever listens to me will live in safety and be at ease, without fear of harm," and Psalm 12:7 reads, "You, LORD, will keep the needy safe and will protect us forever from the wicked."

SCHOOL SAFETY IN ACTION

© Andre Lefrancois/Shutterstock.com

Periodically, parents will approach a principal—especially after their child has been a victim of violence or has experienced an injury on campus—and will demand a guarantee that their child will be safe in the future. The principal may respond, "School is one of the safest places for your child to be, but I cannot guarantee that any child will never suffer harm while at school." Parents do not usually like that answer, but the truth is that no one can guarantee a child's safety in all situations, although all caregivers are obligated to strive to that end. School is indeed one of the safest places a child can be. Most schools implement standard security measures, and there are few places a child can go on campus without an adult being present nearby. Parents should have the confidence that school is one of the safest places for their children, but safety cannot be guaranteed at school any more than a parent can guarantee the safety of a child while driving home in the family car. Educators should have the same perspective regarding school safety that they have with their own children—to do everything within their power to protect their students.

Schools in and of themselves are not dangerous places but are reflections of society and, as such, are not immune to the problems experienced in their communities. If there is crime in the community or those who want to do harm to children, harm can find its way into the school. If children in the community want to fight, get involved in drugs, or commit a crime, these acts can find their way into schools. Many of the questions and concerns regarding school safety are also questions about our society as a whole.

Schools in and of themselves are not dangerous places but are reflections of society and, as such, are not immune to the problems experienced in their communities.

Even though it is possible to implement plans and strategies to reduce the number of accidents and human acts of violence, there is little that can be done to prevent natural disasters. In 2011, a tornado struck the town of Joplin, Missouri, destroying six schools and devastating the community. The effects on the schools were both immediate and long term, both direct and indirect. Thanks in part to school and community leaders, students were given hope in a situation that seemed hopeless. After the rescue efforts turned to rebuilding efforts, education leaders began aggressive efforts to resume classes as soon as possible. Getting the schools up and running became an important part of the recovery effort, both physically and emotionally. In the aftermath of widespread death and destruction, the school system gained national admiration for its resilience and for the commitment of school leaders toward recovery.

Whenever there is a large-scale school catastrophe that includes injuries and/or fatalities, news media make the situation public within minutes. However, individual emergencies, even fatalities, occur at schools across the nation almost daily. The number of individual students experiencing medical emergencies during the school day has increased significantly in recent years. The American Academy of Pediatrics (2008) estimated that up to 25% of injuries among children occur while they are at school but that most schools do not employ medical professionals or maintain adequate medical equipment on-site.

What can school leaders learn from these and other catastrophes that happen in schools across the country almost daily? Although it may not be possible for school leaders to prevent all emergency situations, there are strategies that can effectively reduce the possibilities, or reduce the severity of the outcomes of school emergencies.

Private schools are not immune to the aforementioned crises. Obviously, inclement weather or accidents would have the same potential effect on a Christian school as on a public school. Regarding human behavior, however, research cited by the Council for American Private Education (2010) concluded that students enrolled in private schools are more likely to have a safer experience than those in public schools. It is important, however, to note some of the reasons for these statistical differences. Not only do private schools possess more latitude in which students they select to enroll, they also have more leeway in suspending and expelling students whose conduct may contribute to an unsafe environment. Because private schools rarely hire resource officers, they may not consistently report criminal incidents as frequently as public schools do, choosing to handle them in house.

From a Christian school perspective, one might deduce that differences in safety, violence, or criminal behavior incidents from those in public schools can and should be the result of beliefs in biblical standards of morality and respect for others and their possessions. In a Christian school, lessons on values and character may be supported by the ultimate authority on these issues, the Word of God. If biblical values are not used as the basis for moral education, then what standard is used when addressing these issues in a public school setting? These discussions become much more challenging in a public school setting, where students are often taught that all life forms evolved from the same organisms, that human life carries no more value than that of an animal, and that there are no absolute values. Whereas secular society seeks an explanation as to why school violence and tragedies occur, Christians understand that many of the tragedies experienced in society are ultimately the result of sin and are part of living in a fallen world (Kennedy, 1999).

Proactive Measures

Emergency Preparedness Plans

One of the first steps in school safety and crisis management is preparation of a written plan. Most schools and districts have some form of written plan in place, although the types and names of plans vary significantly. Some of the common names of school emergency plans include crisis management plan, emergency management plan, school safely plan, or some other variation. Although there is an assortment of names for these plans, most of them have one thing in common, and that is a goal of keeping students and employees safe.

A common misconception regarding written emergency plans is that more is better. Some schools try to develop detailed procedures for every conceivable scenario. They produce bulky documents with multiple-step procedures and plans that are complicated and possibly even confusing.

A common misconception regarding written emergency plans is that more is better.

They have drills, run-throughs, and practice emergencies; they plan, debrief, discuss, rewrite, and conduct more drills. Although a thorough plan might be expected when it comes to something as serious as school safety, these plans can become so unwieldy that, in a true emergency, it would be difficult to follow such plans.

An example of this occurred at a large urban high school upon testing its intruder alert procedures. The school had developed a color-coded intercom announcement (code red, code yellow, and code green) that would indicate to the faculty the seriousness of the alert. For the most serious situations, administration would announce over the public address system that the superintendent was in the building. This was supposed to alert the faculty, who knew the superintendent was never announced when in the building, while not alarming the students, who were not supposed to know the code. This was often ineffective, as many faculty members would forget the meaning of the announcement, and many students knew what it meant. In addition to the announcement, instructions were placed on the back of each classroom door. The instructions stated what students and teachers should do in case of an intruder alert; instructions included locking the door, turning off the lights, remaining silent, and moving the students into a corner in the classroom away from the door. On the back of the classroom doors, beside the instructions, were laminated color-coded cards in an envelope. If the situation inside the classroom was safe, the teacher was to place a green card under the door to be seen from the hallway. If, however, there was a dangerous situation in the classroom, a red card should be placed under the door to indicate the problem. These were just the first steps among many subsequent ones for a potential intruder alert.

None of these strategies are wrong in and of themselves, and it may be that many schools have effectively incorporated similar strategies into their emergency plans. At this particular school, though, administration developed concerns during the first few intruder alert drills of the newly adopted plan. The drills did not go smoothly to say the least. In general, many of the teachers did not follow the instructions. Some teachers reported that they had not heard the announcement, some had lost their materials, others claimed they were given incorrect information, and a few admitted that they were simply confused. To compound the situation, there were complications securing the portable classrooms; cards got blown by the wind, intercoms were difficult to hear, and many students could not be located—just to name a few of the problems.

After the drills, administrators, school resource officers, and lead teachers joined together to debrief. There was a brief summary of the many problems that were reported or observed, and the discussion quickly evolved into an argument of how best to fix the problems. Some began to suggest additional instructions to make the expectations clearer. Some recommended scenarios that had not yet been considered, and therefore proposed yet even more steps to the plan. Still others advocated disciplinary actions toward those teachers who failed to follow the instructions. After several more drills that year, the problems persisted—not always the same people and not always the same problems, but problems nonetheless.

A young assistant principal at the school recalled thinking, "If this school ever has an actual intruder, it's unlikely that the faculty will remember this plan because it's been changed so many times." If the steps mentioned previously were the only steps in the plan and if an intruder were the only potential emergency, the staff might possibly have performed well in the emergency situation. However, there were many more steps to the plan than those listed here, and a potential intruder was only one of the numerous possible emergency situations in the school's written plan.

Subsequently, how does a school develop an emergency plan that covers the most common crisis situations while not making it cumbersome or convoluted? The key is to be concise. Classroom teachers are often taught to develop three to five general classroom rules that cover most of their expectations. If a teacher implements 15 to 20 rules, they become difficult to manage. The same principle applies to a crisis management plan. Include general directions for the most common emergencies but avoid multistep processes for every conceivable scenario. The truth is that there is wisdom in planning, but every situation is different and will require some discretion, reaction, and decision making on the fly.

Because there are so many factors determining what a school emergency plan looks like and what details are important, plans may vary greatly among school districts and even among schools within the same district. One example of a factor that may significantly change emergency plans between schools is the age of students. What might be expected of first-grade teachers and their students would be significantly different from the expectations for a high school teacher with 17- and 18-year-old students. Other factors that might be considered when developing a plan include the availability of and relationship with local authorities, the size and location of the school, and available resources. Many schools develop some kind of safety team or committee that involves stakeholders from various groups. This not only allows for diverse perspectives in developing the plan but also develops cooperation and support when there is a school emergency.

Brunner and Lewis (2004) suggested developing a safety checklist in which the primary components of the emergency plan are reviewed annually. An annual review can be beneficial when considering that many schools experience changes in personnel, school policy, laws, and building codes from one year to the next. The best starting point is with an emergency plan audit, or checklist. There are many templates online if your school does not have one in place. There are also experts who can evaluate school safety and procedures, but these audits as well as the recommendations often focus on facility issues and can produce expensive proposals.

Building Security

Securing school buildings has become increasingly important. Many schools adopt security measures from the business world by adding security cameras, access cards, one-way doors, and alarms (McLester, 2011). It is not unusual to see a school secure all exterior doors except for one main entrance. Visitors are usually required to check in at the front office and may even need to press a button (similar to a doorbell) to alert school personnel to open the door. Increasing numbers of schools are equipped with cameras and alarms to monitor building access. Schools are secured in order to keep unauthorized personnel out of the building, as well as to keep students inside, where they can be properly supervised.

© Sasin Paraksa/Shutterstock.com

Building security varies significantly between elementary and secondary schools. In an elementary school, students rarely go very far without the direct supervision of an adult. Students often travel as a class or a group and are not allowed outside of the building unless accompanied by an adult. Additionally, elementary schools are usually smaller than secondary schools and it is easy to differentiate between students and adults. Such a structured environment would make it more difficult for an intruder to enter the building or for a student to leave the building unnoticed.

Conversely, securing a secondary campus can be a significant challenge. Envision a high school with over 3,000 students in which upperclassmen follow abbreviated schedules that permit them to arrive later in the morning or leave early in the afternoon. Many students drive their own vehicles, and there might be multiple streets where the students can enter and exit the parking lot. During a typical day, there may be six or seven transitions where students are traveling from one class to another—to or from lunch, jobs, clubs, sports, dentist appointments, and so forth. During these transitions, doors throughout the building are opened and closed incessantly. Even if students are directed to use the main entrance or main driveway and to follow proper check-in and checkout procedures, the opportunity for someone to enter the building without properly checking in or for a student to leave without permission is significantly great than for an elementary building. Furthermore, in a school with thousands of students, there are likely more than a hundred adults. In this environment, it is less likely that a visitor would be noticed, and a young adult visitor might even be mistaken for student.

Equipment to secure a large building that is highly populated can be costly. Although helpful in maintaining building security, electronic access, security cameras, and extra personnel on hand to supervise hallways and parking lots are high-ticket items. In times of shrinking budgets, however, school leaders can still improve building security through awareness education and staff development. One of the most effective resources in maintaining a safe building is improving safety procedures and building awareness among faculty and staff. When faculty and staff consistently wear proper identification, such as a name tag or badge, it becomes more apparent when someone is in the building who has not properly checked in. Furthermore, increased faculty awareness might cause a school employee to question someone without proper identification or students who do not appear to be where they are supposed to be.

Building security is an issue for which school leaders can really set the tone. If they do not, the faculty will likely develop a casual attitude. It is not uncommon for a faculty member to prop a door open to avoid having to walk around the building. In the teacher's mind, this may not be an act of rebellion but merely reflects a lack of seriousness or understanding regarding the security of the building.

Facility Maintenance

Proper maintenance of school facilities is an important, yet often overlooked, aspect of keeping a school safe. Building maintenance is related to school safety in at least two ways. First, a well-maintained building supports many aspects of a crisis management plan. Some examples include lighting and communication systems. If an announcement must be made during an emergency situation, a faulty intercom system may hinder dissemination of critical information. Many facility and equipment issues may be taken for granted on a daily basis, but neglect can cause significant problems during a crisis. Some common facility or equipment issues that should not be overlooked include the following:

- Smoke detectors, fire alarms, and fire extinguishers
- Intercom system
- Well-maintained doors and locks
- Proper lighting in hallways, secluded areas, parking lots, and sidewalks
- Severe weather warning system (with battery backup)
- Two-way radios for key personnel
- Emergency lighting for power outages
- Clearly identified and maintained emergency exits

In addition to the support aspects of well-maintained buildings during a crisis situation, some emergencies can be caused by the building itself. A gas leak or a faulty electrical system may result in a dangerous situation at a school. In such a case, students should be removed from these dangers immediately. Most dangerous facility issues can be avoided or eliminated. Exposed sharp objects, slippery floors, and elevated areas without railing are examples of potentially dangerous situations that can be avoided. It is unreasonable, however, to expect that students can be protected from any and all potential harm. Students will experience injuries in school from playground equipment, stairs, food on the cafeteria floor, and many other accidents. It is important that school and district officials make issues of safety a top priority when allocating resources for building repair and maintenance. Although accidents in schools can never be totally avoided, a well-maintained building can reduce the probability of such incidences.

For many years, it was the responsibility of the school and school district administration to set standards for building maintenance. Today, most schools are inspected and monitored by a government agency, such as the local fire marshal. Although the expectations of these government agencies may not be consistent nationwide, they are at least likely to address the most egregious safety concerns. At the other end of the spectrum are government inspectors who attempt to alleviate any and all potential dangers to students, sometimes making it difficult for the schools to meet strict guidelines.

Types of Crisis Situations

Natural Disasters

Natural disasters are among the most frightening school emergencies because of the potential magnitude of the dangers and damage that may occur. In recent years, numerous natural disasters have devastated communities and affected schools either directly or indirectly. Tornadoes, hurricanes, floods, and earthquakes can turn a typical school day into a nightmare within minutes. The results of a natural disaster on the school or community can be anywhere from an inconvenience to a life-altering calamity.

One of the advantages educators have in dealing with natural disasters is that there is often a warning of potential danger before the event. Several powerful hurricanes have come ashore in the United States in recent years, and although the storms decimated schools and communities, because there were hours and, in some cases, even days of advance warning, there was usually time to evacuate the community for those who heeded the warnings. For this reason, hurricanes rarely cause a crisis situation during a storm. The school crisis in these situations usually lies in the aftermath of the wind-damaged or flooded school buildings. School crisis management in these situations may involve helping to provide food, shelter, and clothing to community members. It may be difficult to conduct school when community members are still facing many difficult challenges.

Tornadoes are another common natural disaster for which schools must prepare. Because tornadoes are more prevalent in certain areas of the country, many schools develop some type of tornado preparation plan. Although tornadoes may spontaneously occur with little or no notice, meteorological technology has improved warning systems and can give schools precious minutes, sometimes hours to prepare for potential storms. Schools in high-risk areas operate early warning systems that indicate a tornado has appeared or that conditions are favorable for one to develop. When the threat of a tornado occurs during the school day, a common response is to move students into the safest areas of the building, away from doors, windows, and high roof areas. Tornadoes are a unique type of storm in that they can destroy one building while having no effect on a building just across the street. If a tornado does strike a school building, the storm will likely dissipate within minutes; therefore, decisions have to be made quickly, often more as a reaction than as a result of a detailed plan. Moving students to safety in such circumstances is only the first part of a crisis management plan that may need to be sustained for hours, even days, after the storm has passed. School leaders, along with faculty and staff, should immediately begin evaluating the situation to provide medical attention where needed and to reduce any potentially dangerous situations or additional harm to students.

Medical Emergencies

Medical emergencies are common occurrences in most schools. These emergencies can range in seriousness from minor injuries to life-threatening conditions. At a minimum, schools should have in place a process for dealing with minor medical emergencies such as cuts, scrapes, headaches, and stomach aches. School leaders should communicate very clearly the process for addressing the needs of students experiencing a minor medical emergency. Questions such as the following need to be answered:

- When should a student be sent to the office?
- When should a parent be called?
- What emergencies can and should be handled by faculty?

Some schools benefit from the services of a school nurse in the building. In these cases, the medical professional can help determine the seriousness of the emergency. Although many medical issues are easy to categorize as minor, one of the difficulties in dealing with medical emergencies lies in identifying what constitutes a more serious medical crisis. Even an issue that may be considered a serious medical emergency in one situation might be considered minor in another. For example, students who are diabetics, experience seizures, have serious allergies, or have medical disabilities may have frequent and ongoing episodes. Many of these students learn how to self-monitor and prevent problems associated with their medical conditions. Additionally, when caregivers are aware of the issues and are trained in how to deal with a medical emergency involving the student, the chances of experiencing a major emergency are significantly reduced.

Unfortunately, not all medical emergencies can be anticipated, and some may be life-threatening. If a student experiences a serious or potentially life-threatening medical emergency, a quick response will be required. In many cases, one of the first actions to be taken in a health-related emergency is to seek out a medical professional. In some of these situations, the decision to call 911 can be a matter of life or death. The minutes between the time a call is made and the arrival of first responders can be critical. Therefore, if there is a school nurse, this person would be the obvious first contact. In schools where nursing positions have been cut because of budget limitation, training faculty in basic first aid becomes increasingly important. School leaders should identify and train key personnel in the use of cardiopulmonary resuscitation (CPR), automated external defibrillators (AEDs), and/or basic first aid. School personnel have avoided numerous fatalities by implementing CPR or using an AED while waiting for an ambulance.

One of the more disconcerting trends regarding medical emergencies in schools is the increasing expectation for educators to provide medical services. Traditionally, it has been common for teachers, office personnel, or school nurses to distribute student medication or provide basic first aid. There seems to be, however, an increasing expectation that educators will be trained to respond to even more complicated health conditions. Many teachers are accepting this responsibility for the sake of the students, but others are uncomfortable accepting responsibilities for which they have insufficient experience or training. These concerns are exacerbated by an increase in the number of students who come to school with complicated medical conditions. A study by Garrow (2011) estimated that over 2 million school-age children in the United States have serious food allergies and that the number of food allergies is increasing. Furthermore, approximately one out of six students with food allergies will have an allergic reaction while in school. Not only does this raise concerns about school personnel being qualified to deal with allergic reactions, but also how educators can best prevent students from coming in contact with substances that cause these reactions in the school setting.

Threats and Cyber-Threats

Another situation that that falls into its own category is incidents involving threats and, more specifically, cyber-threats. Threats can occur on or off campus and may result in a school crisis regardless of whether students are actually in danger or not. They are exceptionally difficult for a school leader to deal with because they often necessitate addressing an emergency that has not yet occurred and may or may not actually happen. Threats can happen at all age levels but usually become more frequent and serious at the secondary level. A threat from one individual to another can be a significant disruption to the school day. Rumors of a fight can quickly result in classroom disruptions, non-school-related conversations, and the congregation of groups of students waiting to watch the anticipated event. This scenario can become intensified when the threat involves more than one student. The situation can quickly get out of hand when parents begin to catch wind of the situation and try to get involved at the school or in the community.

Threats may occur at school or in the community, and both can cause serious concerns. Most educators are aware of news stories regarding students who have threatened to bring a weapon to school to harm another student or a group of students. There have also been numerous incidents of students writing "hit lists" of others on campus they plan to harm. School leaders must take all of these threats seriously, even when the chances of a student being harmed seems unlikely. In many cases, parents are understandably quick to become upset and demand that something be done immediately. However, threats often require lengthy, detailed investigations to determine the actual chain of events. The perpetrator of a threat often claims it was merely a joke and not a genuine threat. Regardless of what conclusion the administration comes to in this type of situation, at least one parent is likely to remain upset.

In recent decades, use of electronic communication has complicated the process of dealing with threats. Today, making a threat is as easy as a few clicks of the mouse and is often referred to as a cyber-threat. Students can threaten each other using email, text, social networks, and many other electronic media. Furthermore, students seem to experience an increased sense of boldness in their threats because of the perceived anonymity of the Internet and the reduction of face-to-face conflict. For a school leader, investigating a threat becomes more complicated when the origin of the threat is electronic. The ability of the school leader to address cyber-threat issues may depend on whether the threat was sent during the school day or on a school computer, or from an off-campus location outside of the school day. Developing a clear, written policy, including potential consequences, reduces the impact of these disruptive situations.

Off-Campus Emergencies

Off-campus emergencies are some of the most difficult situations school leaders face. One of the primary challenges is determining if an off-campus crisis is even appropriate for the school to address. Some school leaders may want to avoid off-campus situations altogether by taking the stance, "If it does not happen at school, it is not my problem." This, however, is not a reasonable or wise position to take. The reality is that there are many potential off-campus situations that may affect the school setting. Guidelines are necessary for dealing with off-campus emergencies.

The tragic death of a student or school employee is an example of an off-campus situation. In a matter of minutes, a school or community can be turned upside down by the loss of a classmate or coworker. This is more common at the secondary level because such fatalities are often automobile related, but elementary schools are not immune to such tragedies. Despite the number of years an administrator may serve, these types of tragedies are never easy to deal with, and there is no policy manual with sufficient guidelines to dictate how to respond in every type of loss.

As is the case in most crises, the first step in addressing a school fatality is to provide for the needs and well-being of the student body, staff, and faculty. When a life is lost during the school year, leaders can expect the next few days or weeks of school to be very difficult for students and faculty. It is common for schools to bring in extra counselors, community members, and even local church staff to provide additional support. The number of people who will need additional support is often unknown, as students and communities respond differently in different situations. It is also important for school leaders to communicate with faculty regarding what is expected of them. Teachers need to know what changes will be made to the school day, how they should conduct the class, and how to respond to students and colleagues who are having exceptional difficulties dealing with the situation.

As a high school principal, I received a call from a local pastor late one Saturday night, just a few weeks into the school year. The pastor informed me that there had been an automobile accident involving several of our students and that there was one fatality. I immediately drove to the scene of the accident where emergency crews were still on hand and a number of students had gathered just a few hundred feet from the accident. Although I had experienced these types of situations numerous times as an assistant principal, I was not sure what to expect when Monday morning arrived. The student was a football player, so I had already met with the football team and many of the parents on Sunday afternoon. Much of that afternoon and evening had been spent communicating with community members and district office personnel to prepare for Monday morning. I also called a faculty meeting for first thing Monday morning to inform the faculty of the situation and to instruct them on procedures for that day. As a relatively new school, the faculty had not yet experienced such a tragedy as a group. The emphasis of my message to the faculty was to be sensitive, to be flexible, and to meet the needs of the students as best possible. As the students began to arrive on campus, we invited them to report directly to the auditorium, where we had small-group counselors available while faculty members throughout the building were involved in less formal counseling situations. Students were allowed to leave class if they needed to, and those who wanted to cope with the situation by continuing with their routines were encouraged to do so. It was not easy, but many in the building turned to their faith, and almost everyone turned to others, for support.

Leading from a biblical perspective can truly make a difference when guiding a school through the loss of a student, teacher, or other community member. One challenge in dealing with young people in a public or private school setting is that they often have a sense of invincibility, living for the here and now, with little concern for the years to come or, more important, for eternity. When a school community experiences the loss of a loved one, it is often a wake-up call both for students and adults, reminding them that tomorrow is not guaranteed. In a Christian school setting, prayer services, biblical encouragement, and support from local churches will most likely be an important part of the initial response to the loss. Members of the public school community may also become more open to spiritual matters than they are in most situations. Local churches and religious organizations, as well as Christian faculty members, can be an important part of supporting students during this type of a crisis.

There are many other emergency situations that can occur off campus but still have a significant impact on a school. For example, a school that is located in a high-crime area may experience community issues that overflow into the school. The concerns may be anything from the destruction of school property to gang activity near the campus. Although the criminal activity may not be as prevalent during the school day, the fears and anxieties of the students do not disappear when students walk through the school doors. A study by Milam (2010) indicated that exposure to perceived safety concerns and community violence had an adverse effect on the academic performance of students, even at the elementary level.

An off-campus natural or man-made disaster may have a significant impact on a community but not a direct impact on the school building. School leaders must still be prepared to address students who are affected by this type of crisis, some whose families and homes may have been affected. In those situations it is in order for the school to be a place of support and normalcy. The school may also be able to play a major role in supplying basic needs to families such as food, shelter, and clothing. An example of a man-made disaster might be a chemical spill or an explosion in the area. Although it is common to have a plan in place for inclement weather, it is difficult to plan for an almost unlimited number of man-made-crisis scenarios.

From the examples just discussed, it should be clear that school leaders are responsible to respond to off-campus situations. However, there are many other potential situations in which the expectations of the school's involvement are not as clear. What if the student is seriously injured in a fight that took place off campus? How should the school deal with a threat to harm students that occurred off campus? What is a school leader's responsibility regarding emergencies involving students waiting at a school bus stop, driving to or from a school event, or skipping school? Although answers to these questions may vary from one district to the next, it is important for school leaders to understand their role in off-campus emergencies.

Human Relations in Crisis Management

The Human Element

The unpredictable nature of a natural disaster adds to the difficulty of dealing with the crisis, but human behavior potentially adds an unpredictable element as well. To respond to this factor, school leaders can improve the emergency preparedness process through effective communication and relationship building. From a preparation standpoint, students and faculty need to feel that they can trust leaders in a crisis situation. A consistent pattern of open communication and sincere caring for the well-being of students establishes a climate of trust. When students and faculty believe that school leaders hear and address safety concerns appropriately, effective communication is more likely to occur.

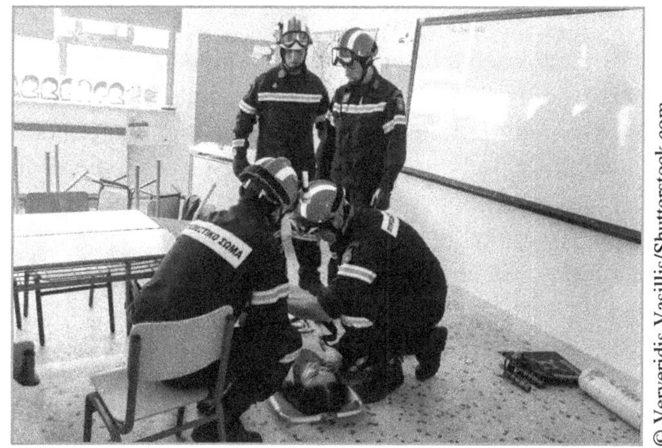

Accompanying most stories of a school tragedy are examples of adults and students who reacted in a heroic manner. When student safety is threatened, there are often those who put their own safety at risk to protect and care for others. These selfless individuals are an important part of dealing with a school crisis and serve as positive models of how the human element may be beneficial in times of crisis. Conversely, a negative aspect of the human element during a crisis situation is that humans can respond in an inappropriate, even harmful, manner. One such situation involved a bomb threat at a high school. Because of the seriousness of the threat and the location of the school, students were not only evacuated from the school but were relocated to an alternate site, which was a church several blocks from the school building. As students were escorted from the school to the church, numerous students attempted to exit the school grounds in a different direction or to run across the street to their personal vehicles. This resulted in an unsafe situation as students crossed a busy street. Once most of the students had settled in at the church, panicked parents began to arrive, demanding they be allowed to take their students home. With 2,500 students spread throughout the church building, it was difficult to find students or to determine if in fact the adult requesting to take the child was actually the child's parent. The conflict between school personnel wanting to protect the students and parents demanding access to their children was a challenge throughout the afternoon. Similar situations transpire during any school crisis, as parents are immediately made aware of the situation via cell phone, text, or social media, such as Facebook and Twitter. Parents may often arrive on campus within just minutes of the crisis. Fortunately, schools are beginning to use technology to their benefit by communicating with parents through email, text, and websites to broadcast information instantaneously regarding emergency situations.

Ensuring procedures are in place to communicate with parents before, during, and after a crisis situation is an essential component of any school emergency plan, but even more critical is a communication plan for students. Such a plan may be instrumental in preventing a student-initiated crisis by increasing awareness and providing resources for troubled students. Although not all acts of school violence involve troubled students, many school tragedies are carried out by students who have shown signs of disturbing behavior. To be proactive in identifying and responding to these signs, schools should have in place a process for students to report school safety issues such as bullying, sexual harassment, and any criminal behavior that negatively impacts the school climate. Two effective measures in this process are (1) training adults to be aware of signs that indicate disturbing behavior and (2) providing a specific place for students to discuss concerns. Programs to educate students in personal safety and crime prevention may also be helpful.

Another preventive measure to reduce human-initiated school emergencies is a clear and consistent behavior management plan. Although students may not always admit it, they feel safer when firm discipline guidelines are in place. Firm discipline must be tempered with common sense and caring, but dealing with minor discipline issues quickly and consistently will reduce the likelihood of the development of more serious disciplinary problems. The contrary is also true; when students receive only minor consequences for violence or weapon possession, they are more prone to become repeat offenders. Although zero-tolerance policies are occasionally implemented without a reasonable amount of common sense, the point has been made in many schools that weapons of any kind will not be tolerated.

Although school administrators cannot prevent every instance of evil in their schools, they can indeed implement both proactive and reactive measures to minimize them. One misconception that school leaders often have is that all school crises are distinct instances to be dealt with individually and in a reactive manner. However, Cornell and Sheras (1998) found that most crisis situations are the culmination of a series of individual instances that have been improperly handled, which in turn creates a campus culture ripe for such an unfortunate incident. For example, a school that does not deal with fighting, weapons, or bullying in a serious manner invites the escalation of more serious incidents in the future.

Although school administrators cannot prevent every instance of evil in their schools, they can indeed implement both proactive and reactive measures to minimize them.

Collaboration with Outside Agencies

In the case of a serious emergency, the first call may be to an organization outside of the school. A call to 911 summons assistance from police, the fire department, or medical personnel in a matter of minutes. Building a positive relationship with these organizations improves communication and ultimately improves the probability of a quick and adequate response.

One of the benefits of building a relationship with outside organizations is familiarity with the school. For example, if police were called to a large high school campus to deal with an act of violence, familiarity with all entrances and exits, access to the building, navigation of hallways, and so on shaves precious moments off their response time. Furthermore, familiarity with emergency personnel reduces student anxiety and increases cooperation during a crisis situation. It is also beneficial to request emergency personnel to assist in the preparation of the crisis management plan.

Full-time school police officers, often referred to as school resource officers (SROs), have become common, especially on secondary campuses. Although the SRO program began in the 1950s, it gained prominence in the 1990s in response to several school shootings. Today, over a third of all public schools report having an SRO (Weiler & Cray, 2011). These officers are often mistakenly perceived as serving dual roles. They are employees of the local police department but are also often mistakenly perceived as employees of the school by teachers, students, and parents. When officers are placed in a school setting on a full-time basis, their effectiveness can be increased through relationships and familiarity with students, faculty, and facilities. When SROs interact with students on a daily basis, the students are often more comfortable interacting with them during a crisis situation than they would be with officers with whom they are unfamiliar. Another proactive benefit of a police officer on campus is that students might share concerns or information when they otherwise would not have contacted the local police department.

There are many other outside organizations that interact with schools during school emergencies or to help prevent them. Social services and mental health facilities can work with students and families to help avert dangerous behaviors. Organizations such as the Red Cross, Salvation Army, and local churches provide much-needed assistance after a crisis or disaster. Building positive relationships with outside organizations benefits both the school and the outside organization. Common partnerships, for example, involve local fire and police departments. In such partnerships, firefighters and police officers visit campuses to conduct safety seminars and to mentor students who express an interest in serving as a future firefighter or law enforcement officer. These relationships are positive public relations for public safety entities and also reduce the anxiety that students sometimes feel around emergency personnel.

Communication

One of the most important aspects of dealing with a crisis situation is communication. As mentioned in the section on developing a crisis management plan, communicating in a clear and concise manner is crucial. Putting a plan in writing is just the beginning of communicating emergency preparedness plans. When communicating emergency procedures, administrators must make sure that the right people are getting the necessary information. For instance, students need to know the location of the nearest exit and understand the procedures for exiting the building in an orderly fashion, but they do not need to know where the bullhorn or two-way radios are located.

Crisis management information should be provided to different groups on a need-to-know basis. Neither students nor parents need to possess a copy of the entire crisis management plan. They do, however, need to understand certain procedures, locations, and contact personnel. Emergency information can be distributed to students during an assembly in a small school or through classroom teachers in a larger environment. Most schools provide practice activities, such as fire or tornado drills, to familiarize students with common emergency situations. Students may also be instructed on what to do during a lockdown, evacuation, intruder alert, or severe weather.

Teachers and support personnel need to understand emergency procedures at a much higher level. This information may be communicated to teachers at faculty meetings, through personal communication, or via electronic communication for less urgent matters. Teachers need to be instructed on how and where to direct their students, what part they will play in securing the building, what will happen after the emergency is over, and how they will find and convey information. Because teachers are most likely to be an integral part of managing a crisis situation, they may be asked to care directly for an entire class of students. Teachers need to be familiar with the basic aspects of an emergency plan and may also need information on emergency equipment such as fire extinguishers and AEDs as well as whom to contact for support. The larger the school, the more important the role of the teacher will be, as the administration cannot be in every classroom. It is important that the teachers have enough information to deal with the situation appropriately, but not so much as to confuse their role.

School leaders, primarily principals and assistant principals, often carry the responsibility of providing and managing school emergency plans. Furthermore, they will most likely be an integral part of guiding, directing, and making decisions during a crisis situation. It is important that key leaders throughout the school are familiar with the entire crisis management plan.

Media Relations

"Never have a school emergency on a slow news day" is an adage that principals might wish they could follow but over which they have no control. The media is quick to report a school crisis, especially one that is dramatic. What constitutes a news story may not always be consistent, depending on the day and location. A school emergency in a small town may be newsworthy, whereas a similar situation in a large city might go unreported. Likewise, a school emergency on a typical day might not make its way into the news at all, but on a slow news day, the same situation could become a prominent story.

A concern for school leaders is that the media may not accurately report a crisis situation. For lack of accurate information, comments and opinions from students and parents may be used to fill in the gaps, and this information may or may not accurately reflect the situation. The most effective strategy for school leaders to avoid one-sided reporting is to ensure the media have accurate information from the standpoint of the school. Rarely does a school leader improve the situation by refusing to make comments to the media. There are occasions in which information may be delayed during an investigation or comments may be deferred to district office personnel, but the key is to be reasonably cooperative with the media and to share appropriate information when it is available.

School leaders also gain favor with the media by building positive relationships during noncrisis situations. Sharing information and providing positive stories about your school builds goodwill among media outlets and with the community. Inviting members of the media into the school for special events can be a win-win situation for the school and members of the local media. School leaders who seem friendly and cooperative when called upon by a reporter improve their chances of receiving the benefit of the doubt when an emergency situation is reported.

Funding of School Safety

There are many ways to improve school safety at little or no expense to the school or school district. Developing an emergency preparedness plan and providing information to school faculty may require little more than the time involved to develop and disseminate the information. Unfortunately, there are also many potential safety needs that are difficult to address without significant funding.

Funding needs may include personnel expenses such as hiring a school nurse or a school resource officer. These are ongoing expenses that would need to be included in a school's annual budget. There are also facility and program issues that require a recurring expense or at least a one-time purchase. For example, installing railings on a stairway might be a one-time expense, whereas installing additional lights in the parking lot would result in a one-time expense as well as an ongoing electrical expense.

School leaders may be required to make difficult decisions regarding dollars spent on safety. Leaders can also impact safety funding by being advocates for their schools before district-level officials or school boards. The principal should communicate school safety needs to those making financial decisions within the school district. If principals believe there is a safety need, but there are no district funds available, they may need to pursue outside funding sources such as grants, business partners, or fundraising events.

CONCLUSION

Crisis management is one of the most difficult aspects of school leadership. Although school leaders can prepare general guidelines for some of the most common emergencies, most occur unexpectedly with little or no time to plan—only time to react. Even when thorough crisis management plans are in place, they may not be appropriate, as every crisis is different. They do, however, need to be thorough and yet reasonable, prepared and yet flexible. Then, when school leaders find themselves in a crisis situation, they are better prepared to be decisive but cautious, firm but caring—always acting in the best interest of the students.

Although increased media attention has heightened anxiety in students and parents regarding safety, school campuses continue to be one of the safest places a child can be. Despite media attention given to school violence, it is not on the rise. In fact, incidents of school violence have been declining in the past two decades (Neuman, 2012).

A reasonable approach to school safety is needed. School leaders cannot totally eliminate the possibility of a school crisis, and trying to anticipate every possible safety scenario will cause anxiety and confusion. Educators may be better served when they try not to make schools like prisons or develop excessive emergency plans and procedures. Just as automobile drivers will buckle their seat belts and try to drive in a safe manner—all the while understanding that an automobile accident is always a possibility—educators should manage schools with a similar attitude, adopting reasonable precautions and guidelines to make school as safe as possible but also praying for God's protection in situations that are out of the administrator's control. As stated in Psalm 4:8, "For You alone, O Lord, make me to dwell in safety."

Discussion Questions

1. What are the expectations in your community regarding the school's responsibility for dealing with an off-campus crisis involving students?

2. Does your school system take a hands-off approach to off-campus incidents, or does it address any issue that may flow over into the school setting? What do you feel is a reasonable approach?

3. To what extent should parents be involved in a crisis management plan? What parts of the plan should you communicate with parents, and how should that information be conveyed? What types of emergency situations require parent contact, individually or school-wide, and by what means would you contact them?

4. Consider a school that you are familiar with. Based on the information in this chapter, describe the key aspects of the school emergency plan that you would implement in the school. What might you add to your plan that is not included in this chapter?

5. As a principal, how would you address safety issues on your campus that you feel are not being adequately addressed by your school district? If the reasoning for not addressing these issues was a lack of funds, would that change your approach?

CASE STUDIES

Case 1: Bomb Threat

You are the principal of a suburban school consisting of approximately 1,000 students. On a beautiful spring Monday, the school receives an afternoon call that there is a bomb in one of the school restrooms that will explode in approximately 20 minutes. You immediately evacuate the school and notify the authorities. After a thorough search by the police, no bomb is found and the students return to class just before afternoon dismissal. On Wednesday of that same week, the school receives a similar call and the school is once again evacuated, with the same results. On the next day a third bomb threat is received.

1. Do you evacuate the building for a third time? What other information might help you in making your decision?
2. Several parents complain to school board members regarding your decision to (or not to) evacuate the school after the third bomb threat. What are the key points you would present to the board member and/or parents to defend your decision?
3. What might you do to help prevent similar situations in the future?

Case 2: Burning Candle

All the schools in your district are required to have at least one fire drill each month. Midway through the year, a small fire was started by a holiday candle that was left unattended in a teacher break room. The fire alarm was set off by the smoke and the building was quickly evacuated. An alert teacher quickly extinguished the flames with a small fire extinguisher, and the fire department arrived shortly thereafter to ensure that there was no further danger. After classes resume, an assistant principal brings it to your attention that several teachers remained in the rooms during the entire situation. When addressed by the assistant principal, the teachers stated that they thought it was just a drill and that they did not have students at the time because it was their planning period.

1. How would you address the teachers who remained in the building?
2. Would you address the rest of the faculty regarding this situation? If so, how would you address the issue, and what would you say?

Case 3: Criminal Activity

At a Parent–Teacher Association (PTA) meeting, some parents express concern about an increase in criminal activity in the neighborhood surrounding the school. Although there have not been any problems on campus during the school day, there have been some incidents of minor vandalism after school hours. As the principal of the school, you have also had concerns about crime in the area. Although you were not prepared to make a formal presentation to the parents, you have already made some small changes to improve security around campus.

1. What are some basic strategies you might have implemented in previous weeks to make the campus more secure?
2. How might you respond to the parents regarding their concerns?
3. How might the parental concerns affect how you approach campus security in the weeks and months to come?

Case 4: Crisis Management Plan

You are hired as the principal of a small rural school that contains less than 1,000 students in grades K–12 and is the only school in the district. Shortly after you are hired, the superintendent tells you that one of your first projects is to develop a school crisis management plan. He informs you that the current plan was developed piecemeal, is outdated, and needs to be totally revamped.

1. With very little direction from the district office, what would be your first few steps in developing a school crisis management plan?
2. Who might be involved in the development of this plan?
3. What are some of the key elements that would be included in your plan?

REFERENCES

American Academy of Pediatrics. (2008). Medical emergencies occurring at school. *Pediatrics*, *122*(4), 887894. doi: 10.1542/peds.2008–2171

Brunner, J., & Lewis, D. (2004). A checklist for school safety. *Principal Leadership*, *5*(1), 65–66.

Cornell, D. G., & Sheras, P. L. (1998). Common errors in school crisis response: Learning from our mistakes. *Psychology in the Schools*, *35*(3), 297–307.

Council for American Private Education. (2010, September). Students safer in private schools. *CAPE Outlook, 357*, 3. Retrieved from http://www.capenet.org/pdf/Outlook357.pdf

Garrow, E. (2011). Managing food allergies in school: What educators need to know. *School Business Affairs*, *77*(4), 8–10.

Kennedy, D. (1999, June). The "missing link" to school violence? Retrieved from http://www.christiananswers.net/q-aig/aig-school-violence.html

Koltko-Rivera, M. (2006). Rediscovering the later version of Maslow's hierarchy of needs: Self-transcendence and opportunities for theory, research, and unification. *Review of General Psychology*, *10*(4), 302–317. doi: 10.1037/1089–2680.10.4.302

McLester, S. (2011). Designing safe facilities. *District Administration*, *47*(8), 71–78.

Milam, A. (2010). Perceived school and neighborhood safety, neighborhood violence and academic achievement in urban school children. *Urban Review*, *42*(5), 458–467. doi: 10.1007/s11256-010-0165-7

Neuman, S. (2012, March 16). Violence in schools: How big a problem is it? Retrieved from http://www.npr.org/2012/03/16/148758783/violence-in-schools-how-big-a-problem-is-it

Weiler, S. C., & Cray, M. (2011). Police at school: A brief history and current status of school resource officers. *Clearing House*, *84*(4), 160–163.

Chapter 9

Partnering with the Community

Shanté Moore-Austin

Coming together is a beginning, keeping together is progress, working together is success
—Henry Ford—

OVERVIEW

It is imperative that school administrators understand the significance of community relations. Because of the increasing responsibility they bear for student success, it is incumbent upon administrators not only to collaborate with those employed in the same building but also to build partnerships with those in the community. The task of addressing the educational needs of all students in a particular school is simply too vast for any one person to administer without community support. This chapter will discuss the background, biblical perspectives, and present trends associated with community relations. It will present suggestions for collaborative strategies with parents, community members, business owners, and local government leaders and will address policy implications for the future.

Objectives

By the end of this chapter, the reader should be able to do the following:

1. Promote understanding, appreciation, and use of the community's diverse cultural, social, and intellectual resources.
2. Build and sustain positive relationships with families and caregivers.
3. Build and sustain productive relationships with community partners.

INTRODUCTION

The daily challenges administrators face can cause the task of leading a school to be quite stressful at times. This stress may be associated with an overwhelming need for more instructional resources, the need for volunteers to assist in classrooms and after school events, or the need to garner parental involvement in student learning. These needs may be resolved to a great degree by building partnerships with agencies, businesses, and individuals in the community. An administrator may start by asking "How can relationships be improved among all stakeholders?" The ability to find answers to this question and to sustain such healthy relationships is key in the process of becoming a successful educational leader.

The problem of rallying support and of maintaining a positive perception of schools within a community is ongoing, as are many aspects of school administration. Obviously, administrators cannot accomplish such a daunting task alone. Especially for new administrators stepping into a situation of weak community relations, improved community relations will require committing to longevity of service in that position and persistently rallying stakeholders both internal and external to the school organization. With increasing federal mandates that place emphasis on standardized testing and stronger accountability, there continues to be a need for administrators to build partnerships with parents and community leaders in order to meet the conditions of these mandates. Before this chapter introduces recommended strategies to build partnerships, it will first provide a brief background of school–community relations.

BACKGROUND

Historical Background

In colonial and early America, parents strongly supported teacher and school efforts, but as education began to reflect the industrial business model, the parental role diminished. It was not until the early 20th century, however, that administrator expectations entailed definitive responsibilities relating to community relations (McLaughlin, 1990). Gestwicki (2013) traced the evolving partnership between schools and the extended community to the Great Depression, at which time, parents—especially those from lower-socioeconomic circumstances—began to interact with schools through partnerships with federal programs such as the Works Progress Administration. Later, during World War II and a period of immigration from global regions other than the familiar Western Europe, parents of diverse cultural and ethnic backgrounds responded positively to efforts to provide family development services. A shift occurred in the 1960s, when schools began to implement interventionist strategies that focused on identifying deficits within families and compensating at school for those deficits. The educational professionals held more control in this model than the parents had previously held. Therefore, the partnership was not one in which families were on equal footing with the educators. Yet, there still existed the need to gain the support of parents and members of the community—particularly for the growing Parent–Teacher Association (PTA). The community became a resource for guest speakers, school–business partnerships, volunteers, and financial resources. In the 1960s, the need for more assistance continued, as McLaughlin and Shield (1987) noted, "In the mid-1960s, educators and policymakers focused on parent involvement as a promising way to improve educational outcomes for poor and underachieving students" (p. 157).

Another shift in family–school relations occurred in the 1970s as women increasingly entered the workforce and necessarily altered the manner in which they interacted with teachers and school officials (Gestwicki, 2013). Educators may have perceived this altered home–school relationship as parental disinterest. Whether it was or not, the boundaries of responsibility, communication, and partnership indeed became blurred with questions being pondered such as "How much weight should be given to parental ideas based on their commitment to their own children?" and "How much weight should be given to the judgment of the professional staff based on professional training?" This tentative era of relations was overshadowed in the 1980s by the accountability movement that defined parents as consumers of education with certain rights that the schools were responsible to meet. Although a return to a tone of partnership and collaboration marked the 1990s, the field of education is currently clarifying its relationship to parents and the broader community. A healthy acknowledgement has arisen that, in different ways, both parents and educators are experts in the education of children. Despite their knowledge of educational processes or lack thereof, parents possess cultural capital that can benefit schools. Additionally, educators are gaining an increased awareness that parents who are physically uninvolved in campus activities may be just as invested in their children's education as those who maintain a frequent campus presence by volunteering in classrooms and extracurricular events. Collaborative efforts and a respect for parental rights are becoming more prominent core values in recent years.

Theoretical Perspectives

To gain a better understanding of the importance of community relations and parental involvement, future administrators will find it beneficial to explore various theoretical perspectives. These theories offer explanations as to why certain schools and communities are successful in their relationships, whereas others are not. Two theories will be presented: ecological systems perspective and the social system perspective.

Ecological Systems Perspective

According to Bronfenbrenner (1979),

> The ecology of human development involves the scientific study of the progressive, mutual accommodation between an active growing human being and the changing properties of the immediate settings in which the developing person lives, as this process is affected by relations between these settings and by the larger contexts in which the settings are embedded. (p. 21)

This ecological systems perspective may be illustrated as a set of concentric circles nested one within the other as shown in Figure 9.1.

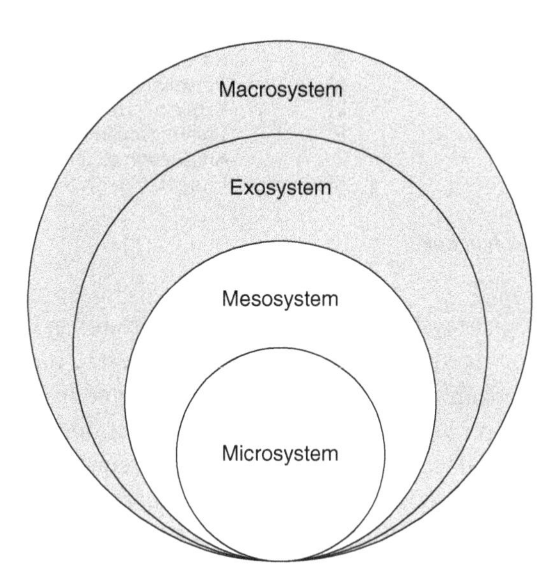

Figure 9.1. ***Moore-Austin's representation of Brofenbrenner's ecological model.***

The two nonshaded inner circles represent the most personal aspects of community interaction. The microsystem is the model's most inner circle, which involves the relationship between a person and those within his or her immediate environment. The mesosystem, the second nonshaded concentric circle, represents the relationship between the settings in which each person participates. This would include a person's work and home or, as in the case of a student, it might represent home and school. Nevertheless, these two nonshaded inner circles represent the most personal aspects of interaction among humans in a community.

The outer shaded concentric circles signify the context external to the personal individual—those community issues that may impact individuals but are less personal. The exosystem, for example, denotes indirect influences that affect the person without the person actually being involved. For instance, community crime levels, a parent's job status, and city zoning laws may all have an indirect impact on a child although the child is not directly involved with any of these factors. The last and final circle within the model is the macrosystem. This level is composed of all the overarching beliefs and values in which all the relationships and interactions represented by the other concentric circles occur. The macrosystem might also be described as being similar to a shared worldview or a metanarrative by which groups function in a cultural system. It is through this macrosystem that communities filter actions, decisions, and expectations. When a reference is made to the Bible Belt, for example, it is a reference to the macrosystem of communities in that area. The same is true when assumptions are made about city life, New England, the Midwest, and other regions identifiable by their ways of living, governing, and relating to others in the community.

Brofenbrenner's model relates specifically to parent–teacher relationships. Parents and teachers develop and function personally within their own ecological models. The items listed in Figure 9.2 pertain to the qualities of the parent-as-person and the teacher-as-person. These qualities have developed within each of their microsystems. The quality of "professional knowledge and skills" indicates knowledge and skills specific to the field of education. Although professional knowledge and skills is listed as a quality only possessed in the teacher's microsystem, there are, of course, many parents with varying levels of educational knowledge and skills. Just as it is important for both parties to acknowledge how all the qualities develop distinctly in the other, it is helpful for teachers to acknowledge that many parents have been exposed to information about teaching and learning or may have an intuition or spiritual giftedness toward teaching. A mutual respect regarding this particular quality will enhance individual parent–teacher interactions. Each parent and teacher is operating from a mesosystem that represents what he or she personally brings to all interactions in the school and community. The two outer circles represent the societal influences, which could include but are not limited to workplace, laws, and customs.

Parent-as-Person	Teacher-as-Person	Qualities
☑	☑	Cultures and Values
☑	☑	Role Understanding
☑	☑	Sense of Efficacy
☑	☑	Personality Characteristics
☑	☑	Expectations
☑	☑	Communication Skills
☑	☑	Knowledge of Children
	☑	Professional Knowledge and Skills

Figure 9.2. *Ecologies of parents and teachers.*

The child is central to the ecological systems perspective, as illustrated in Figure 9.3. The child is the joining factor as parent and teacher partner together for the child's best interest. Often, one party or the other adopts an approach contradictory to a partnership model. Parents may be tempted to view themselves more as consumers and to treat teachers as service providers. The attitude of parents operating from this model may be that the "customer is always right" and that teachers should fulfill their requests. "After all," some parents declare, "our tax dollars pay your salary." Commonly, private school teachers and administrators hear statements such as "My tuition dollars pay your salary" or "It's the least you can do after all the money we've contributed to this school." Such adversarial approaches are not in the best interest of the child.

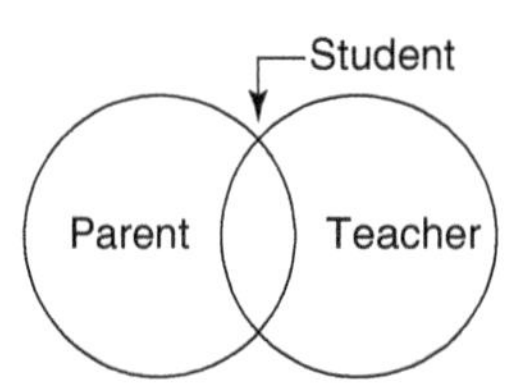

Figure 9.3. *An illustration of the child in the model.*

Neither is it beneficial for educators to disregard the cultural capital, professional knowledge, and spiritual giftedness of parents. The tactic that "I'm the professional here and am the one qualified to make educational decisions for your child" undermines the parental role and hinders a meaningful partnership. It also violates the biblical principle that children are God's blessings to parents, are placed in family structures for their lifelong development, and are to be educated primarily by their parents (Genesis 2:20–25; Psalm 127: 3–5; Proverbs 22:6; Deuteronomy 11:19–20). When parents—because of work responsibilities or the inability to educate their children in certain areas—delegate education to the school, they do not abdicate their authority as parents. Ultimately, they are the ones responsible to God for decisions regarding their children, and not educators in schools run by the government, the church, or independent associations. Therefore, the most constructive relationship between parents and teachers is one of partnership.

Social Systems Perspective

Getzels's (1978) social system perspective, as illustrated in Figure 9.4, provides a model for the interaction among participants and how they impact one another within the environment. Each person has expected roles, which are influenced by societal factors as well as personality dispositions. When parent and teacher meet together, they share a common interest, which is the child. Both participants bring their own views, beliefs, and ideas to the table, which may lead to behaviors resulting in a partnership or in an adversarial relationship.

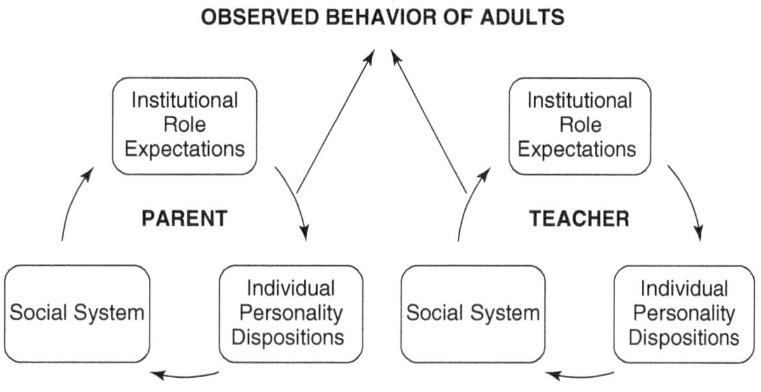

OBSERVED BEHAVIOR OF ADULTS
Institutional Role Expectations
PARENT
Social System
Individual Personality Dispositions
Institutional Role Expectations
TEACHER
Social System
Individual Personality Dispositions

Figure 9.4. ***Moore-Austin's representation of Getzels's social system perspective.***

Communication. Keyes (2000) integrated both Bronfenbrenner's ecological systems perspective and Getzels's social systems perspective together to underscore the importance of communication among stakeholders. This merger of theories is best illustrated by parent–student–teacher interactions. As previously established, parents and teachers have expected roles within society. Teachers are expected to conduct themselves as educational professionals, to interact with parents and community, to set a good moral example, and to protect the interests of students. Also, society expects parents to protect children, to interact with educators, and to ensure their children's needs are met academically, socially, emotionally, and physically. In a Christian school, an added societal expectation is that both teachers and parents serve as spiritual leaders who cultivate children's faith. As home and school carry out their roles, their relationship may be either enabled or constrained by cultures and values, personalities, expectations, and the knowledge of the children being served.

Keyes (2000) combined the ecological and social systems perspectives also to signify the role that administrators play within community relations—specifically regarding communication. How administrators communicate with stakeholders will, to a great degree, decide their success in present and future partnerships. Figure 9.5 illustrates that effective communication is comprehensive and thus encompasses networking to assist the home, to improve the community, and to make decisions. Just as there are various audiences for communication, there must also be multiple avenues to reach each audience with the intended message. Traditional methods of parent–teacher conferences, phone calls, and print newsletters continue to be valuable means of communication. They are no longer, however, sufficient without two additional means: community

> How administrators communicate with stakeholders will, to a great degree, decide their success in present and future partnerships.

service and technology. If schools are not involving their staff and students in serving the community, they are being negligent in developing a sense of social responsibility. Service conveys that the school's role in the community is one of reciprocity—that it is not simply standing with its hands out ready to receive from the community but is also contributing to meeting social needs.

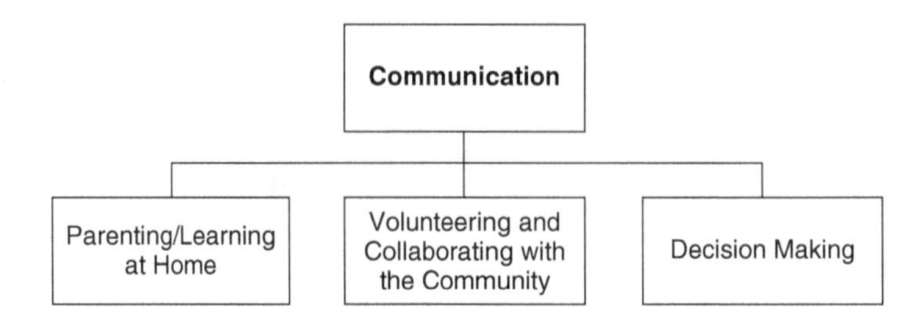

Figure 9.5. ***Framework for school–community communication.***

The pervasive nature of technology requires administrators to engage it as a tool for effective communication. Radio, television, and print media are technologies that schools are accustomed to using, and most schools have built a presence on the Internet. Handheld devices and other technologies make it incumbent upon school leaders to incorporate them if they wish to strengthen communication with parents and the greater community. A note of caution is to avoid adding to the problem of information overload. Rather than to spam all school messages to all audiences, it is best to target messages to those most interested in them. For instance, instead of maintaining just one social media site for the school, maintain several that target specific community subgroups. Some in the community might be interested in sports information, whereas others would be more concerned with academics, service education, music, or volunteer opportunities.

Biblical Perspectives

What does God's Word say about building relationships and partnerships? In *The Maxwell Leadership Bible,* John C. Maxwell (2007) included important facts, notes, and steps to become effective leaders within any organization, and he indicated three specific principles relating to collaboration with others. The first is found in Proverbs 13:20, which states, "He who walks with wise men will be wise, but the companion of fools will be destroyed" (New King James Version). Collaboration is important, but not at the sacrifice of the school's welfare. Fools will inevitably gravitate to a school community. These fools may be unethical, unprincipled, selfish, power hungry, or simply misguided. They may have worldly wisdom to offer, but their aims or approaches just do not align with the heart of the school's vision. If administrators partner too closely with such individuals, they are on the road to destruction professionally and personally and are putting the school's well-being at risk. It is essential that an administrator's closest partners be those who sincerely support the interests of the school and its students. Nominees for board members, for instance, should have a record of supporting the school and reputations as persons of wise discretion. Every school, both public and private, is blessed if they have partners that are influential community leaders with power and monetary resources. Those qualities, however, should be secondary to the qualities of integrity and a sincere passion to empower students to learn.

The second principle is found in 2 Samuel 21:1–14 and is illustrated by David's interaction with the Gibeonites. In this portion of Scripture, there is a famine over the land, and so King David asks the Lord about it. The Lord told David that the famine had occurred because Saul and his family were guilty of murdering the Gibeonites. David then addressed the Gibeonites to ask what could be done to atone for the wrongdoing. Instead of being gracious that David was attempting to appease them, the Gibeonites exploited the situation by making unreasonable demands of him. They remained so bitter that Saul had tried to wipe them out that they requested, among other things, that seven men be hanged. David struggled with how to meet their demands in a fair and just way. This Scripture illustrates what it is sometimes like for leaders to deal with complex situations and demanding people—especially when there seems to be no clear, easy solution.

Not everyone on an administrator's team will think or solve problems the same way; neither should they. This diversity will, at times, result in conflict. How are administrators to cope with these team members, parents, community leaders, and superintendents who have ideas and personalities that are not in line with the majority of the team? Maxwell (2007) presented various types of personalities and how leaders are to deal with them:

Personality Type	Description	Strategy
The Sherman Tank	Rides over people	Consider the issue; stand up if important.
The Space Cadet	Lives in another world	Find and develop their unique gifts.
The Volcano	Explosive, unpredictable	Remove from crowd; listen and be direct.
The Thumb Sucker	Self-pities, pouts	Don't reward; expose them to real trouble.
The Wet Blanket	Always down	Be honest, don't cater; don't let them lead.
The Garbage Collector	Attracts the worst	Challenge their statements; force honesty.
The User	Demands lots of time, energy	Set boundaries, require accountability

(derived from Maxwell, 2007, p. 408)

The personality types listed here are common, and administrators are well served if they react to them appropriately.

The third principle is found in Romans 12:9–21, where Paul spoke about how followers of Christ should behave. The following is a list of the characteristics Paul describes (Maxwell, 2007, p. 1409):

1. **Avoid hypocrisy:** be sincere and genuine.
2. **Be loyal to colleagues:** treat others like brothers or sisters.
3. **Give preference to others:** honor the desires of others above your own.
4. **Be hospitable:** look for ways to meet the needs of others.
5. **Return good for evil:** act, don't react, when others hurt you.
6. **Identify with others:** treat others' needs or victories as your own.
7. **Be open-minded toward others:** seek to connect with anyone you speak to.
8. **Treat everyone with respect:** this is a compliment to any person.
9. **Do everything possible to keep peace:** choose wisely which hills to die on.
10. **Remove revenge from your life:** let God judge others; you love them.

RESEARCH IN COMMUNITY RELATIONS

Research Strands

Studies relating to school–community relations span a variety of topics and are based on various theories and definitions of what constitutes an effective relationship between school and community. One strand of research focuses on the school's role to work for social justice and to engage the community, especially in the democratic process. It is based on the assumption that John Dewey's notion of social progress best represents effective school–community relations. An example of a study based on this notion was conducted in Chicago Public Schools (Sabia, 2012). It pointed to schools whose facilities became community centers of democratic activity as models for progress toward social responsibility. These schools not only opened their facilities for social activist groups but also set up local school councils (LSCs) consisting of six parents, two community representatives, two teachers, the school's principal, and an additional nonvoting student for high schools. Members of the LSCs were elected every 2 years and held substantial influence in the hiring and firing of principals, allocation of discretionary funds, and involvement in the planning and implementation of school improvement.

Another strand of research focuses on public perception. It is based on the notion that schools are performing much better than the media and the general public acknowledge and that they will experience more favorable perceptions if they are more successful at communicating their strengths while minimizing negative public relations. One such study indicated the significance of front-office staff in parent perceptions (Thomson, Ellison, Byrom, & Bulman, 2007). The study described office staff as "a conduit between the home and the school" with "their mediation potentially troublesome" (p. 145). In addition to front-office personnel, the front-office environment was also identified as a strong influence on parent perception. The following factors were found to increase positive perceptions: a clearly marked entrance to the facility, a welcoming and informative foyer, and signage with positive language.

A final example of a strand of research relating to school–community relations has become increasingly prominent in recent years, especially with the nation's prolonged recession. It examines schools that have been successful at acquiring resources from sources external to the school environment. The assumption behind this strand of research is that stronger partnerships will result in increased financial resources outside of the general budget. Scanlin (2008) studied this phenomenon in private schools that were soliciting support beyond school families into the community at large and found that schools that enrolled traditionally marginalized students were more successful at broadening financial support.

Best Practices

Joyce Epstein (2012) is perhaps the foremost researcher in school–community relations. She established the National Network of Partnership Schools in 1995 and has published over 100 works on the topic. Through her research, she consistently found the following key strategies to be effective for engaging parents:

1. **Communicating:** Whether communication is in the form of email, newsletters, phone calls, or social networking sites, all community leaders, administrators, faculty, and parents must know what is going on within the schools. As in any cooperative endeavor, communication is the highest priority.
2. **Helping at home:** Some parents would like to assist their children with homework but do not have the skills to do so or may need additional resources. When schools provide these resources to enable parents to help their children with homework, parents become more connected to the school because they feel as though the school has an interest in them as well as in their children. Successful initiatives to accomplish this include the following:
   - A clear homework policy endorsed by the whole school
   - Homework with instructions that are clear and concise so that parents can assist with the process
   - Class websites that include homework assignments, instructions, examples, and due dates
3. **Attending school events:** It is common for many parents, especially at the secondary level, to limit their involvement at school functions. The challenge for administrators is to make it worthwhile for parents and community leaders to attend parent–teacher organization meetings or other events to support the school community. The following strategies have been shown to increase attendance at such events:
   - Create a welcoming and memorable meet-the-teacher night.
   - Provide advance notice for key events.

- Encourage all parents to attend parent–teacher interviews; reach out to those who cannot attend.
- Encourage both parents and students to attend events together or create events for both parents and students.
    - Concerts
    - Academic nights (e.g., science, literacy, or music nights)
    - Sporting events
    - Seasonal events
- Leverage some events for participation first and then add a component of fundraising.

4. **Building parenting skills:** One approach to build parenting skills is to solicit community leaders who work in the area of social services, medicine, and other related fields to speak to parents on topics of effective parenting. Such meetings should be friendly, engaging, and informative, and should be void of any tone that could be interpreted as implying that the parents are not already caring well for their children. Other suggestions include the following:
    - Establish a parent resource center that contains books, DVDs, pamphlets, and other materials.
    - Organize guest speaker events that focus on topics that are of interest to the parents.
    - Partner with other schools to develop and share parenting resources.
5. **Volunteering:** Many parents, retired teachers, school board members, and others may desire to volunteer at the school but are either hesitant to initiate the offer or do not know how they may be of benefit. Administrators can lead the charge in recruiting these volunteers for specific tasks such as the following:
    - Recruit volunteers and recognize them for their efforts.
    - Encourage teachers to identify key roles for volunteers.
    - Field trip supervisors
    - Math or science helpers
    - Plan separate volunteer meetings.
6. **Leveraging community resources:** Creating a directory of agencies and private services will make referring families much easier. A link to these services may be placed on the school website or on a flyer to be distributed when a need arises. It is best to be prepared when parents are seeking a family counselor, social services, tutoring, or other resources.
    - Seek out community resources.
    - Bring local business owners to school events.
    - Form relationships with local services, including the police department, firefighters, student assistance agencies, and so forth.

COMMUNITY RELATIONS IN ACTION

Community Relations in the News

In Virginia, Lynchburg City Schools—in cooperation with the city government and other community organizations—established an annual event called Walk to School Day. As part of a Safe Routes to School program, this collaborative initiative promoted a safer and more accessible walking and bike-riding experience for children on their way to and from school each day. On a designated day each year, parents, teachers, and administrators accompanied the students as they walked or rode their bikes to school. Parents reported that they looked forward to the annual event and believed that it heightened safety awareness for children who provide their own transportation to school rather than riding the bus or being driven by parents. The program encouraged both parents and school personnel to walk and talk with children as they travelled to and arrived at school. The Virginia Department of Transportation joined the program to fund the installation of sidewalks, crosswalks, and signaled pedestrian crossings (Pounds, 2012).

The Reality Store is another example of a cooperative program that many schools across the nation have conducted. Marshall County Kentucky is one community that successfully implements this program each year. The Reality Store provides an opportunity for administrators, teachers, community leaders, and students to come together to grasp the realities of life—"from learning how to balance a budget and juggle a career with family, as well as hearing from a fellow classmate whose family has had a lifetime struggle with drugs and addiction" (Drew, 2013, para. 1). In one particular Reality Store event, eighth-grade students from three Marshall County middle schools were transported by bus to one school's gymnasium, where they explored booths sponsored by community leaders representing the employment commission, universities, grocery stores, hospitals, insurance agencies, and others. Upon arrival, students received a card that assigned them a career and a corresponding salary. The Reality Store experience taught students how to budget their money and to see how far it would actually go with life's everyday expenses. Various testimonies exposed students to the realities that accompany self-destructive behaviors, such as drug addiction, that can detract them from reaching life's goals. Organizations that joined Marshall County Schools to sponsor this event included the Youth Service Center, the 4-H Council, the University of Kentucky Cooperative Extension Service, and a variety of local business (Drew, 2013).

The Walk to School Day and the Reality Store are only two examples of school–community events that are commonly broadcast in the news. These particular events are regarded by their communities as being highly successful and as means to help bring communities, administrators, parents, and students together for a worthy cause. There are many other events, such as fall festivals and parents' lunch with children, that will help to build positive relationships with all stakeholders.

Common Mistakes in Community Relations

After investing a great deal of effort arranging group partnerships, administrators often assume that community members will support programs simply because the cause seems worthy and that results will benefit students. The valuable outcome of the cause notwithstanding, administrators must still reach out to connect with influential individuals on a personal level beyond official organizational communiqués. Although teachers may interact with parents and the community on variety of levels, administrators often find themselves at a personal distance with stakeholders. They may over-rely on mass communication through newsletters, websites, emails, and group meetings, rather than employ face-to-face interaction to build positive relationships. Whatever the reason for the distance, it is important for administrators to overcome barriers that may hinder them from networking in personal, meaningful ways with community leaders. New administrators particularly will find it beneficial to visit community entities in order to introduce themselves and open-endedly ask how the school may partner with that specific entity.

Another mistake that administrators make is that they all too often throw in the proverbial towel when collaborative efforts do not seem initially successful. When outcomes do not meet expectations, they may assume that the effort had no effect whatsoever. Frequently, they are mistaken. Even when programs do not result in the expected outcomes, they display to the community the administrator's and school's desire to collaborate. Perseverance will accentuate this desire and will serve to draw more partners for future efforts. A time of apparent failure is a time to work all the harder to network with community leaders and parents. They eventually will realize that school personnel are truly interested in a reciprocal partnership.

As administrators consider community partnerships, they should avoid the mistake of limiting their approaches, depending solely on methods that have proven profitable over a period of time. An innovative twist on a longstanding tradition may revitalize it in unexpected ways. A bit of variety, creativity, and fun go a long way in making programs meaningful and winsome to the community. The following suggestions include social activities that might draw parents and community members to the school. Once they are drawn to the campus and begin building relationships, more meaningful partnerships for even greater causes may result.

- Back-to-School Meal Night: At each table, assign hosts to sit with groups of parents during the meal. The hosts may be faculty and staff, or they may be members of the school leadership team, city council, or school board. In a Christian school, hosts might include senior pastors, youth pastors, or other spiritual leaders. During the meal, hosts collect questions from each group and address them in a panel discussion after the meal.
- Barefoot Book Break: During an outdoor lunchtime in the spring, invite parents to bring a picnic lunch, a blanket, and a favorite book to read aloud to their children.
- Community Service Day: Collect a list of community needs from faculty, staff, parents, and students. Have a committee assign the needs to classrooms and arrange a specific day of service to meet the needs. Projects should be assigned to grade levels as they are appropriate to the age of the students. If this becomes an annual event, the community will begin to contact the school throughout the year with suggestions for the day of service.

As administrators build positive relationships, they must avoid certain pitfalls. Some effective ways of doing so are to invest time in becoming familiar with individuals and groups within the community, persevere even when efforts appear unsuccessful, plan creative outreach events, and remember to be approachable and welcoming to all stakeholders.

Policy Implications

Thus far, this chapter has addressed the importance of parental involvement and community relations, discussing possible activities, effective communication, and newsworthy exemplary programs. At this point, the question posed is "How might an administrator establish an effective school–community relations program?" As indicated earlier, the administrator is not solely responsible for ensuring the success of this program. Who, then, will be involved in the ongoing process of community relations? How much money will be allocated for such efforts? In developing positive relationships with parents and the community, it is necessary to work with the school board officials, appoint a director of a school–community relations task force, determine a budget, and work strategically to link families and communities to student performance.

School Board

School board officials are elected to serve for a specified amount of time. Understanding that schools within the district must meet the academic needs of all students, they are accountable for the allocation of funds and other resources to accomplish this task. It is incumbent then upon building-level administrators to become acquainted with those officials who serve on the school board. These individuals are usually community leaders and can be a tremendous asset in the development of an effective school–community relations program. Ideally, parents should also become familiar with the school board, but they rarely see the need, believe they have the political savvy, or feel informed enough on the issues to participate at that level. Also, parents who are unhindered by practical restraints are more likely to be involved at the practical level with local teachers and principals than with district school board members. Nevertheless, the local school boards, as they adopt policies, set much of the tone for school communities. If members of the community believe that the school board is not interested in their needs, it may be that community members are not making their voices heard or that they are not as active in electing members to the board who will properly represent them. Consideration of the following questions (Bagin, Gallagher, & Moore, 2008, p. 56) may assist a community in assessing the degree to which it is holding its school board accountable: The school board . . .

1. Cooperates with the news media.
2. Communicates systematically with residents.
3. Makes deliberate advance communication efforts on major policy issues through surveys, advisory committees, or public hearings.
4. Represents the total public interest in decisions, not self-interest.
5. Designates representatives of the board to meet with other local governing bodies and community groups to discuss matters of mutual concern.
6. Adheres to channels of communication through the superintendent for concerns, complaints, and criticisms.
7. Makes facilities and resources available to the community.
8. Plans communication in the event of crisis.

Director of School–Community Relations

In most schools, the school improvement team is responsible for developing strategies to increase parental involvement and to build positive relationships with community leaders. The director of school–community relations, however, is a special position that is usually appointed either to an assistant principal or to one of the lead faculty members. This person is typically responsible for recruiting others to serve on a committee to navigate school–community relations programs.

Determine the Budget

According to Bagin et al. (2008), there are several ways to determine how much money is to be allotted to school–community relations. Because varying amounts of money are allocated to schools, this is an area that the director of the school–community relations committee should discuss with the administrator. Depending on the size of the school and the district, the amount of money allocated for public relations will vary. One method of determining the budget is by setting a fixed percentage of the total school budget, which may be 0.5%. With the activities that need to be planned throughout the year, it is imperative that the budget be set early in the process.

Linking Family and Community to Student Performance

It is vital that families be included in the overall learning process because they have a direct influence upon student achievement. Guthrie and Schuermann (2010) presented various strategies for schools to work with communities for the purpose of improving student achievement. Some of these suggestions are as follows:

- Adopt a family–school–community partnership policy. The philosophy behind it should see the total school community as committed to making sure that every single student achieves at a high level and to working together to make it happen.
- Identify target areas of low achievement. Work with families and community members to design workshops and other activities to give them information about how to help students learn. Provide materials for families to use at home and get ideas about how to help their children learn at school.

- Offer professional development for school staff on working productively with families and community members.
- Assess the current family–school–community involvement program to determine how it is linked to learning. Work with faculty and community constituents to create activities that will foster a learning community. (p. 352)

CONCLUSION

Because students are influenced by their parents and families, administrators need to find ways to involve parents in the education of their children. Community leaders are also beneficial in the overall learning process because they have the resources needed to provide a more enriching educational experience. To these ends, this chapter argued the benefits for administrators to engage parents and community leaders in the learning environment, as it is imperative that everyone work together to meet the needs of students.

Because students are influenced by their parents and families, administrators need to find ways to involve parents in the education of their children.

Discussion Questions

1. Apply Bronfenbrenner's ecological model to your local learning environment by completing an illustration displaying all of the stakeholders and where each person fits in within the model.

2. Discuss how Getzels's social system model relates to parent–teacher partnerships.

3. Explain the importance of Proverbs 13:20 to school administrators. Give an example of an actual school scenario that illustrates this verse.

4. Explain the following personalities: Sherman Tank, Wet Blanket, Volcano. Provide an example of how an administrator might relate to each of these.

5. What are the key strategies for engaging parents as discussed by Joyce Epstein? Which of the strategies do you believe to be the most effective? Explain why you selected these strategies.

6. Other than the ones already mentioned in the chapter, what are some common mistakes administrators make when working to improve parental involvement and public relations within their schools? How could these be avoided?

Activities for Enrichment

1. Develop a plan for the upcoming school year to increase parental involvement at your school.
2. Interview an administrator from an elementary, middle, and high school. Begin with the following questions and then develop some of your own:
    - How do you work with your faculty and staff to improve parental involvement within your school?
    - What are some of the strategies that you use to maintain a positive relationship with those in your community?

- Do you have a parental involvement and community relations plan established at your school? If so, explain the nature of it.
- What suggestions would you give to an aspiring administrator to ensure that parents and community are involved in the education process?

3. Compare public relations plans from two schools. List their similarities and differences. Evaluate their strengths and weaknesses.
4. Describe an example of an effective parental involvement and community relations plan utilized in your school district.
5. How are people recruited for the parental involvement and community relations committee in your school district? Who are the people who serve on this committee?
6. Determine the process for evaluating the effectiveness of community relations plans in your school district.

CASE STUDY: TROUBLE AT PINEVILLE MIDDLE SCHOOL

It was a cold winter evening when Dr. Chiles walked the campus at 7:00 p.m. to check the attendance for the monthly Parent–Teacher Night. All of the teachers were in their classrooms anticipating the parents' arrival. Dr. Chiles greeted the teachers and then returned to her office. Sitting on her desk was a spreadsheet containing comments from the previous year's parent survey, so she opened it, thinking, "What better time than Parent–Teacher Night to review what our parents think of Pineville Middle School?" She hadn't read far when she began to be concerned by the number of negative comments. The following are a few samples of what she read:

- The teachers don't have enough resources to teach each student properly. In my child's math classes there were 24 students, but the teacher only had four calculators available.
- It seems like the teachers and administrators don't want parents on campus. We don't feel welcome.
- My son played on the basketball team last year, but I was surprised at how few parents and faculty members attended. We're considering enrolling next year in a private school that has a very established sports program.
- My child was disappointed that there was no yearbook last year. The sponsor told us it was because students didn't work hard enough to get advertisers. How sad!

The more she read, the more disturbed Dr. Chiles became. This was her first year as the principal, and she knew things had to change. Mr. Day interrupted her thoughts as he popped his head through the office door: "Is it okay if we teachers pack up and leave early? Most of us didn't have many parents show up."

The two of them left the office and walked down the hall, where they saw a number of teachers gathered. From a distance, they heard the teachers commenting about Parent–Teacher Nights being a waste of time. "There's no need for us to come if parents don't care about it," one teacher said.

Not seeing Dr. Chiles and Mr. Day approach, Mrs. Battle—who had been at Pineville for 17 years—spoke up. "I thought I'd never teach anywhere else," she said, "but I'm seriously considering putting in a transfer request for next year."

Dr. Chiles stopped in her tracks and returned to her office. "What have I gotten myself into?" she wondered. Concerned about the future of Pineville Middle School, she knew that in order to boost the morale of the teachers and to gain the support of parents and the community, something had to be done.

Analyze the Case

1. Rank the comments from the previous year's parent survey from most significant to least significant.
2. Offer suggestions for Dr. Chiles to handle each of the parent comments about Pineville Middle School.
3. What are some of the steps that Dr. Chiles can take to boost the morale of the teachers?

Discuss the Larger Issues

1. What steps should Dr. Chiles take to ensure that an effective plan is in place to improve parental involvement and community relations at Pineville Middle School?
2. What steps should be taken to evaluate the effectiveness of a parental involvement and community relations plan?
3. As she develops the parental involvement and community relations plan, whom should Dr. Chiles recruit to assist her? How should she garner support and input from teachers?

Problem Solving

Step into Dr. Chiles's shoes and write a description of how you would approach your faculty members about the problems at Pineville Middle School. Make plans for effective changes to any plans that are already in existence at the school pertaining to parental involvement and community relations. You may wish to speak with the faculty about each of the comments noted in the parent survey as well as the lack of attendance at Parent–Teacher Nights. Discuss how you would resolve the issues at Pineville Middle School.

Test Your Solution

To test some of your ideas and suggestions, role play one or more of the following situations in class:

1. A meeting between Dr. Chiles and the faculty and staff of Pineville Middle School and the discussion of the comments and complaints about the school
2. A meeting between Dr. Chiles and community leaders about possible ways to gain their support and receive more resources for classroom instruction
3. A meeting between Dr. Chiles and the parental involvement and community relations improvement committee

REFERENCES

Bagin, D., Gallagher, D. R., & Moore, E. H. (2008). *The school and community relations.* Boston, MA: Pearson Education.

Bronfenbrenner, U. (1979). *The ecology of human development.* Cambridge, MA: Harvard University Press.

Drew, M. (2013, March 27). Students learn vital life lessons in "Reality Store" program. *Marshall County Daily.* Retrieved from http://www.marshallcountydaily.com/index.php?option=com_content&view=article&id=6234:a-dose-of-reality-students-learn-vital-life-lessons-in-reality-store-program-hear-from-fellow-student-whose-family-stuggles-with-addiction-&catid=1:latest-news&Itemid=50

Epstein, J. (2012). Eight key strategies and ideas for engaging parents in education. Retrieved from http://www.parentinvolvement.ca/eight_strategies.htm

Gestwicki, C. (2013). *Home, school, & community relations* (8th ed.). Belmont, CA: Wadsworth.

Getzels, J. W. (1978). The communities of education. *Teachers College Record, 79*(4), 659–682.

Guthrie, J. W., & Schuermann, P. J. (2010). *Successful school leadership planning, politics, performance, and power.* Boston, MA: Allyn & Bacon.

Keyes, C. R. (2000). Parent-teacher partnerships: A theoretical approach for teachers. Retrieved from http://ecap.crc.illinois.edu/pubs/katzsym/keyes.html

Maxwell, J. C. (2007). *The Maxwell leadership bible.* Nashville, TN: Thomas Nelson.

McLaughlin, M. (1990). History of parent involvement. Retrieved from http://www.schoolengagement.org/TruancypreventionRegistry/Admin/Resources/Resources/2004ParentalInvolvementWorkshop.pdf

McLaughlin, M., & Shields, P. (1987). Involving low income parents in the schools: A role for policy? *Phi Delta Kappan, 69*(2), 156–160.

Pounds, J. (2012, February 22). Lynchburg elementary schools to get "Safe Routes to Schools" grant. *The News & Advance.* Retrieved from http://www.newsadvance.com/news/local/article_6e61eb53-96b1-5b05-b344-6c7e5692d661.html

Sabia, D. (2012). Democratic/utopian education. *Utopian Studies, 23*(2), 374–405.

Scanlin, M. (2008). Caregiver engagement in religious urban elementary schools. *Marriage & Family Review, 43*(3), 308–337.

Thomson, P., Ellison, L., Byrom, T., & Bulman, D. (2007). Invisible labor: Home-school relations and the front office. *Gender and Education, 19*(2), 141–158.

Chapter 10

Political and Legal Context

Andrea P. Beam

The clearest way to show what the rule of law means to us in everyday life is to recall what has happened when there is no rule of law.

—Dwight D. Eisenhower—

OVERVIEW

Building upon the previous chapter's discussion of the importance of partnering within the community, this chapter will provide an overview of educational law and how political, social, and cultural changes are directing how courts act and react. The global mindset present in the nation's highest courts has directed and will continue to redirect how the courts view many judicial rulings, and from those considerations, a new set of legal precedents will emerge that will affect how those courts view educational systems. This chapter will present public and private school law and include a discussion of how the courts have traditionally ruled in various educational incidents. Federal, state, and local laws will be discussed along with federal and state court systems, including a discussion on the amendments—specifically those that apply to education. Other components that will facilitate the reading are basic definitions of legal jargon, historical background, critical issues, and biblical perspectives.

Objectives

By the end of this chapter, the reader should be able to do the following:

1. Ensure that each student is treated fairly, respectfully, and with an understanding of each student's culture and context.
2. Ensure that each student has equitable access to effective teachers, academic opportunities, and other resources necessary for success.

3. Develop policies that address misconduct in a positive, fair, and unbiased manner.
4. Confront and address biases and low expectations associated with race, class, culture and language, gender and sexual orientation, and disability or special status.
5. Act with cultural competence and responsiveness in interactions, decision making, and practices affecting student learning.
6. Address matters of equity and cultural responsiveness in all aspects of leadership.

INTRODUCTION

By studying educational law, administrators are better prepared to understand and navigate constitutional demands, restrictions, and provisions—especially as they relate to religious freedoms and limitations. It would benefit leaders greatly to devote time to this study because much of today's growing societal unrest with education appears to be connected to the religious unrest throughout the nation and the world.

Blackstone (1908), a legal authority and Christian leader, wrote,

> The doctrine of the law then is this: that precedents and rules be followed, unless flatly absurd or unjust; for though their reason be not obvious at first view, yet we owe such a deference to former times as to suppose that they acted wholly without consideration. (p. 52)

It is therefore imperative for school leaders to have a firm grasp on case precedent and the impact past decisions may have on current cases.

Several important points are worth noting before readers approach the information in this chapter:

1. Anyone may sue another person for any reason whatsoever, as long as the plaintiff has sufficient funds to file suit. It does not necessarily mean that the plaintiff will prevail, but—whatever the outcome—the defendant will indeed experience some degree of stress, legal expense, and exertion of time and energy toward the defense.
2. The plaintiff is responsible to provide the burden of proof. The defendant only has to respond to the complaints brought forth.
3. There is not a binding precedent case for every incident that comes before the court. As a result, different courts may produce different rulings. Several items of consideration include the jurisdiction of the court, the surrounding community and its practices and beliefs, the perspectives of the judge, and the judge's moral and/or ethical compass. For example, one might expect a court in a conservative jurisdiction to rule against a teacher who was terminated for posting pictures of a party where he or she consumed an alcoholic beverage, whereas in a more liberal jurisdiction, the case might not even be adjudicated.
4. Legal cases will sometimes get overturned upon appeal, depending on which judge is hearing the case and where that court is located.
5. In the event that there is a precedent or common law for a particular incident, one can expect the precedent to carry weight when a judge considers the decision.
6. Educators are held to a higher standard than is the common person and are thought to make better decisions with regard to the safety of students. They are expected to foresee possible dangers and make decisions to avoid possible negligence. As a matter of fact, judges will often defer to educators when making decisions, as they are viewed as experts within their field.

BACKGROUND

American Legal System

Written'in 1787, the U.S. Constitution was designed to provide legal principles by which society was to live. The first 10 amendments of the Constitution, also known as the Bill of Rights, and the 14 Amendment represent those primary rights ensuring that citizens' freedoms are not infringed upon. The U.S. Constitution and the Bill of Rights were not written with education in mind; therefore, the courts have interpreted certain amendments as the basis for deciding educational matters. Because it is not addressed at all in the Constitution, the function of education itself is reserved to the power of the states by the 10th Amendment. Which stipulates, "The powers not delegated to the Unites States by the Constitution, nor prohibited by it to the States, are reserved to the States respectively, or to the people" (Bill of Rights, 1789).

Because it is not addressed at all in the Constitution, the function of education itself is reserved to the power of the states by the 10th Amendment.

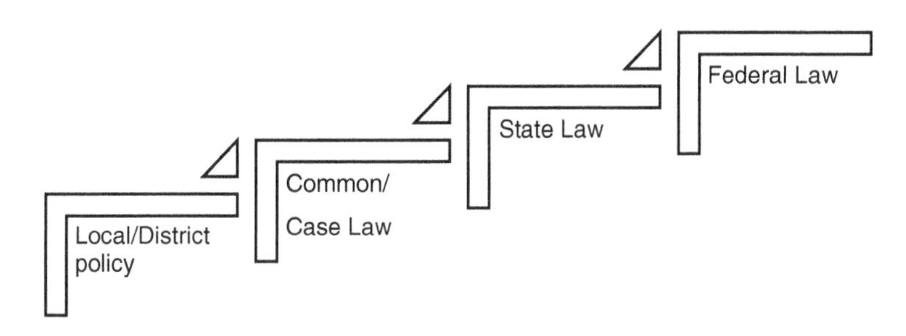

Figure 10.1. *Beam's staircase model of the U.S. legal system.*

Regarding the law, one should visualize a tiered series of steps, such as the one depicted in Figure 10.1. The steps begin with federal law, then comes state law, followed by common law (also known as case law), and end with local or district policy. Federal law provides the foundation for policymaking and is followed nationwide. No other level is to deviate from the federal Constitution, as all statutes enacted on other levels are subordinate to it. Common federal laws that educators must comply with include the 2015 Every Student Succeeds Act (ESSA) and the Individuals with Disabilities Education Act (IDEA) of 2004.

Beneath the federal Constitution are the state constitutions, which provide the basic source of law for individual states and prescribe funding and operational structures for public schools. State laws address the same subject matter found in the U.S. Constitution, such as due process and individual rights. State constitutions must meet the basic requirements of the federal Constitution but may exceed its coverage.

Case law immediately follows state constitutions. Case law is also known as judge-made or common law, and uses precedence as a basis for decisions. Case law consists of judgments, opinions, and court decisions that adopt or enforce preceding customs and usages. Because education is regulated and overseen by state government, one state does not necessarily follow another state's precedence regarding similar disputes.

The final and lowest tier of law is that of state statutes, also known as local or district policy. State statutes are the most abundant source of law affecting public schools, providing the basis for school district policies, rules, and regulations. Unless there is a direct conflict with the U.S. Constitution, federal law, or state constitutions, statutes are rarely brought into court because school boards are given the authority to adopt and enforce reasonable rules and regulations to operate and manage schools. Local and district policy is derived from the state board of education and allows districts to do the following:

- Establish educator licensure standards, graduation requirements, and testing requirements
- Regulate preparation programs for teachers, administrators, and school counselors

- Review and approve the state budget
- Develop rules and regulations for administering state standards

State boards of education are recognized by courts to hold authority to regulate student and school personnel conduct. Again, the policies enacted by the local school boards are the basic sources of law and are legally defensible as long as they do not conflict with the federal Constitution or state constitutions, statutes, or case laws.

Law is an interesting phenomenon in that it is not clearly a black-and-white issue. As a matter of fact, there is oftentimes more gray than the clear-cut "yes or no" or "right or wrong" answer that one would hope for when discussing legalities, and this is true specifically in the field of school law. Although education was not at the forefront of the founders' minds when writing the Constitution, there are several key amendments that the courts have referenced when making legal decisions. The following list outlines the most referenced amendments and the concepts contained in each:

1st Amendment: freedoms of students and school personnel, including speech, press, assembly, and religion.

4th Amendment: search and seizure; right to privacy and protection from unreasonable intrusions into person or property.

5th Amendment: protection against self-incrimination in cases when life, liberty, or property is in jeopardy.

8th Amendment: protects individuals against cruel and unusual punishment.

10th Amendment: limits federal government power; reserves education as a function of the states.

14th Amendment: addresses due process rights of students and school personnel to ensure equality and fairness.

Now that the amendments have been addressed, it is important to understand the actual court system and the proceedings. The court system is made up of federal (i.e., district, appellate, and the U.S. Supreme Court) and state courts with the purpose being to settle disputes by applying the law to factual circumstances, interpreting legislative enactments, and determining the constitutionality of the law. Using a similarly tiered system and working from the lower courts to the higher courts, one might begin court proceedings in a trial or district court and then move to the court of appeals and finally on to the U.S. Supreme Court.

Trial and district courts address constitutional issues within their territories and deal with parties from different states. If either party appeals the lower court's decision, the case will be heard in the appellate court. The appellate court reviews proceedings from the lower courts and looks for irregularities, constitutional misinterpretation, and inappropriate application of evidence. From the appellate court, one could then appeal to the highest state court—the state supreme court. State courts are also a part of each state's judicial system and hear cases related to constitutional law, state statutes, and common law. Many of the educational cases are heard in the state courts.

The highest court in the United States is the Supreme Court. Very few cases actually make their way to the Supreme Court, and should the justices decide not to hear the case, they send the case back to the lower court and the lower court decision stands. It is important to note that there is no appeal beyond the decision of the Supreme Court and that its rulings can only be overturned by an amendment to the U.S. Constitution.

Before delving too far into specific educational issues, one must first understand how the law has evolved from noneducational topics to the point where it began to be applied specifically to educational concerns. For example, the issue of the 14th Amendment began to surface as one of the primary matters in the schools in the 1940s and 1950s. Although cases relating to the 14th Amendment did not early in the nation's history include school issues per se, such applications have now become common.

In 1891, *Plessy v. Ferguson* was among the first landmark cases dealing with segregation. Homer Plessy was considered in his day an octoroon, which was defined as a person who was 7/8 white and 1/8 black. The son of free African Americans, Plessy entered a railroad car designated for white passengers only. When asked to leave, he refused. Following his arrest, Plessy challenged the case in court, as he believed it was a clear violation of his 14th Amendment rights. Unfortunately, Plessy did not prevail because the courts upheld the separate but equal doctrine. In 1955, however, the concept of separate but equal was challenged in *Brown v. Board of Education* and was reversed. The court ruled that the notion of separate but equal was inherently false and should be abolished. As a result, segregation in public schools was determined to be unconstitutional according to the 14th Amendment.

Although these two cases bookend a discussion on segregation in the public schools, several additional cases had a critical impact on the educational system. Later in this chapter, various cases that have had a major influence on educational practices will be discussed, along with their implications for the school setting.

Biblical Perspectives

No matter a person's religious faith or lack thereof, one would be negligent not to acknowledge that the United States was founded upon Judeo-Christian principles—many of which are still influential in American jurisprudence today. As previously mentioned, rulings for incidents that may be similar in nature are not always consistent across the nation, as it depends on the court hearing the case and the community in which the laws were allegedly broken. Although rulings may vary, those who follow Jesus Christ rely heavily on the laws and teachings found in one of the oldest books known to humankind. Christians observe the Bible as a blueprint by which to live their lives. For the non-Christian as well, living an ethically based lifestyle grounded in biblical truth aids in developing a moral citizenry. Regardless of how educators might identify themselves, all should attempt to do what is morally upright, and the root of those actions as they relate to the law begin with the Bible.

Regardless of how educators might identify themselves, all should attempt to do what is morally upright

Equality and Fairness

Examples abound of biblical principles that relate to educational law. Equal treatment under the law, for example, is a value that many, if not all, Americans embrace. The Bible supports the concept of equality in Galatians 3:28 (King James Version), where it states, "There is neither Jew nor Greek, there is neither bond nor free, there is neither male nor female: for ye are all one in Christ Jesus." People should be seen as equal, regardless of their gender, age, ethnicity, nationality, or religious affiliation. When suits are brought forth in court, the plaintiff assumes that judges will be fair in their rulings. Those settling disagreements (i.e., between plaintiff and defendant) hope that the mediator (i.e., judge) will listen to the facts and only the facts, laying aside any biases or personal assumptions. Christ also placed a higher expectation on those called to such professions to remain fair. Several other biblical references support the importance of fairness:

"Open your mouth, judge righteously, defend the rights of the poor and needy" (Proverbs 31:9).

"But if you show partiality, you are committing sin and are convicted by the law as transgressors" (James 2:9).

Honesty

Honesty is another important element in legal matters. All parties involved—plaintiffs, defendants, judges, juries, and attorneys—need to be honest in all that they do and say. The apostle Paul commanded that this trait be present in Christ followers when he wrote, "Therefore, laying aside falsehood, speak truth each one of you with his neighbor, for we are members of one another" (Ephesians 4:25). Throughout Scripture, the principle is repeatedly affirmed that those who are honest will be blessed but that those who are dishonest will come to ruin. One such affirmation is found in Proverbs 10:9 that states, "He who walks in integrity walks securely, but he who perverts his way will be found out." Honesty in everyday actions, regardless of who may or may not be watching, is as important as honesty in the courts of law: "Providing for honest things, not only in the sight of the Lord, but also in the sight of men" (2 Corinthians 8:21). Finally, arbitrators must listen to the facts of each case and stand by the decision made, without vacillation: "Above all, my brothers, do not swear—not by heaven or by earth or by anything else. Let your 'yes' be yes and your 'no' be no, or you will be condemned" (James 5:12).

Judgment and Justice

Wherever proper judgment is withheld, therein lies injustice. With law and legal issues comes the sinful nature of humans to use judgment inappropriately, which corrupts not only the justice system but also personal relationships. To avoid such corruption, God calls people not to judge hypocritically, for there is a Higher Authority who will serve as the ultimate Judge in all matters:

> Judge not, that you be not judged. For with the judgment that you pronounce, you will be judged: and with the measure you use it will be measured to you. Why do you see the speck that is in your brother's eye, but do not notice the log that is in your own eye? Or how can you say to your brother, Let me take the speck out of your eye when there is a log in your own eye? You hypocrite, first take the log out of your own eye; and then you will see clearly to take the speck out of your brother's eye. (Matthew 7:1–5)

The Bible teaches the principle of justice not only for society but also for personal daily actions. For example, the Lord commanded Israel through the voice of Amos to "let justice roll down like waters, and righteousness like an ever-flowing stream" (Amos 5:24). God desires for His people to do good deeds, not just when they think others are watching but especially when they do not realize the eyes of others are on them. Through the prophet Isaiah, God implored His people to "learn to do good; seek justice, correct oppression; bring justice to the fatherless, plead the widow's cause" (Isaiah 1:17). If people followed these decrees more closely, the docket of legal cases would not be as nearly overloaded as it presently is. As stated earlier, however, the sinful nature of humans is a corrupting force. Therefore, a legal system is necessary to bring about justice, and it is more likely to do so effectively if individuals in the system follow the Lord's directive to "render true judgments [and to] show kindness and mercy to one another'" (Zechariah 7:9).

SCHOOL LAW IN ACTION

Objectives Relating to School Law

The chart in Figure 10.2 is provided to facilitate an understanding of how specific objectives relate to samples of legal cases mentioned thus far in this chapter. Many of the cases listed in this chart have set clear precedent and therefore should be familiar to all educational leaders—although it is not expected that they know the names of every case.

Objective	Illustrative Cases	Issues and Rulings
1. Ensure that each student is treated fairly, respectfully, and with an understanding of each student's culture and context.	*Brown v. Board of Education of Topeka (1955)*	Separate but unequal is unconstitutional. Schools may not be racially segregated.
	Pierce v. Society of Sisters (1925)	Compulsory education laws must allow options other than public schools.
2. Ensure that each student has equitable access to effective teachers, academic opportunities, and other resources necessary for success.	*Pickering v. Board of Education of Township High School District 205 (1968)*	As citizens, educators may express opinions regarding public issues without fear of termination.
	Wisconsin v. Yoder (1972)	Established religious beliefs trump the state's interest in compulsory education beyond the eighth grade.
	Safford Unified School District #1 et al. v. April Redding (2009)	Reasonable suspicion is required before a strip search may be conducted.
3. Develop policies that address misconduct in a positive, fair, and unbiased manner.	*Criminal cases regarding the suicides of Megan Meier (2006) and Phoebe Prince (2010)*	Cyber-bullying may result in criminal charges.

Figure 10.2. *Relation of chapter objectives to court cases*

Objective	Illustrative Cases	Issues and Rulings
4. Confront and address biases and expectations associated with religion, culture and language, gender and sexual orientation, and disability or special status.	*Engel v. Vitale (1962)*	School personnel may not endorse, require, or encourage official prayers.
	Lee v. Weisman (1992)	School personnel may not arrange for prayer at graduation ceremonies.
	Good News Club v. Milford Central School (2001)	Equal access must be granted to school facilities regardless of the religious content of the activities.
	Gavin Grimm v Gloucester County School Board, 2015	Schools may decide how transgender issues are handled regarding restroom facilities.
	Highland School District v US Department of Education, 2016	The student's gender identity shall dictate the sexual treatment that the school is mandated to follow
	Student v Arcadia Unified School District, 2013	Schools shall treat transgender students in accordance with their gender identity
	Whitaker v Kenosha Unified School District, 2017	The student's gender identity shall dictate the sexual treatment that the school is mandated to follow
5. Act with cultural competence and responsiveness in interactions, decision making, and practices affecting student learning.	*Owasso Independent School District No I-011 v. Falvo (2002)*	The Family Educational Rights and Privacy Act (FERPA) is not violated by students grading each other's assignments and calling out grades.
6. Address matters of equity and cultural responsiveness in all aspects of leadership.	*Tinker v. Des Moines Independent Community School District (1969)*	Students maintain a degree of freedom of expression without being disciplined so long as the expression does not disrupt the school or violate others' rights.
	New Jersey v. T.L.O.(1985)	Search and seizure of personable student property is acceptable under terms of reasonable suspicion.
	Bethel School District No. 403 v. Fraser (1986)	The 1st Amendment freedom of speech rights do not protect lewd and indecent language.
	Vernonia School District v. Acton (1995)	Random drug testing of school athletes is permissible.

Figure 10.2. *(Continued).*

Current Issues in School Law

Court rulings related to education may vary greatly from state to state, depending on community standards and past practices; however, some rulings remain constant regardless of locality. As previously discussed, there is no appeal beyond the U.S. Supreme Court; only by amendment of the Constitution may a Supreme Court decision be overruled. Several cases, therefore, remain as precedent in today's courts and serve as a framework for school administrators as they make decisions. The following subsections discuss legal issues and cases that are at the heart of the school law discussion and that continue to impact education in every locality.

1st Amendment Rights

One of the freedoms protected by the 1st Amendment is the expression of religion in the public arena, which would include public schools. It specifically states, "Congress shall make no law respecting an establishment of religion, or prohibiting the free exercise thereof; or abridging the freedom of speech, or of the press; or the right of the people peaceably to assemble, and to petition the Government for a redress of grievances" (Bill of Rights, 1789). Note that in addition to protecting the free exercise of religion, the 1st Amendment also prohibits the establishment of religion. Applied to the public school, this has been interpreted by the courts to mean that school officials may not arrange for any religious activities that are proselytizing, indoctrinating, or worshipful in nature, especially in an environment where students or their families are compelled to attend. Violating either the establishment clause or the free exercise clause may lead to litigation. School administrators who are aware of how to avoid these violations are less likely to experience such litigation. As the following 1st Amendment issues are considered, it is important to keep in mind that religious rights are protected for both students and school personnel in public schools. The religious rights of teachers and other school officials, however, are restricted far more than those of students.

it is important to keep in mind that religious rights are protected for both students and school personnel in public schools.

Religious expression in public schools. Time set aside specifically for meditation or voluntary prayer in the public school is in violation of the 1st Amendment (*Engle v. Vitale,* 1962; *Wallace v. Jaffree,* 1985). School officials may, alternatively, lead students in a moment of silence; this is permissible as long as it is for a secular purpose, such as personal reflection or to honor the memory of people who have died. Also, public schools may not display religious exhibits or other visual materials in the hallways or classrooms unless they are part of a secular study of world religions or cultures. Even then, the school should be careful that nothing visual serves to proselytize, indoctrinate, or lead students to worship. Additionally, programs or assemblies during school hours or any time students or their families are compelled to be in attendance may not be strictly religious in nature. It may be appropriate, however, for public school teachers to acknowledge and explain various holidays of all cultural and religious groups as a unit in cultural heritage or some other related subject or to hold a program that encompasses many secular and religious traditions. For example, a musical concert may include a variety of songs—both secular and religious—in order to acknowledge influences on a particular group of people or at a particular season. A Christmas-season concert may include carols about the birth of Jesus only if it also includes songs representing Hanukkah, winter solstice, secular winter traditions, and so forth.

Another example would be programs highlighting student-created artistic expressions, such as paintings or poetry. Courts have consistently ruled that presentations of student-created work are considered open forums in which speech or symbolic expressions may not be discriminated against based solely on their religious nature. In other words, preference may not be given either to secular or religious speech in an open forum for students. Preference to secular speech violates the free exercise clause, and preference to religious speech violates the establishment clause. The key is to ensure that a secular purpose is served.

If conducted in a proselytizing, indoctrinating, or worshipful manner, the observance of holy days by public school officials is clearly an unconstitutional activity. The 1st Amendment prohibits states from either aiding religion or showing preference for one religion over another. For this reason, the issue of neutrality and nondiscrimination is important (*Freiler v. Tangipahoa Parish Public Schools*, 1999; *Lee v. Weisman,*

1992). Finally, materials in school libraries may not be removed based solely on the religious nature of the content. Just as the Koran is allowed in public school libraries, so is the Bible. These items are viewed as reference or supplemental materials. Because they serve a secular instructional purpose by supporting the state curriculum, religious materials may be housed in public school libraries just as they are in tax-supported community libraries.

Religious expression at graduation and other events. Establishing constitutionality is somewhat confusing regarding student-led prayer or Scripture recitation in public schools. When the venue is graduation or athletic events, the issue becomes even more convoluted. Student-initiated and student-led religious expressions—such as praying, quoting Scripture, or sharing a spiritual testimony—are usually acceptable under the following conditions:

1. It is not requested or arranged by school officials.
2. It is in an open forum in which the student choosing to make a religious expression has been given a degree of latitude in the content of the expression.
3. It is not disruptive.

Regarding the final condition, courts have consistently ruled that simply because speech or symbolic expressions may be offensive to others, they are not deemed to be disruptive. To disrupt, in this context, means to interrupt planned activities or to incite violence. If the school has created an open forum for student expression, the only expressions that may be discriminated against are those deemed disruptive or socially unacceptable—for example, profanity, hate speech, and sexually graphic content.

To be clear, schools may not arrange for there to be prayer at any government-sponsored event (*Santa Fe Independent School District v. Jane Doe,* 2000). This includes graduations, athletic events, performances, and assemblies. It is therefore a violation of the establishment clause to schedule a benediction or to allow graduating seniors to vote for their choice of a pastor to open up the ceremony. Both of these examples give preference to religious speech over secular speech. An acceptable alternative would be to permit seniors to vote for any community member to offer words of encouragement or inspiration to the graduating class. The school is then providing a constitutionally protected open forum for speech or symbolic expression. At that point, the school may not show preference to or discriminate against the speech's content based on either its secular or religious nature. Valedictorian speeches also fall under the protection of an open forum. Consequently, administrators who prohibit valedictorians from making religious references, reading Scripture, or even praying in their speeches have violated the free exercise clause.

Student rights. As mentioned earlier, students have many more rights in the public school than do school employees. One of those rights relates to student religious clubs, which must be granted the same opportunities to access school facilities as other noncurricular clubs enjoy. Similar to the open-forum concept discussed previously, this notion is referred to as equal access. If the school opens its doors to any clubs or activities, it has created a situation in which equal access must be granted to religious groups (*Colin v. Orange Unified School District,* 2000; *Good News Club v. Milford Central School,* 2001). To disallow them would be a clear violation of the free exercise clause, as it would be showing preference to secular speech over religious speech. If a school does not wish to allow religious groups to form or meet, it would need to disallow all other clubs and groups as well.

Regarding students' general freedom of speech, the situation varies depending on instructional versus noninstructional time. In either setting, however, students maintain certain rights. During noninstructional time, student speech may only be limited if it does any of the following:

- Interferes with the rights of others.
- Is unacceptable because of school rules or societal norms regarding profanity or sexually graphic content.
- Includes hate speech.

Otherwise, students may speak freely on religious issues and distribute religious literature during noninstructional time (*Jones v. Clear Creek Independent School District*, 1992). The distribution of religious literature, however, must comply with school rules. Many schools will permit distribution during noninstructional time to friends or to small groups of students for whom the content of the literature is relevant. If the school has a rule regarding the mass distribution of literature to random students, the school may limit distribution based on the parameters of the rule but must consistently do so for both secular and religious literature distribution, without showing preference to one over the other. If the rule or the manner in which it is enforced limits only the mass distribution of religious literature, it is a violation of the free exercise clause.

During instructional time, student speech may be limited to the subject matter being discussed. Speech within the subject matter, however, may not be restricted because of its religious nature. In sum, student speech may not be restricted unless it causes substantial interference with school operations. Students are allowed to speak freely on various topics, such as religion, abortion, and presidential elections, to name a few. They may speak on such issues without fear of repercussion, but the line is drawn when their speech carries over to vulgar or profane language. Schools have the right to restrict speech or edit content in the school newspaper if it is deemed obscene. They may not, however, do so without a valid educational reason (*Bethel School District No. 403 v. Fraser,* 1986). This particular ruling holds true for both public and private sectors.

Rights of school personnel. Despite a great number of prohibitions, teachers are indeed afforded religious rights within the walls of the public school—albeit on a limited basis. Their rights may vary depending on the time and place, just as they do with students. For instance, during any time public school personnel are functioning in an official capacity, they are prohibited from praying or reading Scripture in a devotional manner in the presence of students. Also, they are not permitted to distribute religious materials on school premises. Such practices would clearly violate the establishment clause.

The Bible, though, may be taught in public schools if it is not offered in a manner to proselytize, indoctrinate, or worship. It may be taught to facilitate an understanding of other literary works, historical events, and figures of speech. Teaching biblical content is indeed justifiable as long as it supports the established curriculum and is implemented for secular purposes. Thus, the academic subjects most likely to reference the Bible will be English and social studies. A public school teacher may teach about religion in an objective manner, but should avoid promoting belief in any particular religion and should likewise avoid degrading or showing hostility toward any religion. Teachers may answer student questions about personal religious beliefs only as they relate to the subject matter and should take into account the children's developmental ability to separate a teacher's personal beliefs from the established curriculum.

Regarding extracurricular groups, teachers may sponsor Bible clubs, Fellowship of Christian Athletes, or other religious clubs. They may attend the club meetings and offer counsel but are not to provide leadership or participate in the club's religious activities. They are to be seen as a sponsor only. Teachers may not publicly participate in programs such as "See You at the Pole" but may be present for student supervision.

With other school personnel, teachers may freely discuss religion and religious topics before school, after school, between classes, in teacher lounges, and so forth. They may also gather to pray with other teachers but may not invite students or encourage their participation. After school hours, off school property, and when teachers are not functioning in an official school capacity, they are citizens with the same protections as anyone else and may engage in any protected behavior. At such times, they may pray with and proselytize students and their parents and may invite them to church or youth groups.

Other rights afforded to teachers, within certain limits, include freedom of speech, freedom of association, and freedom of expression. It is no surprise that teachers, like students, enjoy the opportunity to express themselves freely. When outside the school environment and speaking as a public citizen, all school personnel would be wise to qualify public expressions as representing their own opinions and not any official position of the school. Even though some parties may not find particular discussions preferable as teachers express themselves, such expressions are, nonetheless, completely acceptable and legal (*Pickering v. Board of Education of Township High School District 205,* 1968).

Academic freedom is a concern for teachers. Although it may vary depending on the educational site, public school teachers are indeed granted a degree of academic freedom. One limitation, for instance, is that teachers in P-K–12 settings must focus on established curriculum and keep their discussions, within reason, to the topics at hand. Students as minor children are viewed as impressionable, so their educators need to ensure that they remain focused on the established curriculum. On the other hand, at the university level, professors have much more academic freedom because their students are adults.

Another liberty that teachers enjoy is the freedom of association. Teachers are able to associate with others and assemble with a multitude of various groups. The only limit, however, is affiliation with "hate" groups. Whereas it is legal for teachers simply to be associated with these groups, their involvement in illegal activity is impermissible. Equally acceptable is an educator's right to hold office. An educator may run for office in political venues and even hold a political position. Such educators may be requested by their superiors to take a leave of absence, though, if such endeavors interfere with normal day-to-day routines within the school.

The rights of private school teachers—especially of those in Christian schools—may differ greatly from those in public schools. As private religious entities, these schools are constitutionally protected in their ability to limit activities of their teachers that might not be limited in public schools. If a limitation or requirement is grounded in religious Scripture or doctrinal teaching, the school may be permitted to enforce it. There are certain protections, however, that remain constitutionally protected and cannot be superseded by any religious doctrines. Private schools, for example, may not discriminate based on race, gender, age, handicap, ethnicity, ancestry, national origin, or military status. If they are found to have discriminated based on any of these characteristics, they are at risk of losing their tax-exempt status. Unlike their public school counterparts, however, they may use religious grounds to discriminate based on religion and sexual orientation. They may also discriminate based on marital status in the following instances:

The rights of private school teachers—especially of those in Christian schools—may differ greatly from those in public schools.

- A single person is cohabiting with another.
- A single female teacher is or becomes pregnant.
- The divorce of a married teacher does not comply with established doctrinal teachings documented by the school or its sponsoring church.

Personnel employed at a Christian school typically sign a statement of faith indicating that they are in compliance with certain doctrinal teachings espoused by the school and, if applicable, by its sponsoring church. Although they typically have the freedom to teach the Bible in subject-matter courses, teachers may be limited as to how they teach certain doctrines. Depending on the policies of the school, teaching contrary doctrine could be grounds for disciplinary action or termination.

There are many other matters of lifestyle that Christian schools may limit, and they are free to do so as long as there is a sound doctrinal rationale as the basis. Examples of such lifestyle limitations include prohibitions on alcohol, smoking, and adult entertainment. Schools that are most successful at defending challenges to these limitations in court are those that have established clearly written policies and that require their personnel to sign a statement agreeing to abide by the policies. Lifestyle and religious practice policies may extend beyond the faculty and staff to school board members, parents, and students.

4th Amendment Rights

The topic of 4th Amendment rights is one that administrators, especially secondary principals, are certain to deal with on a regular basis. Specifically, the issue of search and seizure originates out of the 4th Amendment, which states that individuals have an inherent right to privacy and protection from unreasonable intrusion into their person or property. In some situations, school officials have more freedom than other public officials (e.g., police officers), especially when it comes to searches on school grounds. Whereas police officers acting in their capacity as school resource officers must have a warrant and probable cause to conduct a search, a school administrator only needs reasonable suspicion. This suspicion can come in many forms, including but not limited to student reports of wrongdoing, eyewitness accounts, or unusual student behaviors. At any rate, school administrators are granted broad powers to search. Because of the former No Child Left Behind Law, administrators must act swiftly to keep schools safe at all times. However, according to *Tinker v. Des Moines Independent Community School District* (1969), "Students possess the same constitutional rights as adults and that these rights do not end at the school house door." School leaders must therefore be prudent as searches are conducted.

Reasonable suspicion. Searches within the school take many forms. Some searches involve administrators searching book bags or purses (*DesRoches v. Caprio,* 1997, whereas others include locker searches (*Isaiah B. v. State of Wisconsin,* 1993). Still others deal with canine searches and, on rare occasion, strip searches. Regardless, the search must reasonably match the infraction; the intrusiveness of the search, too, must match. An example of an intrusive search not matching the infraction would be a strip search of middle school students when looking for ibuprofen (*Safford Unified School District #1 et al. v. April Redding,* 2009). *New Jersey v. T.L.O.* (1985) is the landmark case that serves as precedent in nearly all search-and-seizure cases regarding reasonableness. In this case, two students were suspected of smoking in the girls' restroom. One girl confessed to smoking, whereas the other (identified in the case only by the initials T.L.O.) denied doing so. When school administrators began questioning T.L.O., she said she was not smoking in the bathroom, but because of reasonable suspicion, administrators began a simple search of her purse. While looking for cigarettes and other paraphernalia, leaders came across additional items such as rolling papers, marijuana, and letters and ledgers detailing money owed. The question before the Supreme Court was, "Did the search violate the 4th Amendment?" Because school officials are granted broad powers and it is their duty to uphold a safe school environment, the search was ruled as reasonable at its inception.

Metal detectors. Although courts have ruled metal detector searches as acceptable, schools should have a history of violence or unlawful activity within the community before installing such devices. To set up metal detectors in a building without a history of drugs or weapons would send a red flag to the community that the school is unsafe.

Canine searches. Canine searches are also permissible and are standard practice in many districts. Dogs may sniff lockers, student belongings, or cars on school property (*Zamora v. Pomeroy,* 1981). They may never search students, however, as this practice has been ruled as too intrusive and not reasonable (*Horton v. Goose Creek Independent School District*, 1982; *Jones v. Latexo Independent School District,* 1980).

Random drug testing. Random drug testing is a debatable topic. Because students follow compulsory attendance laws, it is unlawful randomly to drug test the typical student body. It is appropriate, though, to drug test student athletes or those in extracurricular activities. Students involved in extracurricular programs are oftentimes perceived as leaders in the school and may be held to a higher standard. It is important, then, to remember that these students do not fall under compulsory laws, as extracurricular activities are optional and voluntary. Students may be randomly drug tested, whether parents are in opposition to this practice or not (*Board of Education of Independent School District 92 of Pottawatomie County v. Earls,* 2002; *Vernonia School District v. Acton,* 1995).

Locker searches. School officials may conduct a locker search only if there is reasonable suspicion that the student has in his or her possession something that violates school policy. It is not permissible, though, for administrators to conduct random locker searches. This is true for both public and private institutions. Although lockers are the property of the school, students are expected to have some measure of privacy with their desks and lockers (*Tinker v. Des Moines Independent Community School District,* 1969).

Strip searches. Finally, the issue of strip searching is one that is becoming more common in the courts. Although there are some cases where administrators have prevailed in court (*Cornfield by Lewis v. Consolidated High School District No. 230,* 1993), the practice is not an advisable one. There are far too many scenarios where strip searches have gone wrong (*Oliver v. McClung,* 1995; *Safford Unified School District #1 et al. v. April Redding,* 2009).

14th Amendment Rights

The 14th Amendment addresses due process rights of students and school personnel to ensure equality and fairness. It is set forth to ensure that students' and teachers' voices are heard before removal from the school setting or position. Whenever students or teachers are suspected of misconduct, they possess a legal right to explain their side of the story (*Goss v. Lopez,* 1975). To deprive them of this opportunity would be a clear violation of their 14th Amendment rights.

Compulsory Attendance

The age of compulsory attendance for students varies from state to state, with most states requiring students to attend school until the age of 16. There are no laws requiring parents to send their children specifically to public schools, private schools, or even home schools; parents retain this right of school preference (*Pierce v. Society of Sisters*, 1925). There are a few religious exceptions that allow students to withdraw from school based on their religious practices—one being based on the *Wisconsin v. Yoder* (1972) ruling, which permitted Amish students to withdraw from school after the eighth grade.

FERPA

From Public Law 93-380 came the Family Educational Rights and Privacy Act (FERPA), which was established to protect the confidentiality of student records. For those students in P-K–12, parents make the final decision regarding their child's records and the confidentiality of them. They can determine if any information is released or if certain identifiable information is to be held behind a secure folder. Once a child reaches the age of 18, though, or attends a postsecondary institution, parental consent is no longer required. The child, now adult, is the one who decides what information is shared. As a matter of fact, students who attend higher education facilities must grant parental permission to review their records, including grades. This is in effect for any school, public or private, that receives federal funds.

Individuals with Disabilities

According to the Individuals with Disabilities Education Act (IDEA), students with disabilities (SWD) are guaranteed a free and appropriate public education (FAPE) from the ages of 3 to 21, and sometimes 22, depending on when the student's birthday occurs in the school year. They may receive services not only in P-K–12 but also in higher education. When students are of school age (i.e., P-K–12), they fall under the federal law of IDEA. After students graduate from P-K–12, they fall under the Americans with Disabilities Act (ADA). These students have far more resources available in the public schools than they do in private schools. Private schools are not required to provide special education services to SWD; however, if a private school student wishes to receive services, the neighboring public school will be required to provide the necessary services.

As stated, public schools are required to provide a FAPE. Failure to do so could result in the public school being required to pay tuition for students whose families choose to enroll them in a private school. Public schools are not required to maximize the programs for SWD, but they are responsible for providing a free and appropriate education (*Board of Education of Hendrick Hudson Central School District v. Rowley,* 1982; *Florence County School District Four v. Shannon Carter,* 1993; *Forest Grove School District v. T.A.,* 2009).

Negligence

Although many may think of teachers and administrators as "the common person," they are oftentimes held to a higher standard in the eyes of the courts. They are believed to be able to make predictions, foresee possible dangers, and act appropriately when students face hazardous situations. Consequently, the previous No Child Left Behind (NCLB) of 2001 mandated that schools keep students safe at all times. This means that school officials are to keep students safe from harassment, predators, and other such situations (*Davis v. Monroe County Board of Education,* 1999). Additionally, the former NCLB, combined with the concept that educators hold more responsibility as trained caregivers than the common person, requires educators to act as *in loco parentis*, that is, to act in the place of parents and keep the students safe to the greatest extent possible. School personnel thus can be held liable if they act in a negligent manner, either intentionally or unintentionally. Educators are human, nonetheless, and have received leniency from the courts in some respects. Although educators try to provide a safe learning environment for students at all times, the courts agree that they cannot possibly foresee all potential hazards and dangers that arise in a school setting (*Gathright v. Lincoln Insurance Company,* 1985).

Some intentional torts (i.e., wrongdoing) include assault, battery, libel, slander, defamation, false arrest, malicious prosecution, and invasion of privacy (Essex, 2012). This type of tort requires proof of intent. The unintentional torts, on the other hand, do not require the same proof of willfulness. These torts occur when someone fails to exercise a degree of care in doing what is permissible.

School Law in the News

© Zebor/Shutterstock.com

With the advent of the 24-hour news cycle, not much time or effort are needed to know what is going on in society, especially when it comes to problems in schools. One need only go as far as the local newspaper or the Internet to learn of plenty of mishaps and controversies. A quick perusal using one's Internet search engine will yield a multitude of stories dealing with child abuse, assault, and illegal sexual encounters in a matter of seconds. For instance, in Fresno, California, a teacher faced disciplinary measures after she tied up one of her fifth-grade students for acting out in class. The child's disruptive act was a refusal to sit down in class (Gates, 2013). In Virginia, a teacher was arrested and charged after he allegedly struck a male student in class (Maclauchlan, 2013). In Atlanta, Georgia, a former superintendent and over 30 district personnel were indicted for conspiring to alter and destroy documents to make it appear that student standardized test scores were higher than they actually were (Strauss, 2013). In addition to such reports of misconduct and corruption, many other stories regularly flood the Internet with tales of illegal sexual activity between teachers and their students.

No matter what type of school—private or public numerous events display wrongdoing by students, teachers, and administrators. Unfortunately, this is not new, nor is it a trend likely to disappear anytime soon. For those striving to move into educational leadership, it is important to keep such reports at the forefront of the mind so as not to repeat unscrupulous behaviors. School administrators would be wise to remain current in educational news, both the good reports and the bad. They should understand that misconduct must not be ignored but must be addressed swiftly, especially if it is unethical or unlawful. It is also prudent to understand that even if a person is found innocent, his or her reputation may be marred beyond recovery. To avoid even accusations of wrongdoing, educators should practice such precautionary measures as keeping doors open at all times when in the company of students. Although these words of wisdom cannot guarantee immunity, they may at least curb thoughtless behavior.

Common Mistakes in School Law

The field of education is certainly not immune to the types of corruption found in other fields, such as business, law, and politics. Some educators will continue to make poor judgments, break ethical codes, and violate the law. In addition to situations of educators cheating on standardized tests, becoming involved sexually with students, and working under the influence of various narcotics and intoxicants, there is a multitude of other issues that can land teachers and administrators in the proverbial hot water. Most times, violating educators are cognizant of the law and that their behaviors are inappropriate. Nevertheless, they somehow justify their conduct or believe that they will not be discovered.

It is a mistake for administrators to neglect to cultivate an environment of legal and ethical accountability. For whatever reason, they may be uncomfortable discussing certain issues, believe the faculty under their supervision are morally superior to those in other schools, or assume that the faculty

It is a mistake for administrators to neglect to cultivate an environment of legal and ethical accountability.

already are informed and have a heightened awareness of liabilities. Accountability and awareness go hand in hand. Open discussions with faculty and periodic reminders about legal and ethical integrity will alert school personnel of the administrator's expectations and will discourage carelessness that could lead to infractions of the law.

Rarely does the study of school law hold a prominent role in a university's teacher preparation program. Even in most principal preparation programs school law is limited to a single course that typically serves as an overview of the topic. It is a mistake, then, for administrators to ignore the study of legal trends and issues. For instance, many administrators are unaware that if they employ a canine unit for a search of the school premises, it is acceptable for the dogs to search lockers, cars, and student materials that are in clear view. It is, however, never appropriate for the dogs to search the students, as this deemed excessively intrusive. If the dogs are searching the school, students should be outside or in the classrooms with the doors closed while the dogs walk the halls sniffing the lockers. The dogs may also sniff student materials (e.g., book bags, purses) in classrooms as long as students themselves are not in the same classroom—they must be in the hallway or outside. This holds true both for public and private schools.

Another tentative situation involves random locker searches. Although the lockers are property of the school, it is still not permissible for teachers or administrators to search a locker without a reasonable suspicion. School resource officers (SROs) are allowed to conduct searches only after obtaining a warrant or identifying probable cause to conduct the search. Administrators need only reasonable suspicion to conduct the same type of search. Students have a property right to their lockers, so unless there is an allegation of drugs, weapons, or other illegal paraphernalia contained in the locker, educators are not permitted to search randomly. This holds true both for public and private schools.

Regarding special education, a mistake in public schools is not providing a free and appropriate public education. If students with disabilities have been identified and are to receive special education services, they have specific needs, and those needs must be met appropriately and without cost. If those needs are not met, the school could be held responsible for fees, even including those for private school tuition. The school, though, is not required to provide a specific accommodation exactly as it is requested by the parents. For example, a parent may request a sign language interpreter, but if the student progresses well with a frequency-modulation system, the school is not obligated to comply with the request for a sign language interpreter. As long as the school is providing appropriate accommodations, that is all that is necessary. Schools are not required to provide a more costly or complicated accommodation if a less costly or simpler accommodation is sufficient. If, however, a student requires a specific accommodation in order to progress satisfactorily through the curriculum, the school is obligated to provide it. Otherwise, the parent may remove the student and place him or her in private school, and the public school may be required to pay the tuition. In short, public schools must provide a FAPE.

Educators sometimes run into trouble for simply not knowing what they do not know. Ignorance is never an excuse, especially because educators are considered professionals. If they are unsure of the law, administrators should consult an attorney before moving forward rather than making decisions based on intuition. It is much cheaper to pay for counsel than to pay for damages on the back end. Most school divisions or private school associations have attorneys on retainer who stand ready to provide counsel for such tentative circumstances.

Implications for the Future

Now that basic components of law and case precedents have been discussed, it is necessary to consider implications for the future. Many of the situations that educators and youth face today were not even a concern just two decades ago. This is evidenced by some of the more current cases involving issues such as cyber-bullying and strip searches. Other issues not yet addressed are covered in the following subsections.

Homosexual and Transgender Issues

One future implication regarding school law involves how schools respond to openly homosexual and transgender students and teachers. Regarding homosexuality, as long as the behavior does not impede the duties of a public school teacher, that teacher cannot be dismissed. In Christian schools, as long as a policy exists requiring conduct and beliefs to comply with biblical doctrine, teachers may be terminated for homosexual activity or for coming out as gay or lesbian. As with all lifestyle requirements for employees, students, or parents, Christian schools will be more successful defending their policies in court if the policies are (1) written, (2) voted on by the school board, (3) supported by established religious doctrines of the Bible or of the sponsoring church's denomination, (4) disseminated in a handbook, and (5) acknowledged by signature of all those affected by the policies.

Regarding homosexual students, whether in public or Christian schools, they must adhere to the policy and procedures of the student handbook. Any violation of this would warrant disciplinary measures, just as it would for heterosexual students. In public schools, no policies may be adopted that would require a student to be disciplined simply for claiming to be homosexual. Christian school policies may vary on this. Some Christian schools may permit students to claim a gay or lesbian orientation, whereas others may refuse enrollment or may expel students for such open claims. Unlike public schools, many Christian schools adopt policies—sometimes called "lifestyle agreements"—relating to personal conduct outside of school hours. There may be separate codes of conduct for students, teachers, and sometimes even parents. Typically, these codes address sexual activity. It is recommended that policies related to sexual activity be the same both for homosexual and for heterosexual activity. For instance, if students and single teachers are requested to sign a lifestyle agreement prohibiting sexual activity, there should be no difference in how the policy is administered concerning homosexual or heterosexual activity. The stipulations and disciplinary actions should be the same for both.

Schools have been dealing with transgender parents for a time, but most recently are beginning to grapple with the treatment of transgender students. One conundrum is to decide which restroom they should use. It would be problematic for a biological male parent who identifies himself as a woman to use a girls' restroom when on campus for a school function. A common solution is for schools to identify a general faculty restroom as unisex. Parents are then directed to use that particular bathroom when on campus. This alleviates any confusion for students who may observe a male entering a female restroom or vice versa. For transgender students, the problem is yet more convoluted; therefore, schools are experimenting with a variety of solutions, none of which has become standard (Gavin Grimm v Gloucester County School Board, 2015; Highland School District v US Department of Education,2016; Student v Arcadia Unified School District, 2013; Whitaker v Kenosha Unified School District, 2017).

Prayer at Graduation

As a longstanding tradition, graduation ceremonies are by nature rich with symbolism and customs. Communities rally around commencement exercises, finding unity in the celebration of the accomplishments of their youth. Yet, in such a unifying event, controversy prevails over which rituals to retain and which ones might violate the constitutional rights of some community members. Prayer is one of those rituals. Although it clearly established that public school officials may not pray or arrange for prayer at graduation exercises, the Supreme Court has yet to rule on the issue of prayers offered in an open forum by students or guest speakers. At present, the understanding is that just as valedictorians and guest speakers may quote poetry or other inspirational literature, they may read or recite prayers of their own choosing.

Cyber-Bullying and Sexting

Sure to have policy implications in the future are the issues of cyber-bullying and sexting. Just a few years ago, nobody even knew what the terms *sexting* and *cyber-bullying* meant. In a nutshell, cyber-bullying is defined by KidsHealth (2013) as, "The use of technology to harass, threaten, embarrass, or target another person." There has always been bullying in the schools, but that behavior often ceased once students were back safe in their homes. Today, students are facing bullying from multiple venues at all hours of the day. It follows them on their phones, computers, and iPads. Because bullying is becoming even more pervasive, urgent action must be taken to avoid more children being psychologically wounded by this phenomenon. Students do not always feel comfortable talking to adults at school or even at home, but educators must encourage them to seek help and—once they are aware of it—do everything reasonable to put an end to the bullying. Although the law may be unclear on the responsibility of educators regarding cyber-bullying, they do have a moral, ethical, and spiritual obligation to intercede on the behalf of victims to bring it to a halt.

Sexting, another technology-based problem, includes sending sexually explicit photos or words through one's cell phone or instant messaging service (Matte, 2013). Young people often do not understand the damage this action may cause to themselves and to others. Students must be informed that whatever is placed on the Internet does not go away; it can follow them from adolescence into adulthood and could potentially hinder them when seeking employment. Teenagers do not always think about the consequences of their actions, but this type of behavior is sure to have policy implications in the future.

Although there are currently no laws on sexting or cyber-bullying, that will most likely change soon. As more and more children who are caught up in the drama and trauma of these actions commit suicide (e.g., Megan Meier) or respond with violence, it is only a matter of time before lawsuits make their way into the judicial system and schools are forced to respond with new policies.

Technology in the Schools

As students become more and more technologically savvy through 21st-century learning, educators need to ensure their understanding of law specifically as it relates to technology. As mentioned in earlier sections, students have many individual rights within the school setting. They also have legal entitlements at home. For instance, when students are at home, working from their own computers, they are able to do just about anything, such as make fictitious social media accounts or talk to classmates using an alter-ego. Some leaders mistakenly believe that they can take disciplinary action within the school based on what students do outside of school. This may be the case in Christian schools but is rarely accurate for public schools. If students make a fictional account of their teachers or administrators at home on a personal computer, there is very little that administrators can do. School personnel would have to prove that harm (e.g., substantial disruption) was done by the fake account, which is oftentimes extremely difficult to prove in the court of law (*Beussink v. Woodland R-IV School District,* 1998; *Emmett v. Kent School District No. 415,* 2000; *Killion v. Franklin Regional School District,* 2001). However, there have been cases when, after much review and litigation in the court system, the school has been able to demonstrate a substantial disruption to the school environment (*J.S. v. Bethlehem Area School District,* 2002).

CONCLUSION

Although the majority of this chapter focused on public school law, it is important to remember that some laws do not apply the same way in private schools—either because they have a religious exemption or because they may not receive federal funds. Private schools indeed have the ability to require certain lifestyle agreements from employees, students, and parents that public schools cannot require. There are certain rights, however, that apply equally in private schools as they do in public schools. Protecting a student's privacy rights regarding search and seizure would be one example. It is key, in whatever arena administrators serve, to pick battles carefully and to determine the degree to which a conflict is worth the resources it might take to respond to litigation. At times, the cause and the cost are well worth the end result. In those instances, educators must proceed prayerfully to do what is right for their students.

Discussion Questions

1. What course case do you believe to have impacted educators most in recent years? Explain your answer.

2. What current events in your state or community have related to the religious rights of students and/or teachers? What actions did administrators take? Do you agree with those actions? Cite court cases in your answer.

3. Review topics of the other chapters in this book and relate them to school law concepts discussed in this chapter. What connections do you notice, for example, between legal issues and school safety, finance, or ethics?

4. Review the Constitutional Amendments mentioned in this chapter and discuss how an awareness of these amendments may benefit educators.

5. Describe scenarios in which it would be appropriate for a principal to search a student's property or person. When would it be inappropriate to do so?

Activities for Enrichment

6. Pull a recent article from the news that deals with an educator being removed from employment (e.g., search the words "teacher fired" on the Internet). After reviewing the details of the case, determine if the school administration or central office acted appropriately in the firing of the employee. Include what the leaders could have or should have done differently that could keep this case from litigation, and make a prediction of what the outcome would be if or when this case went to court. Support your prediction with case precedent.
7. Examine the discipline policy for your school or school district as it applies to students covered by IDEA. Compare your policy to those of other schools or districts. Summarize how your discipline policy adheres to or fails to adhere to the guidelines of IDEA.
8. Conduct a Socratic seminar on any topic regarding law. The topic may include any aspect of law or a comparison of private versus public institutional practices. It may also be used to exhaust a required reading assignment for class. Regarding the Socratic seminar, divide the class into two groups. Group one will be the "inner circle" and group two will be the "outer circle." While the inner circle is meeting, the outer circle is listening and taking notes. Members of the outer circle are not allowed to participate

in the inner group's discussion. Group one will begin the discussion on the selected topic as the inner group. This is not a "round robin" activity. All participants share during this exercise. The discussion could begin with student thoughts or reactions based on the topic—how the topic relates to law or personal connections of the topic to one's worldview. While group one is discussing the assigned topic, group two is listening and taking notes. After a specified amount of time (e.g., 15 minutes), the groups switch roles. Group one becomes the outer circle and group two becomes the inner circle. The second group will build upon the first group's discussion and add to the conversation. At the end of the session, the instructor may tie up loose ends or make connections between the discussion and topic. This activity elicits critical thinking of all participants.

CASE STUDIES

Case 1: Cone of Shame

An administrator in a secondary school employed a veteran teacher who was well liked by the students, faculty, and community. When students arrived to class late or without completing their homework, this teacher made the offender wear a cone-shaped dog collar (like the ones veterinarians place on animals after surgery so they do not bite infected areas) and named this device the "Cone of Shame." Although many students thought this practice was quite funny and video recorded the action on cell phone devices, some parents got wind of these events and did not find them humorous. The teacher was released from his position.

1. Do you agree with how the situation was handled by school administration? Explain why or why not.
2. Do parents have the right to be outraged and to sue based on the teacher's actions? If so, on what grounds? Based on court precedent, what do you anticipate the ruling would be?
3. What other factors would you consider if you were the principal?
4. Did the principal follow correct procedures? Explain.

Case 2: Mr. Mann

Mr. Mann, a secondary teacher, was arrested and charged with unlawful contact with a minor, sexual abuse of children, indecent exposure, open lewdness, criminal attempt to possess child pornography, and corruption of minors. The teacher allegedly sent sexually explicit text messages to two students, a 14-year-old and a 13-year-old. He asked one victim to send pictures of herself to him via cell phone, and he exchanged pictures with another student via text. The particulars of the case unfolded when the 13-year-old student reported to two other teachers that Mr. Mann had sent her inappropriate text messages one evening. One of the teachers involved confronted Mr. Mann the following day and inquired if perhaps he had inadvertently sent the messages to the student by mistake. This teacher stated that Mr. Mann became teary-eyed and said that the texts were no mistake. When approached by the school superintendent about the allegations, Mr. Mann did not deny sending the texts but did state that he had been drinking and had been trying to send the text messages to an older female. He was immediately suspended from the school system awaiting the outcome of his court case. While investigating these charges, police soon discovered that Mr. Mann had exchanged nearly 300 text messages. Many of these included nude pictures of himself, and others included nude pictures of the 14-year-old girl.

1. What would you have done differently, if anything, if you were the teacher who was approached by the student?
2. What do you believe the principal should do in this situation? Justify the reasons for your answer.
3. Should Mr. Mann receive different consequences if he can prove that he has a substance abuse problem?
4. Did the superintendent handle this situation appropriately? Explain.
5. How might the outcome be different if the students were of 18 years of age instead of minors?

REFERENCES

Bethel School District No. 403 v. Fraser, 478 U.S. 675, 106 S. Ct. 3159, 92 L.Ed. 2d 549 (1986).

Beussink v. Woodland R-IV School District, 30 F. Supp. 2d 1175 (E.D. MS 1998).

Bill of Rights. (1789). Retrieved from http://www.archives.gov/exhibits/charters/constitution.html

Blackstone, W. (1908). *Commentaries on the laws of England.* Philadelphia, PA: J. B. Lippincott Company.

Board of Education of Hendrick Hudson Central School District v. Rowley, 458 U.S. 176, 102 S. Ct. 3034 (1982).

Board of Education of Independent School District 92 of Pottawatomie County v. Earls, 536 U.S. 822, 828, 122 S. Ct. 2559, 153 L. Ed. 2d 735 (2002).

Brown v. Board of Education, 349 U.S. 294, 75 S. Ct. 753 (1955).

Colin v. Orange Unified School District, 83 F. Supp. 2d 1135 (C.D. Cal. 2000).

Cornfield by Lewis v. Consolidated School District No. 230, 991 Vol. II F. 2d 1316 (7th Cir. 1993).

Davis v. Monroe County Board of Education, 526, U.S. 629; 110 S. Ct. 1661; 143 L.Ed. 2d 839 (1999).

DesRoches v. Caprio, 974 F. Supp. 542 (E.D.Va 1997).

Emmett v. Kent School District No. 415, 2000 U.S. Dist. LEXIS 4995 (W.D. Wash. Feb. 23, 2000).

Engle v. Vitale, 370 U.S. 421, 82 S. Ct. 1261 (1962).

Essex, N. (2012). School law and the public schools (5th ed.). Boston, MA: Pearson.

Every Student Succeeds Act (ESSA). (2015). Retrieved from https://www.ed.gov/essa?src=rn

Family Education Rights and Privacy Act (FERPA). (2008). Retrieved from http://www.ed.gov/policy/gen/guid/fpco/ferpa/index.html

Florence County School District Four v. Shannon Carter, 510 U.S. 7, 114 S. Ct. 361, 126 L. Ed. 2d 284 (1993).

Forest Grove School District v. T.A., 129 S. Ct. 2484 (2009).

Freiler v. Tangipahoa Parish Public Schools, 185 F. 3d 337 (5th Cir. 1999).

Gates, S. (2013, February 1). Fresno teacher allegedly tied student to chair because he wouldn't remain seated. *The Huffington Post.* Retrieved from http://www.huffingtonpost.com/2013/02/01/teacher-tied-unruly-student-chair-bakman-elementary_n_2598882.html

Gathright v. Lincoln Insurance Company, 285 Ark. 16, 688 S. W. 2d 931 (1985).

Good News Club v. Milford Central School, 202 F. 3d 502 (2nd Cir. 2001).

Goss v. Lopez, 419 U.S. 565, 95 S. Ct. 729, 42 L.Ed.2d 725 (1975).

Horton v. Goose Creek Independent School District, 690 F. 2d 470 (5th Cir. 1982).

Isaiah B. v. State of Wisconsin, 500. N.W.2d 637 (Wis. 1993), cert. denied, 510 U.S. 884 (1993).

Jones v. Clear Creek Independent School District, 977 F.2d 963 (5th Cir. 1992).

Jones v. Latexo Independent School District, 499 F. Supp. 223 (E.D. Tex. 1980).

J.S. v. Bethlehem Area School District, 757 A. 2d. 412 (Pa. 2002).

KidsHealth. (2013). Retrieved from http://kidshealth.org/parent/positive/talk/cyberbullying.html

Killion v. Franklin Regional School District, 136 F. Supp. 2d 446 (W.D. Pa. 2001).

Lee v. Weisman, 505 U.S. 577 (1992).

Maclauchlan, S. (2013, February 1). Chesterfield teacher arrested, charged with assaulting student. *NBC12.* Retrieved from http://www.nbc12.com/story/20937927/chesterfield-teacher-arrested-charged-with-assaulting-student

Matte, C. (2013). What is sexting and why is it a problem? Parenting: Family technology. Retrieved from http://familyinternet.about.com/od/computingsafetyprivacy/a/sexting_what.htm

New Jersey v. T.L.O., 469 U.S. 325 (1985).

Oliver v. McClung, 919 F.Supp. 1206 (N.D. Ill. 1995).

Owasso Independent School District No I-011 v. Falvo, 534 U.S. 426; 122 S. Ct. 934; 151 L. Ed. 2d 896 (2002).

Pickering v. Board of Education, 225 N.E.2d, 16 (Ill. 1968).

Pierce v. Society of Sisters, 268 U.S. 510, 45 S. Ct. 571, 69 L. Ed. 1080 (1925).

Plessy v. Ferguson, 163 U.S. 537 (1896).

Safford Unified School District #1 et al. v. April Redding, U.S. LEXIS 4735 (June 25, 2009).

Santa Fe Independent School District v. Jane Doe, 120 S. Ct. 2266; 147 L.Ed. 2d 295 (2000).

Strauss, V. (2013, March 30). Scathing excerpts from Atlanta indictment in test cheating scandal. *The Washington Post*. Retrieved from http://www.washingtonpost.com/blogs/answer-sheet/wp/2013/03/30/scathing-excerpts-from-atlanta-indictment-in-test-cheating-scandal/

Tinker v. Des Moines Independent Community School District, 393 U.S. 503, at 511, 89 S. Ct. 733, 21 L.Ed. 2d 731 (1969).

U.S. Constitution. (1787). Retrieved from http://www.archives.gov/exhibits/charters/constitution.html

Vernonia School District v. Acton, 115 S. Ct. 2386; 132 L. Ed. 2d 564 (1995).

Wallace v. Jaffree, 472 U.S. 38, 105 S. Ct. 2479 (1985).

Wisconsin v. Yoder, 406 U.S. 205 (1972).

Zamora v. Pomeroy, 639 F. 2d 662 (10th Cir. 1981).

Chapter 11

Ethics in School Administration

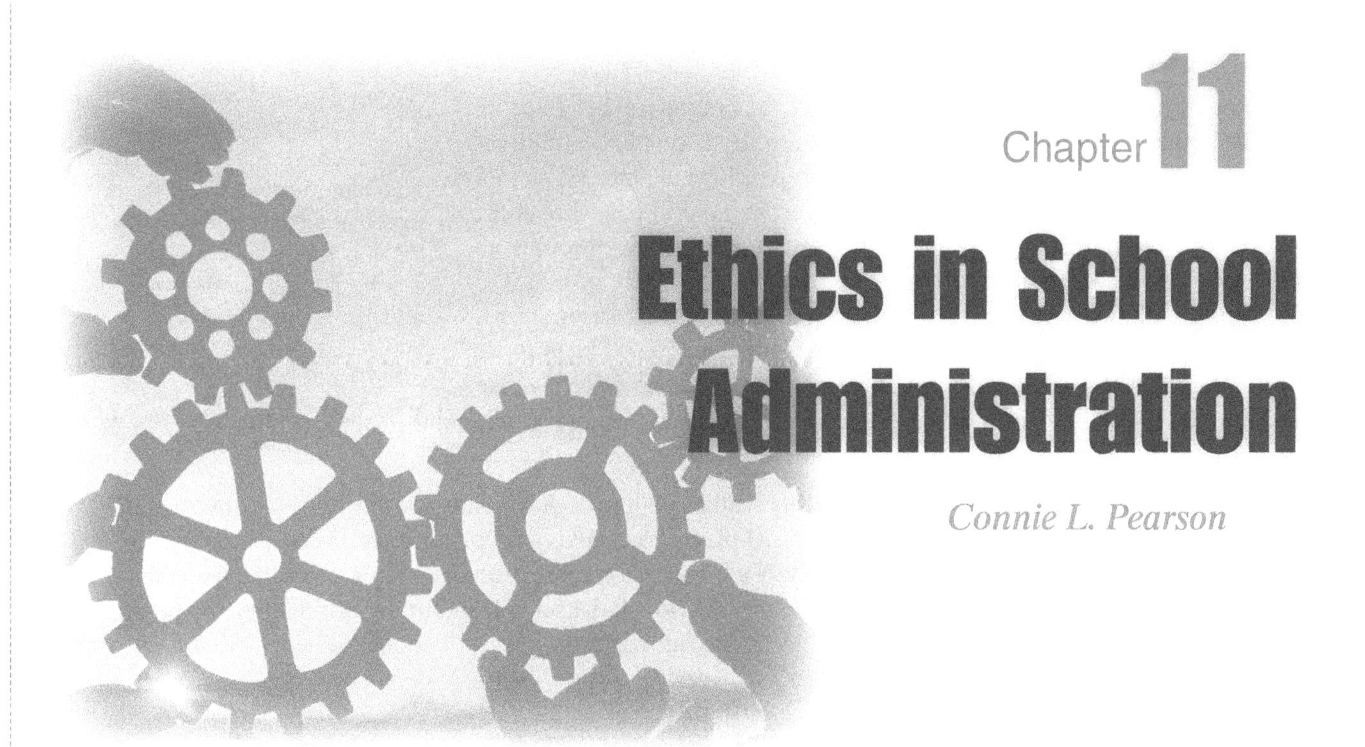

Connie L. Pearson

Educators must become aware of the ethical implications of their work and that they must continually strive to make and be guided by morally sound decisions and to encourage others to do the same.
—Beck and Murphy (1994)—

OVERVIEW

In the last 25 years or more, ethical issues regarding school boards, school administrators, teachers, parents, and even students have come to the forefront. Frequently in the news are incidents of administrators embezzling monies from their schools or school systems, teachers changing student responses on high-stakes tests, teacher candidates falsifying application documents, and students cheating on tests and mercilessly bullying classmates—to name only a few. These high-profile cases must be dealt with at some level, but just as important are those daily ethical decisions that must be addressed by the administrator. This chapter deals with the principles upon which ethical decisions should be made by the Christian educator, whether in a public or private venue. Topics found in this chapter include the theoretical, biblical, and historical perspectives of ethical decision making; particular examples in the news; and policy implications for the Christian educational leader.

Objectives

By the end of this chapter, the reader should be able to do the following:

1. Ensure a system of accountability for every student's academic and social success.
2. Model principles of self-awareness, reflective practice, transparency, and ethical behavior.
3. Safeguard the values of democracy, equity, and diversity.
4. Consider and evaluate the potential moral and legal consequences of decision making.

INTRODUCTION

Because of the rise in inappropriate and unscrupulous behavior in schools in the recent past, there has been a renewed interest in the study of ethics (Noddings, 2002). As addressed in the previous chapter on school law, cheating, theft, bullying, disrespect, anger, and the like have become increasingly problematic. In response, character education has become an important part of the curriculum in many schools. The study of ethics is also being included in educational programs, especially those programs that train school administrators (Shapiro & Stefkovich, 2005). The purpose of ethics education, whether for administrators or students, is to provide the framework for making wise decisions, for responding as appropriate, and for acting ethically. On what precepts are those decisions founded? What determines an ethical decision?

The purpose of ethics education, whether for administrators or students, is to provide the framework for making wise decisions, for responding as appropriate, and for acting ethically.

Ethics is generally defined as that which deals with morality—that which is considered right or wrong. Blum (1991) defined it as "action-guided rules and principles, choice and decision, universality and impartiality, and obligation and right action" (p. 701). For the school administrator, these precepts narrow down to making the right decision, taking into consideration the benefit to the individual, the school, and/or the community; however, this can be very nebulous. What foundation leads one to the right decision? Why does one individual see things from one perspective and someone else from another?

The foundational difference is worldview. The American Family Association (Rusbult, 2009) defined a worldview as "a theory of the world, used for living in the world . . . a mental model of reality—a framework of ideas and attitudes about the world, ourselves, and life, a comprehensive system of beliefs—with answers for a wide range of questions" (p. 1). In society, there are basically two worldviews: a secular worldview, which is primarily grounded in the mores of society, which may change with time; and a biblical worldview, which is established in the Scriptures and is ageless and unchanging. An example of the contrast is the two views of the meaning of human life, especially before birth. God's Word teaches that human life is sacred from the time of conception and that human beings are special creations, like none other. Genesis 1:27 (New International Version) states, "God created mankind in his own image, in the image of God he created them; male and female he created them." He created people in His image and He values them, as reflected in the psalmist's statement to God about His human creation: "You have made him a little lower than the heavenly beings and crowned him with glory and honor. You have given him dominion over the works of your hands; you have put all things under his feet" (Psalm 8:7). Psalm 139:13 proclaims that a fetus is not just a little unborn glob of matter; God forms individuals in the womb: "For you created my inmost being; you knit me together in my mother's womb." This concept of the unborn child, for those with a Biblical worldview, has not changed.

© Brasil Creativo/Shutterstock.com

The secular view of the unborn has progressively changed, and now not only makes the murder of the unborn acceptable but has also legalized the termination of pregnancy in the last few weeks. It has been the impetus behind the attempt to make partial-birth abortions socially acceptable. This was not always so. Up until the middle of the 20th century, there was little argument with the biblical view that the baby before birth was a human being, deserving of respect and protection. Opinion, however, began to shift. Focus was no longer on the right and protection of the unborn but on the will and desires of the mother instead. In 1973, the U.S. Supreme Court case of *Roe v. Wade* ruled that, within a certain time frame, a woman was protected by the Constitution to terminate a pregnancy for almost any reason. Society's views continue to change, dehumanizing the unborn child, even embracing the practice of partial-birth abortion (National Right to Life, n.d.).

When attempting to determine what is right or wrong, one cannot escape the foundational principles found in the Bible. The focus of this chapter is on two basic ethical principles rooted in biblical values: integrity and fairness. *Integrity* refers to the inward character that drives decision making. Throughout Scripture, integrity is highlighted and encouraged. God commended Job when He asked Satan, "Have you considered my servant Job, that there is none like him on earth, a blameless and upright man, who fears God and turns away from evil? He still holds fast his integrity . . ." (Job 2:3, English Standard Version [ESV]). Job's integrity was based on his relationship with God, and that relationship affected his decision making. Job was blameless and honest; those around him could not find fault with him. He was upright; those around him could trust his word. He turned away from evil; he walked with God and sought to keep himself from those things that God called evil. Job's character was rooted in his relationship with God and obedience to God's principles, which led to his existence as a man of integrity.

These character traits must be foundational for ethical school leaders. Effective administrators must be honest, trustworthy, and conscientious—people of integrity. Curren (2008) described the concept of integrity for today's academic administrators as a "set of three cardinal virtues: commitment to the good of the institution, good administrative judgment, and conscientiousness in discharging the duties of the office" (p. 337).

People will not willingly follow leaders unless they see them as possessing integrity. That integrity demands consistency and is best demonstrated in times of adversity (Blackaby & Blackaby, 2011). A person's true colors come out when put under pressure. It is easy to have integrity when there is nothing to lose, but when telling the truth may be costly, it may be much more difficult to do. One's word must be reliable, under all circumstances, or that person will not have the support that might be expected: "The one who lives with integrity lives securely, but whoever perverts his ways will be found out" (Proverbs 10:9, Holman Christian Standard).

A person's true colors come out when put under pressure.

The ethical principle of fairness is also grounded in God's Word, primarily rooted in the Golden Rule, found in Jesus' Sermon on the Mount: "So whatever you wish that others would do to you, do also to them, for this is the Law and the Prophets" (Matthew 5:12, English Standard Version). One must ask, "What would I want to happen to me in this situation? How would I feel about it? How should I respond?" Although considered a hackneyed expression by some, the common adage from the novel *In His Steps*, would be applicable: "WWJD . . . What would Jesus do?" (Sheldon, 1897).

BACKGROUND

Biblical Framework for Ethics

The seminal study of ethics and ethical decision making began with Socrates and Plato in the 4th century B.C. when these philosophers began searching for truth (Irwin, 2008). The foundation of moral behavior, however, is rooted in Judeo-Christian Scripture beginning with God's dissemination of His laws in the book of Exodus at approximately 1445 B.C. These laws are primarily found in the Ten Commandments in Exodus 20. After the first four laws related to the relationship between individuals and God, He added the last six to govern people's responsibility to each other:

- Honor your father and your mother.
- You shall not murder.
- You shall not commit adultery.
- You shall not steal.
- You shall not bear false witness against your neighbor.
- You shall not covet . . . anything that is your neighbor's. (Exodus 20:12–17)

With these final six commandments, God provided the foundation for making ethical decisions.

The New Testament reinforces these principles when Jesus warned that not only these external commands should govern behavior but that they should direct people's thoughts and emotions, which originate in the heart and mind. Motivational thoughts are as significant as the resulting actions themselves. Just as Jesus admonished His disciples, He admonishes people today: "A new commandment I give to you, that you love one another. Just as I have loved you, you also are to love one another" (John 13:34). As He finished His Sermon on the Mount, Jesus presented yet another challenge: "You have heard that it was said, you shall love your neighbor and hate your enemies. But I say to you, love your enemies and pray for those who persecute you . . . For if you love those who love you, what reward do you have? Do not even the tax collectors do the same?" (Matthew 5:43–46). The admonitions culminate in the Golden Rule: "And as ye would that men should do to you, do ye also to them likewise" (Luke 6:31, King James Version).

Why is this important? Its central importance is that, for those who claim to be followers of Christ, the Bible is an initial guide. Followers of Christ trust God's Word to be true, so they begin there to find the principles upon which to base their decisions. One biblical example is Solomon, arguably the wisest man who ever lived (other than Christ), who asked God, "Give your servant therefore an understanding mind to govern your people that I may discern between good and evil, for who is able to govern this your great people" (I Kings 3:9, ESV)? Solomon asked for wisdom to make decisions about discerning between right and wrong behavior and actions. God honored Solomon's request and not only made him wise, but also gave him riches and honor (I Kings 3:12–13). The importance of following God's principles was highlighted in the New Testament. In His Sermon on the Mount, Jesus emphasized that the Old Testament commandments were still essential:

> Therefore whoever relaxes one of the least of these commandments and teaches others to do the same will be called least in the kingdom of heaven, but whoever does them and teaches them will be called great in the kingdom of heaven. (Matthew 5:18–19)

Very simply, the framework for the ethical decision making of a Christian is God's Word. Throughout Scripture, God's admonitions and warnings regarding people's thoughts and actions are pervasive. Imbedded in those pages are the guidelines for making wise and ethical decisions. Solomon assured his readers that "the Lord gives wisdom, from his mouth come knowledge and understanding; he stores up sound wisdom for the upright; he is a shield to those who walk in integrity" (Proverbs 2:6–7).

Very simply, the framework for the ethical decision making of a Christian is God's Word.

Historical Background

In recent history, much attention has been given to decision making by educational leaders. Up until the beginning of the 20th century, it was assumed that "school leaders would embrace values consonant with American ideals, with widely accepted religious beliefs, and with common cultural norms" (Beck, Murphy, & Associates, 1997, p. 2). The American ideals were those rooted in patriotism and the religious beliefs that were found in the Scriptures, the absolutes of God's Word.

In the early 1900s, as the Industrial Revolution was raging, the business and industrial worlds began to influence the educational arena with a focus on productivity, order, efficiency, and stability, and a move away from the overtly religious. Most educational administration programs avoided the study of ethics because it was considered non-empirical and useless (Beck et al., 1997). They instead focused on capitalist-industrialist values (Murphy, 1992), which prepared administrators to manage their schools like businesses or factories.

Soon the emphasis on these values began to shift and affected educational administration programs in the United States. First came the Great Depression of the 1930s, which—with its devastation to the American population—tarnished the luster of the business values that had become so dominant. World War II brought concerns related to democracy and patriotism. The shift was to an emphasis on societal relationships, and as John Dewey arrived on the academic scene, he saw the school as a community of cooperation. Ethical principles that supported the ideals of democracy and collaboration were lauded in institutions that prepared educational leaders (Beck et al., 1997).

During the 1950s, the preparation of educational leaders continued to provide a paradigm shift, attempting to make it a more scientific process and void of value-laden principles (Culbertson, 1988). There were those, however, who believed that educational leadership programs should include the study of ethics (Immegart & Burroughs, 1970). Into the 1970s and 1980s, still little attention was given to the study of ethics in educational leadership programs. Then, Beck et al. (1997) found that about half of the educational programs that were surveyed were giving some attention to ethical issues. Leading into the 21st century, the issue has become not whether or not ethics should be studied but what the study should encompass.

An Ethics Paradigm

The foundation for making ethical decisions should be the absolutes of God's Word, but one must then determine what ethical study should be developed to profoundly affect the life of today's Christian administrator. Administrators must deal with budgets, facilities, and test scores; however, they must also make value-laden decisions regarding personnel, students, parents, and the broader community. They must make decisions that affect people who have many differing perceptions and ideals. Those decisions will be made from the individual's ethical viewpoint, through the lens of the administrator's worldview.

The major ethics paradigms, as they relate to these human interactions, have been narrowed down to three basic suppositions: the ethics of justice, care, and critique (Starratt, 2004). These should not, however, be viewed as separate entities, but parts of a whole, grounded in a biblical worldview.

The Ethic of Justice

To begin with, each of these ethics is imbedded in God's Word. Repeatedly, the Bible teaches the importance of justice and care in dealing with people. It also encourages us to be rational thinkers. First, when God makes decisions about us, He deals fairly and justly. "The works of his hands are faithful and just; all his precepts are trustworthy; they are established forever and ever, to be performed with faithfulness and uprightness" (Psalm 111:7). "The Lord loves justice" (Psalm 37:28).

Because of His just character, God is no respecter of persons; we are all equal in His sight. Romans 2:11 establishes that "God shows no partiality." James 2:13 teaches that it is sin for us to treat people with partiality:

> My brothers, show no partiality . . . If you really fulfill the royal law according to the Scripture, 'You shall love your neighbor as yourself,' you are doing well. But if you show partiality, you are committing sin and are convicted by the law as transgressors. (James 2:1–13)

Administrators must seek to be impartial in dealing with people. Too often they are governed by the politics of their positions, the hierarchy of the societal structure in which they operate, and they struggle with their related decision making concerning issues of fairness, equity, and justice. They must seek to be as impartial and just as they can be, because people often measure their effectiveness by this quality. Strike, Haller, and Soltis (2005) suggested, "Administrators are just as likely to fail because they are seen as unjust as they are to fail because they are seen as inefficient" (p. 15).

Strike et al. (2005) also identified two principles considered to be related to justice and impartiality: the principle of equal respect and the principle of benefit maximization. The principle of equal respect is based on the Golden Rule, that people treat others as they themselves want to be treated. This concept is foundational to all decisions related to human interaction. When considering this tenet, administrators must also realize that they are dealing with people who are free to make decisions and who should be respected as such.

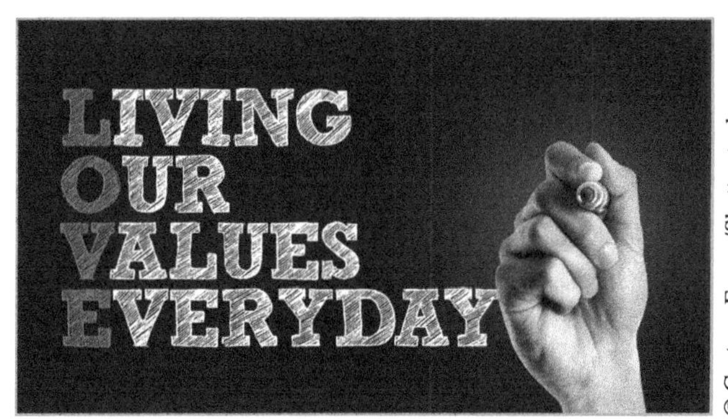

The principle of benefit maximization means that, when making decisions, one should consider what actions would bring the most good to the most people. "Morality is judged by its consequences" is a well-known adage adopted by many. The problem with this adage, however, is that the principle is primarily grounded in situation ethics, which change with the mores of society. The *American Heritage Dictionary of the English Language* (2001) defines *situation ethics* as "a system of ethics that evaluates acts in light of their situational context rather than by the application of moral absolutes" (para. 1).

Situation ethics was very evident in the values clarification movement prevalent in the mid-20th century. It stressed the importance of being aware of one's own values, beliefs, and attitudes (Ali, Allmon, & Cormick, 2011). Its premise was that—as values change with time—students should be taught how to recognize those changes and how they might affect them. Values clarification attempted to elucidate students' own values, not dictate to students what values they should embrace. Although Christian educators strive for students autonomously to develop their own values, they do encourage those tenets to be based on the unchanging Word of God, not on the shifting values of the world. The ideal filter for decision making is a biblical worldview.

The ethic of justice, particularly as it relates to fairness and equity, is foundational in the decisions of successful administrators. Educational leaders must answer questions related to the fairness of policies, the relevance of related laws, the good of the community, and the benefit to the individual. By basing their policies and practices on the ethic of justice, they are more likely to make wise and ethical decisions.

The Ethic of Care

The ethic of care is also rooted in God's Word, which consistently offers assurance of His care. A prime example of this reassurance is found in I Peter 5:7, which states, "Casting all your anxieties on him, because he cares for you." In fact, God loved all humanity so much that He sent His Son, the Lord Jesus Christ, to die on the cross for their sins (John 3:16). As previously mentioned, the Golden Rule should be foundational—not just in the school administrators' professional lives but also in their personal lives. It is the ultimate paragon of human care for each other.

The ethic of care, however, has been belittled by some scholars, primarily males, as being somehow less important than that of justice (Oliver & Hioco, 2012). Feminists challenged the insinuation—because it was related to caring and nurturing and because it was associated more with women—that somehow the ethic of care was less important than that related to the more patriarchal ethic of justice (Shapiro & Stefkovich, 2005). Noddings (1994) placed caring at the top of an educational hierarchy when she said that the primary responsibility of the school was to care for its children.

Beck and Murphy (1994) reported that the ethic of care stresses relationships and connections instead of law and policies. They suggested that administrators should focus more on personal interactions and less on competition. The emphasis on cooperation is intended to help build community, belonging, and collaboration.

The Ethic of Critique

The last ethic to be discussed is that of critique. Upon a cursory observation, this ethic may seem more complicated than the others. The ethic of critique encourages a critical examination of possible conflicts between laws and democracy, between the inequities in society and in the school. It focuses on the analysis of the inconsistencies in thinking and actions (Shapiro & Stefkovich, 2005). Even so, the principles related to this ethic are grounded in God's Word, where discernment is lauded. The writer of Hebrews identified the mature as "those who have their powers of discernment trained by constant practice to distinguish good from evil" (Hebrews 5:14). The quintessential meaning of the ethic of critique is being able to discern between good and bad. Solomon of the Old Testament knew this—that discernment comes by seeking God's guidance. Again, the foundation for the ethic of critique is found in the principles of the Bible and must be carefully and consistently studied and practiced.

The elements of an ethics paradigm—such as the elements of justice, care, and critique—need not be considered as separate entities. Shapiro and Stefkovich (2005) recognized this when they discussed care: "Attention to this ethic can lead to other discussions of concepts such as loyalty, trust, and empowerment" (p. 16).

Administrators whose character is based on biblical integrity, and who ask for God's guidance, can affectively meld the ethics of justice, care, and critique into appropriate decision making.

Ethics in the News

Examples of ethical issues are in the news daily. One need not look long or hard before finding reports related to ethical practices of school administrators. Especially common are reports dealing with the honesty, or lack thereof, of those in authority—principals and superintendents. For example, a pioneer of the charter school movement was reported to have defrauded the Philadelphia School System of $6.5 million (West, 2012). The accused, along with her colleagues, had allegedly used taxpayer money to operate a string of charter schools, which were ultimately closed because of students' poor academic progress and because of unqualified personnel. The freedom that has been afforded charter school administrators, according to one news commentator (West, 2012), "has meant the freedom to skim taxpayers' money and run scams . . ." (para. 9). Another such scam involved an Oklahoma school superintendent who had been charged with embezzling more than $44,000 from a local school district (Kimball, 2011). Yet another superintendent was arrested for income tax evasion after just having been convicted and sentenced to 6 years in prison for embezzling more than $500,000 from a local school district (Spechko, 2011).

Almost every day, scandals related to educators and their inappropriate actions with children are in the news. In 2012, three high school teachers in Camden, New Jersey, were charged with having inappropriate sexual relationships with female students, and two administrators were charged with covering up the scandal (Mulvihill, 2012). Cases such as this one are not isolated. *The New York Times* reported that, during the first part of 2012, there had been an upsurge in sexual misconduct allegations against school personnel, with a 37% increase over the previous year (Chapman & Monahan, 2012). These same kinds of incidents are found all over our country ("Resignation Made Official," 2012; Stepzinski, 2012).

Not only are there incidents of inappropriate sexual behavior, but also occurrences of other unethical behavior by school personnel. CBS News reported that a 35-year-old teacher in Stockton, California, along with the police officer assigned to the school, was on paid leave for violating the district's code of ethics by running a porn website from her school computer (Glynn, 2011).

Because of pressures put on teachers, some have succumbed to unethical behavior to meet the stressful demands. Examples of infractions were found in the news of the last few months of 2012. CBS Atlanta reported that teachers were helping students cheat on state tests. Approximately 180 public school teachers in the city of Atlanta were implicated in the related investigation (CBS/AP, 2012).

On November 25, 2012, news of a cheating scandal among Southern teachers surfaced. Saninz (2012) reported that for more than 15 years, teachers in three Southern states had paid to have someone else, with fake identifications, take the Praxis exam for them. With the passing of the test, these teachers were awarded the necessary credentials and began their careers as qualified teachers.

The news is replete with articles not only related to the behavior of school leaders themselves, but also related to the decisions they must make regarding the behavior of others. Their responses to inappropriate and even damaging behaviors of students, teachers, and parents often make the news. One of the most injurious actions is the epidemic of bullying, which sometimes leads to tragedy. CNN reported that a 16-year-old male student walked into a California high school with a loaded 12-gauge shotgun, shooting one classmate and missing another (CBS/AP, 2013). In a related article (CNN, 2013), a friend of the teen reported that the youth had been consistently bullied by these two classmates over a long period of time. His comment was: "I was his friend. I don't know why people picked on him. He was misunderstood" (para. 6). Allegedly, the shooter had composed a list of the people whom he wanted to kill. This scenario has been repeated far too often, perhaps not to the extreme of this bullied child, but such incidents are occurring on a regular basis in schools across the country.

These are only a few examples of school administrators who have either violated ethical principles in their own lives—destroying their own credibility—or examples of the kinds of ethical issues that school administrators must deal with on a daily basis.

Common Mistakes

For the Christian educator, the foundation for living ethically and for making good ethical decisions is a personal relationship with Jesus Christ. With that relationship comes the indwelling of the Holy Spirit (1 Corinthians 6:19), Who empowers believers in the decisions they make. Before Jesus' death, He promised His disciples that "[God] will give you another Helper, to be with you forever, even the Spirit of truth" (John 14:16). He also promised, "When the Spirit of truth comes, he will guide you into all the truth" (John 16:14). Galatians 5:16–23 teaches that those who are led by the Spirit will exhibit the fruit of the Spirit, "love, joy,peace, kindness, goodness, faithfulness, gentleness, [and] self-control" (v. 23). Those who are indwelled by the Holy Spirit can then "Ask, and it will be given to [them]; seek, and [they] will find; knock, and it will be opened to [them]. For everyone who asks receives, and the one who seeks finds, and to the one who knocks it will be opened" (Matthew 7:7–8).

The problem, however, is that much of the time Christians do not recognize the relationship they have with the Holy Spirit and do not seek God's direction for their lives. Instead of living lives of integrity and fairness, they find themselves compromising their values and cutting corners. Ultimately, they may find their reputations tarnished and their leadership ineffective. In their book, *Spiritual Leadership*, Blackaby and Blackaby (2011) listed several pitfalls that leaders may fall into. One pitfall is pride. "Pride may be a leader's worst enemy, and it has caused the downfall of many" (p. 313). Leaders whose perspectives have been tainted by pride have a distorted view of themselves. These administrators are tempted to take all the credit for the successes of their lives and their schools. Scripture warns that "pride goes before destruction, and a haughty spirit before a fall" (Proverbs 16:15). Because proud people are always blowing their own horns, Solomon admonished others to "let another praise you, and not your own mouth; a stranger, and not your own lips" (Proverbs 27:2). Pride also closes the minds of leaders to wise counsel. It makes them become unteachable and overly self-confident. They begin to reject any advice offered to them.

For Christian Leaders, a significant danger is that pride will keep them from seeking God's guidance. Again, leaders are warned in Proverbs: "The fear of the Lord is the beginning of knowledge; fools despise wisdom and instruction" (Proverbs 1:7). Blackaby and Blackaby (2011) remind the spiritual leader, "Genuine spiritual leaders never take God's grace, blessing, and presence for granted. When they are enjoying their greatest achievements, they must be vigilant that pride doesn't cause them to fall" (p. 318).

Another pitfall is sexual sin. It seems that when leaders are compromised by pride, they are much more vulnerable to sexual sin. That sin can quickly destroy lives, homes, and ministries. To avoid such sin, Blackaby and Blackaby (2011) suggested five safeguards: (1) be accountable to a friend, (2) listen to one's own counsel, (3) consider the consequences, (4) develop protective habits, and (5) maintain a strong relationship with God.

Another danger for administrators is cynicism. This is a danger for those who have been in leadership positions for a while. After having been repeatedly criticized for decisions and having continuously to deal with problem personnel, leaders have a tendency to develop attitudes of cynicism and pessimism. Rather than concentrate on the positive, they are inclined to see the negative and are apt to respond to people and to most situations negatively. Christians, more than any other people, should be optimistic and positive and thus have no excuse for cynicism.

Leaders' decisions may also be tainted by greed. When money and material wealth become the priority, administrators may compromise their values to attain it. Solomon, a man of great wealth and wisdom, warned how futile and empty the pursuit of material things is:

> I made great works. I built houses and planted vineyards for myself. I made myself gardens and parks . . . I had also great possessions . . . more than any who had been before me in Jerusalem. I also gathered for myself silver and gold . . . And whatever my eyes desired I did not keep from them . . . Then I considered all that my hands had done . . . and behold, all was vanity and a striving after wind, and there was nothing to be gained under the sun. (Proverbs 2:4–11)

Wealth and material blessings are not wrong in themselves, but if they become the focus of life, they may cause leaders to act unethically.

Christian administrators' bad decisions may be swayed by many different influences, but these identified by Blackaby and Blackaby—pride, sexual sins, cynicism, and greed—are primary sources of poor judgment and indiscretions. Leaders must continually be on guard so that they are not tempted to compromise their ethical decision making by succumbing to the attraction of these pitfalls. Proverbs reminds the leader that "the prudent gives thought to his steps" (Proverbs 14:15).

Making Ethical Decisions

To this point, we have discussed the biblical and theoretical foundations for making ethical decisions, ethical paradigms, examples of unethical behavior in the news, and the pitfalls and dangers for the ethical leader. No attempt, however, has been made to provide a practical process for making ethical decisions. In his book *Lessons in Leadership,* Trieber (1996) listed seven ingredients for making good and ethical decisions: (1) faith, (2) the Bible, (3) godly counsel, (4) the will of God, (5) patience, (6) that which is pleasing to the Lord, (7) and experience.

Then, after first asking for God's direction and guidance, the leader may use the nine-step process for decision making provided by Oliver and Hioco (2012):

1. What is the issue?
2. Why is a decision needed?
3. What are the alternatives?
4. What are the potential consequences of each alternative?
5. How likely or unlikely and valuable or adverse is each consequence?
6. Does each alternative comply with laws, policies, and standards of conduct?
7. What are the ethical considerations in each alternative and consequence?
8. What is the decision?
9. Was the decision effective? (para. 24)

Each step should be weighed and examined. The most difficult and the most important is the first step as one clarifies the issue or problem. After defining the question, one must determine whether a decision is really needed. Then, as one determines the alternatives, decisions have to be made regarding their related consequences. Questions 4–7 address those consequences. Finally, question 8 addresses the decision itself and question 9 is an evaluative question after the decision has been made.

CONCLUSION

Many factors are related to the success of school administrators, but none is as important as their character. Nothing affects their success or failure as does their ethical foundation. For Christian leaders, that foundation should be God's Word and a personal relationship with Jesus Christ. Once that is established, the various ethical paradigms may be the impetus for decision making: the ethic of justice, the ethic of care, and the ethic of critique. Administrators must also beware of the pitfalls of their positions—especially pride, sexual sins, cynicism, and greed. These all may taint the decisions of the leader.

Many factors are related to the success of school administrators, but none is as important as their character.

Consistently, the news provides examples of unethical behavior by educational leaders, from embezzlement of school funds to sexual misconduct with students. Also in the news are reports of the rampant incidents of bullying by students and the resultant violence, such as the entrance of gunmen into schools who kill innocent children and adults without any regard for human life. Administrators are tasked with both personally acting ethically and then making wise, ethical decisions when dealing with their students, personnel, and communities. Nothing is more important.

Discussion Questions

1. Describe a system of personal accountability that ensures that an administrator is concerned for students' academic and social success.

2. Discuss how an administrator can model the principles of self-awareness, reflective practice, transparency, and ethical behavior. What biblical principles are foundational?

3. Using biblical and ethical principles, how should a Christian educator respond to the related issues of the December 14, 2012, Sandy Hook School shooting? How can administrators maintain the safety of their children and schools? Should school personnel be allowed to carry concealed weapons?

4. How should a Christian educator respond to the problems of bullying? How might parents be helped in preventing and addressing bullying? How should bullies be handled? How should those students who are being bullied be addressed?

CASE STUDIES

Mr. Rodriguez, principal of Anywhere Middle School, sat at his desk on a warm spring afternoon when Trisha, a quiet, introverted eighth grader, came through the door of his office, accompanied by the school counselor, Ms. Phillips. Trisha seemed distraught and Ms. Phillips was also visibly upset. Ms. Phillips shared that this was the third time Trisha had come to her office in tears. Trisha reported that two girls in her physical education class had been taunting her. The first time had been a week or so prior to this when she had come to class with a hole in the leg of her gym shorts. They made fun of her, calling her "trailer park trash." Then, for the next 2 or 3 days, they just laughed and pointed at her as she walked by. On this day, she recounted that they had made fun of her old tennis shoes and her gray, dingy gym shirt, calling her a variety of derogatory names.

After the first incident, Ms. Phillips had called the girls into her office to discuss the situation, but when confronted, the girls denied that they had said anything to Trisha. They were overly defensive, acting as if she had fabricated the entire story. Ms. Phillips had tried to encourage Trisha to ignore the girls, perhaps trying to avoid getting near them. That seemed impossible for Trisha because one of the girls had a locker next to hers. After the third incident, Ms. Phillips escorted Trisha to Mr. Rodriguez's office.

When asked, Trisha shared with Ms. Phillips and Mr. Rodriguez that she really didn't want to come back to school. She felt like she was needed more at home and—besides—she could no longer handle the taunting at school. She reported that her father had left their family right before school began in August, abandoning her mother with four children. The mother was now behind in her bills and could not afford repairs to their trailer home. To make matters worse, Trisha's mother had lost her job in October and was now supporting her family on a small welfare check either until she could find work or until her husband would begin sending support checks. Trisha felt obligated to try to help.

As Mr. Rodriguez began investigating the incident, he found that the two girls who had been mocking Trisha were not just any girls. One was the daughter of the school district superintendent and the other was a teacher's daughter. Mr. Rodriguez had a real dilemma on his hands.

1. What biblical principles should be considered in this scenario?
2. What ethical or moral issues must Mr. Rodriguez address?
3. How should Mr. Rodriguez approach the situation in general and then specifically with each of the following individuals: Ms. Phillips, Trisha, the two girls, and the parents of the two girls?

REFERENCES

American heritage dictionary of the English language (4th ed.). (2001.) Boston, MA: Houghton Mifflin.

Ali, S. A., Allmon, A., & Cormick, C. (2011). Value clarification. In J. D. Allen, M. R. Worthington, & L. J. Everett (Eds.), *Spiritually oriented interventions for counseling and psychology* (pp. 41–64). Washington, DC: American Psychological Association.

Beck, L. G., & Murphy, J. (1994). *Ethics in educational leadership programs: An expanding role.* Thousand Oaks, CA: Corwin Press.

Beck, L. G., Murphy, J., & Associates. (1997). *Ethics in eduational leadership programs: Emerging models.* Columbia, MO: The University Council for Education Administration.

Blackaby, H., & Blackaby, R. (2011). *Spiritual leadership.* Nashville, TN: B & H Publishing Group.

Blum, L. (1991). Moral perception and particularity. *Ethics, 101*, 701.

CBS/AP. (2012, August 20). School: Teacher helps student cheat because she says they're dumb as hell. Retrieved from http://atlanta.cbslocal.com/2012/08/28/school-teacher-helps-students-cheat-because-she-says-theyre-dumb-as-hell/#

CBS/AP. (2013, January 13). California school shooting: Alleged gunman, Bryan Oliver, pleasds not guilty to attempted murder. Retrieved from http://www.cbsnews.com/8301-504083_162-57564059-504083/california-school-shooting-alleged-gunman-bryan-oliver-pleads-not-guilty-to-attempted-murder/

Chapman, G. B., & Monahan, R. (2012, June 6). Sexual misconduct cases in city schools are on the rise. Retrieved from http://www.nydailynews.com/new-york/education/sexual-misconduct-cases-city-schools-rise-article-1.1090602

CNN. (2013, January 10). Police: Teen shot 1 classmate, missed another in California high school. Retrieved from http://news.blogs.cnn.com/2013/01/10/two-reported-hurt-in-california-school-shooting/

Culbertson, J. (1988). A century's quest for a knowledge base. In N. Boyan, *Handbook of research in educational adminstration* (pp. 3–26). New York, NY: Longman.

Curren, R. (2008). Cardinal virtues of academic adminstration. *Theory and Research in Education, 6*(3) 337–363.

Glynn, C. (2011, November 18). Teacher accused of running porn website from school computer, put on paid leave. Retrieved from http://www.cbsnews.com/8301-504083_162-57327522-504083/heidi-kaeslin-teacher-accused-of-running-porn-website-from-school-computer-put-on-paid-leave/

Immegart, G., & Burroughs, J. M. (1970). *Ethics and the school administrator.* Danville, IL: Interstate.

Irwin, T. (2008, July 7). The development of ethics: A historial and critical study; Volume 1; Socrates to the Reformation. Retrieved from http://ndpr.nd.edu/news/23617-the-development-of-ethics-a-historical-and-critical-study-volume-i-from-socrates-to-the-reformation/

Kimball, M. (2011, April 27). Former Pauls Valley superintendent charged with embezzlement. Retrieved from http://newsok.com/former-pauls-valley-superintendent-charged-with-embezzlement/article/3562499

Mulvihill, G. (2012, October 5). Teachers, bosses charged in NJ school sex scandal. Retrieved from http://www.deseretnews.com/article/765609321/Teachers-bosses-charged-in-NJ-school-sex-scandal.html

Murphy, J. (1992). *The landscape of leadership prepartion: The reframing the education of school administrators.* New Berry Park, CA: Corwin Press.

National Right to Life. (n.d.). Abortion history timeline. Retrieved from http://www.nrlc.org/abortion/facts/abortion-timeline.html

Noddings, N. (1994). *Caring: A feminine approach to ethics and moral education.* Berkley, CA: University of California Press.

Noddings, N. (2002). *Educating moral people.* New York, NY: Teachers College Press.

Oliver, D. E., & Hioco, B. (2012). An ethical decision-making framework for community college administration. *Community College Review 40*(3), 240–254.

Resignation made official for teacher accused of abuse. (2012, October 19). *10tv.com.* Retrieved from http://www.10tv.com/content/stories/2012/10/19/columbus-teacher-resignation-made-official.html Rusbult, C. (2009, January 1). What is world view? Definition & introduction. Retrieved from http://www.asa3.org/ASA/education/views/index.html

Saninz, A. (2012, November 25). Cheating scandal: Feds say teachers hired stand-in to take their certification tests. Retrieved from http://usnews.nbcnews.com/_news/2012/11/25/15430647-cheating-scandal-feds-say-teachers-hired-stand-in-to-take-their-certification-tests?lite

Shapiro, J. P., & Stefkovich, J. A. (2005). *Ethical leadership and decision making in education* (3rd ed.). New York, NY: Routledge.

Sheldon, C. M. (1897). *In His steps.* Chicago: The Henneberry Company.

Spechko, V. (2011, November 7). Former Mullins school superintendent arrested for tax evasion. Retrieved from http://www.carolinalive.com/news/story.aspx?list=195106&id=683650#.UPR2xvIiiSo

Starrattt, R. J. (2004). *Ethical leadership.* San Francisco, CA: Jossey-Bass.

Stepzinski, T. (2012, August 30). Duval school board firing of accused teacher is official. Retrieved from http://jacksonville.com/news/crime/2012-08-30/story/duval-school-board-firing-accused-teacher-official#ixzz2HzLYn2Br

Strike, K. A., Haller, E. J., & Soltis, J. F. (2005). *The ethics of school administration.* New York: Teachers College Press.

Trieber, J. (1996). *Lessons in leadership.* Seminole, FL: Fundamental Press.

West, T. (2012, August 3). Charter schools: A school for scandal. Retrieved from http://www.phillyrecord.com/2012/08/charter-schools-a-schhol-for-scandal/

About the Authors

Courtesy of Samuel J. Smith.

Mark A. Angle currently serves as a School Superintendent. He has taught and served as a principal of both elementary and middle schools and has also been a central office administrator. He has authored and presented on such topics as writing across the curriculum, differentiating with gender in mind, parent–school relationships, and global collaboration. Most recently his research has focused on improving preparation of teacher candidates by integrating educational psychology, assessment, and technology into a single blended course. He holds degrees from Concord University and the University of Virginia.

Courtesy of John C. Barlett.

John C. Bartlett is Assistant Professor at Liberty University, where he teaches courses in school finance, resource management, and educational leadership. He also supervises internships in school administration. He has served as a public school principal in Knoxville, Tennessee, and has authored and presented on topics such as instructional improvement, school culture, brain-based research, instructional technology, school leadership principles, and philosophy of education. He holds degrees from Tennessee Temple University, Tennessee Technological University, and Liberty University.

Courtesy of Ronda Heerspink.

Andrea P. Beam is the Director of Liberty University's Secondary Education Licensure Programs. She has taught in public school special education and has been an administrator in elementary and secondary schools in Virginia Beach. Presently, she teaches courses in special education, school law, and educational leadership and has published on the topics of inclusion, leadership, Brain Gym, school improvement plans, business programs for special education students, and differentiation. She holds degrees from George Washington University, Norfolk State University, and Old Dominion University.

Courtesy of Lee Claxton

Dr. Bunnie Claxton is an educator with over 27 years' experience in public school, private school, home school, and higher education. She earned her B.S. degree in Early Childhood Education from The University of Georgia, M.Ed. in Special Education from Liberty University, and her Ed.D. in Curriculum and Instruction from Liberty University. Dr. Claxton has presented at both state and national conferences and has taught various undergraduate and graduate level courses at multiple universities. She served as the Superintendent of Liberty University Online Academy, which is a K-12 online school serving over 7000 students. Most recently she has been involved in developing an Applied Research Program for Liberty University and teaches research methodology courses.

Courtesy of Anna Harrell.

Russell L. Claxton is a Department Chair in Liberty University's School of Education. He has been a coach, teacher of business education, and a principal at both middle and high school courses levels in the Atlanta, Georgia, area. Presently, he teaches educational leadership. His presentations and publications address such topics as school law, transition programs, school safety, and professionalism in education. He holds degrees from the University of Georgia, the University of West Georgia, and Liberty University.

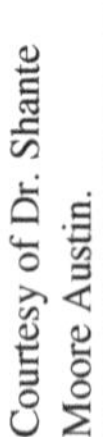
Courtesy of Dr. Shante Moore Austin.

Shanté Moore-Austin is an Assistant Professor of Education at Liberty University. She has been a teacher of mathematics in secondary education on the Eastern Shore of Virginia. Presently, she teaches courses in educational leadership and mathematics. She has published articles and given presentations at national conferences on topics such as promoting diversity in higher education, partnering with the community, and the impact of parent and community involvement on the academic success of students. She holds degrees from the University of Virginia, Regent University, and Capella University.

Courtesy of Delores Beery.

Leldon W. Nichols is an Associate Professor of Education at Liberty University and has leadership experience in elementary, secondary, and higher education. His publications include writing, editing, and producing numerous continuing education programs of study. He has been a keynote speaker for education and leadership conferences in the United States and in seven foreign countries. He holds degrees from Tennessee Temple University, the University of Alabama, and the University of Tennessee.

Courtesy of William Ted Pearson.

Connie L. Pearson is a professor in Liberty University's School of Education. In addition to her experience teaching and administrating elementary through secondary schools in both public and private sectors, she has been a college dean, university vice president, and accreditation commission officer. As an author and international conference speaker, she has addressed topics of teaching pedagogy, gender research, classroom management, differentiated instruction, and educational philosophy. She holds degrees from the University of Tennessee, Illinois State University, and Tennessee Temple University.

Courtesy of Ronda Heerspink.

Samuel J. Smith is the Director of Liberty University's School Administration Licensure Program and teaches historical and philosophical foundations of education. He has taught in both public and Christian schools and served as a P–12 administrator in Texas and Florida. His publications include book chapters and articles on topics such as principal preparation, high-poverty schools, moral education, the phenomenon of teaching as a calling, religious rights in public schools, and special education in Christian schools. He holds degrees from Oklahoma State University, Grace Theological Seminary, and Mid-America Christian University.

Courtesy of Samuel J. Smith.

James A. Swezey is Director of Qualitative Research a Professor of Educational Leadership at Liberty University. In addition to serving as a Christian school administrator, he has been a high school history and Bible teacher and a combat survival instructor for the U.S. Air Force. His publications include book chapters and articles on religion in public schools, worldview, school safety, teacher professionalism, professional development, and the history of the Association of Christian Schools International. He holds degrees from George Fox University, Columbia International University, Simpson University, and the Community College of the Air Force.

CPSIA information can be obtained
at www.ICGtesting.com
Printed in the USA
LVHW022226160520
655746LV00003B/22